Maria Keckler
739-0209

D0016624

ENGLISH GRAMMAR

Language As Human Behavior

Second Edition

Anita K. Barry

The University of Michigan-Flint

Upper Saddle River, New Jersey
07458

Library of Congress Cataloging-in-Publication Data
Barry, Anita K.
  English grammar : language as human behavior/Anita K. Barry.—2nd ed.
    p. cm.
  Includes index.
  ISBN 0-13-032260-1
    1. English language—Grammar. 2. Human behavior. I. Title.

PE1112.B28 2002
428.2—dc21

                                                              2001021856

Editor in chief: Lean Jewell
Acquisitions Editor: Craig Campanella
Editorial Assistant: Joan Polk
Senior Managing Editor: Mary Rottino
Project Liaison: Fran Russello
Production Editor: Terry Routley/Carlisle
  Communications

Prepress and Manufacturing Buyer: Mary
  Ann Gloriande
Marketing Manager: Rachel Falk
Art Director: Jayne Conte
Cover Designer: Bruce Kenselaar

This book was set in 10/12 New Baskerville by Carlisle Communications, Ltd.
and printed and bound by Maple Vail Press.
The cover was printed by Phoenix Color Corp.

Acknowledgment: From BELIEVERS: A NOVELLA AND SHORT STORIES by Charles Baxter.
Specified excerpts, pp. 3, 12, 17, 88, 104, 118, 183, 218, and 222.
Copyright © 1997 by Charles Baxter. Reprinted by permission of Pantheon Books, a division of
Random House, Inc.

© 2002 by Pearson Education, Inc.
Upper Saddle River, New Jersey 07458

Printed in the United States of America

10 9 8 7 6 5 4 3 2 1

ISBN 0-13-032260-1

Pearson Education LTD., London
Pearson Education Australia PTY, Limited, Sydney
Pearson Education Singapore, Ltd.
Pearson Education North Asia Ltd., Hong Kong
Pearson Education Canada, Ltd., Toronto
Pearson Education de Mexico, S.A. de C.V.
Pearson Education Japan, Tokyo
Pearson Education Malaysia, Pte. Ltd.
Pearson Education, Upper Saddle River, New Jersey

For Bill and our family,
Mike, Lani, Ben, Rachel, Hannah, Jim

Contents

Preface

author's goal ?

This book is written for students of English grammar, who come to the task of studying the language with a variety of skills, interests, goals, and expectations, not to mention fears and anxieties. It is addressed primarily to the native speaker of English, and so it is not designed to teach English. Rather, it builds on what students already know to develop an appreciation for how the language works.

The main focus of the book is on language as human behavior. Students are encouraged to view English not as an abstract system of rules, but as an instrument of people who seek patterns and regularity, who use language to communicate their needs and wishes and to exercise power over others, and who are capable of experiencing linguistic insecurity in the face of social judgments about their usage. Students also come to learn that the language they use is the result of people's use over a long period of time, not just a tool for the present, and that English, along with judgments about particular usage, shifts over time. The goal of the book is to make students feel that they are active participants in shaping their language rather than passive victims of grammar rules that someone imposes on them. They are encouraged to be curious about how others use English, and to be flexible enough to understand that there are competing descriptions of language structure, as well as competing opinions about correctness.

In its discussion of English, the book largely adheres to traditional grammatical terminology to keep continuity with our long and rich heritage of grammar studies. At the same time, the grammatical descriptions are informed by the insights gained from modern linguistic analysis. The merger of these two approaches gives students the necessary tools to think about how their language works without becoming entrenched in the mindset of a particular theory. It also provides them with the flexibility to adapt to new terminology they might encounter elsewhere. Lastly, in keeping with the main goal of talking about human behavior, discussion turns to usage and usage questions wherever they are relevant.

The book is designed for a one-semester college course. It covers the basics of English without dwelling on the exceptional or the exotic. It begins with a discussion of the development of a standard English language and the origins of our present day rules of English and attitudes towards usage. Students are invited to explore their own recognition of standard English and to appreciate that people may differ in their judgments. They learn that what is considered "correct" does not always match what sounds appropriate to them. The first chapter lays the foundation for the study of grammar, emphasizing the complex interaction between language rules and behavior. The second chapter talks about how one approaches the study of the structure of a language, including a brief discussion of how languages change over time. It also gives an overview of language structure, explaining the essentially hierarchical as opposed to linear nature of language. From there the book works from the lowest levels of grammatical organization to the highest, starting with an analysis of words and working up to the level of the sentence.

As students and teachers begin to work with this book, they will realize that the material is integrated in ways not apparent from the chapter headings. There is no part of language that is wholly separate from the other parts: it is an organic system in which the parts are interrelated and function together to perform the highly complex task of communicating human thought. Naturally, then, a description of a language cannot consist of wholly separate parts either. In this particular description, there is a good deal of recycling of information. Topics are not necessarily explored in their entirety when they are first introduced and may resurface in other contexts to have new light shed on them. In some cases a theme is introduced early and developed gradually throughout the book. The most commonly recurring themes have to do with the factors that influence people's use of their language: their common needs and preferences, and their shared strategies for turning their thoughts into words.

Each chapter contains three types of exercises. First, there are short **Discussion Exercises** distributed throughout the chapter and designed for group or class work. These typically exemplify and reinforce a newly introduced principle. They give students a chance to check their own understanding in a nonthreatening forum and to spend part of every class period talking about language. On occasion these exercises are used to encourage students to extend what they have learned and to uncover new facts and principles of grammar themselves. In this way, the exercises become an integral part of the text material and serve a teaching as well as a review function. The Instructor's Manual provides additional discussion of these exercises, which may be shared with students to the extent that the instructor finds it relevant and useful.

Second, there are open-ended questions and project suggestions at the end of each chapter, called **Reflections.** These are intended to get students to think about language use—their own and others'—in real-life settings or to ponder some aspect of English structure that eludes analysis. These exercises are intended to stimulate further class discussion and engage students in timely, enjoyable discourse about their language.

Finally, there are **Practice Exercises** at the end of each chapter that integrate all the information presented in that chapter. These are designed for students to work on outside of class. They are intended to be more closed-ended than the other exercise types, and they focus on purely structural material rather than on questions of usage. Answer guides to these exercises are provided at the end of the book. Of course, given the nature of language, these also often lend themselves to discussion.

The exercises taken together are designed to get students to think, talk, and write about English with increasing confidence and sophistication as the term progresses.

As anyone who has ever tried it knows, describing a language is an open-ended enterprise. There is always more that could be said. The goal here is to lay the necessary groundwork for thinking about language so that students can extend what they learn to new situations when the occasion arises, and to apply their knowledge in ways most useful to them, either in teaching the language to others or in their own speaking and writing, or in making sense of the often subtle but always pervasive set of social judgments that accompany language use. This book is a conversation about English that approaches grammar as a process, not a product; and it is a book in which thoughtful explanations are valued over "correct" answers. Above all, it strives to stimulate excitement, enthusiasm, and wonder about English usage that will endure once the course is over.

NOTES ON THE SECOND EDITION

In response to the thoughtful and insightful comments of students, colleagues, and reviewers, I have made certain changes in this edition. Most of these changes involve reorganization and the addition of exercises. The final chapter of the first edition has been omitted entirely, and the material on ambiguity and coordination, originally Chapter 8, has been integrated into other chapters. Clause coordination and clause subordination are treated in chapters of their own. I have tried to respond to the "save the trees" debate by scaling back but not eliminating entirely the use of tree diagrams for illustrating sentence structure.

A minor change in the exercises is that answers are provided for every *other* question in the Practice Exercises, rather than for every question. This should be enough for students to gauge their level of understanding without creating undue dependence on the answers, and it is hoped that missing answers will serve to integrate these exercises into classroom discussions. The remaining answers can be found in the Instructor's Manual.

A more serious concern about the exercises in the first edition was that they did not give students a chance to examine language in its natural context, exactly what they would ultimately be doing when applying their grammatical knowledge. With that concern in mind, I have added two additional types of exercises at the end of every chapter. The first provides an excerpt of literary prose (from Charles Baxter's collection *Believers: A Novella and Stories,* Pantheon Books: New York, 1997) and asks students to identify grammatical structures within the selection. The second is a series of letters written by a fictitious person (me!) that exhibit many of the typical nonstandard features of written English, and students are asked to identify them. The added advantage of both new exercise types is that they are a comprehensive and prompt ongoing review of past material.

With the second edition, students also have the advantage of an extensive online Study Guide, which reviews basic concepts and provides a wide variety of practice exercises with answers for the material of each chapter. The Study Guide appears on Prentice Hall's companion website and provides automatic scoring of the exercises. It is also available for download for students who prefer a regular print format.

ACKNOWLEDGMENTS

I have referred to this book as "a conversation about English." More accurately, it is a contribution to a conversation that has been taking place for hundreds of years among grammarians, linguists, English teachers, dictionary makers, and self-appointed guardians of the English language. This larger conversation is not an orderly one. There are differences of opinion and differences of approach, some minor and some major. Nevertheless, this collective thinking about the English language provides a rich and lively context in which to do one's own exploration. I gratefully acknowledge the work of the many other language scholars whose work has helped to shape my thoughts about English grammar and usage.

As with any particular work, there are some individuals whose contributions stand out above the rest. I wish to thank the editors at Prentice Hall, especially Maggie Barbieri and Kim Gueterman, for their ongoing help and support throughout the preparation of the first edition and Craig Campanella and Terry Routley for their equally valuable support in the preparation of the second edition. I am also indebted to Joan Polk for her many kindnesses throughout the process. A special note of thanks goes to my colleague Jan Bernsten for her very helpful suggestions on the second edition drawn from her own experience in using the book. I am enormously grateful to the reviewers who forced me to clarify my thinking in more than a few places and who added a wealth of information and insight of their own: for the first edition, Nancy Hoar, Western New England College; Kitty Chen Dean, Nassau Community College; and Robin C. Barr, American University; for the second edition, Linda Callis Buckley, California State University, Sacramento; George Settera, California State University, Stanislaus; Lee Thomas, University of Nevada, Reno; Jerry Ball, Arkansas State University; Clifford Wood, Bridgewater State College. Many of the examples and observations in the book are theirs. An additional debt of gratitude is owed to my son, Michael Hochster, for his thoughtful reading of the original manuscript and extremely helpful commentary, especially on questions and negation. Also, I thank Bill Meyer, my husband, friend, and colleague, for his patient and engaged listening while I talked this book into being. I am grateful as well to Charles Baxter, who probably never imagined that people would be using his beautiful prose to hunt for participles. Thanks go also to Arleen Lieberman, perhaps the only person to have read the first edition without being asked to. Finally, no acknowledgments would be complete without recognizing one other group of participants in this conversation about English: the students of Linguistics 244 at the University of Michigan-Flint. For over two decades I have been inspired by their wisdom and good humor. It is with great pleasure that I write this book for them.

I learned from reviewer responses that instructors are using this book for a variety of purposes and a variety of audiences, and so not all of the excellent suggestions I received could be implemented in this revision. I hope that this second edition generally broadens the usefulness of the text and allows enough flexibility for instructors to adapt it to their particular needs and the needs of their students. I accept responsibility for all errors of fact and lapses of judgment in this new edition.

Anita K. Barry
The University of Michigan-Flint

ONE

WHY STUDY ENGLISH GRAMMAR?

NATIVE SPEAKERS AND GRAMMAR STUDY

If you are a native speaker of English, the study of English grammar is not the same for you as the study of Spanish or Japanese grammar, for example. You already know English, and you know it well. You can construct complex sentences, ask questions, give orders, request help or permission, transmit information, express your feelings, make suggestions, scold, promise, apologize, accuse, warn, or say anything else that you want to say without a moment's hesitation. At this point in your life, you can also read and write English, with an even broader range of structures and vocabulary with which to express yourself. So what is to be gained from studying English grammar? What is there to learn that you don't already know? What we learn in this book is that "knowing" a language can occur at several different levels. "Knowing" a language so that you can use it is not the same as "knowing" a language so that you can explain how it works. It is the purpose of this book to teach you how English works. Once you know that, you can explain it to others or use it as a way of understanding and evaluating your own writing or speech.

Another reason people sometimes give for studying the grammar of English is to find out what is "correct." Speakers of English are sensitive to the social judgments that accompany variations in structure, vocabulary, and pronunciation. We are aware that not everyone speaks the same way and, more importantly, we are acutely aware that some forms of English have higher social value than others and bring respect to their users. Linguistically speaking, no one form of English is better than another, but that does not change the social fact that some versions generally signal to us lower class and a lower level of education, while others signal higher class and a higher level of education. Thus it becomes important to all of us to understand how those judgments work and the social consequences of choosing one form of English over another. "Correct" versus "incorrect" English is much too simple a designation

1

for what is in fact a complicated array of behaviors and social judgments. The idea of "correctness" is one of the important themes of this book. It is an idea that defies definition and only becomes clear to us as we explore how English is used and received in a variety of contexts. So, if learning "good grammar" is your primary motivation for studying English grammar, you will need to have patience, because the answers will unfold gradually as our conversation about English progresses.

STANDARD ENGLISH

No one can study all facets of English at once, although they are all worthy of study: the richness of its variation; the complexity of its pronunciation, vocabulary, and sentence structure; its fascinating history; its spread around the world all offer amazing insights into how people have used English for centuries to communicate with one another, to judge others, to exercise power over others, and to express their innermost needs and feelings. In this book we focus our attention on what is known as **Standard American English.** It is that form of English that is expected in public discourse in the United States: in newspapers and magazines, in radio and television news broadcasts, in textbooks, and in public lectures. It is the form of English that is recognized as the English of the educated, irrespective of region, gender, or ethnicity. The written form of English does not vary as greatly as its spoken forms, even from country to country, so we can approach a universal description of the language by focusing primarily on its written form. As our discussion progresses, you will learn what constitutes Standard American English and how we determine whether a particular facet of English does or does not fall within this designation. Of course, we cannot explore these questions without also understanding something about the broader range of variation in English and the historical and social contexts in which it has developed and grown. English, like any language, is not merely a set of rules. It is the product of human behavior over many hundreds of years and will continue to evolve indefinitely into the future. The only reason we assign particular importance to modern Standard American English is that it is the form of English that has the most immediate consequences for us.

When we think about standard English, naturally we also think about nonstandard English. After all, if there were no variation in English, we wouldn't need to talk in terms of a "standard" at all. But all speakers of English recognize some forms of English as falling outside what we consider "correct" or "acceptable" or "normal" (although we may not always agree on just what those are). Sometimes we react to regional differences, which are largely differences in pronunciation and vocabulary. Some may think it curious that many speakers of English, including some New Yorkers and Bostonians, leave out *r*s when they speak, or that some southerners pronounce *pin* and *pen* alike. It may strike some of us as odd that people from other areas of the country pronounce *cot* and *caught* alike, or stress the first syllable of *insurance.* You might be surprised to discover that what you call a *frying pan* other people call a *spider,* or what you call a *faucet* is a *spigot* to others. We experience a range of reactions to these differences, but overall they tend to be relatively mild and nonjudgmental. Furthermore, they are not likely to show up in the written form of the language. New Yorkers may say what sounds like *bawn* or *bahn,* but they write "barn." We make harsher judgments about language differences that we associate with social class. Many of these (but not all) involve sentence structure and may show up in the written as well as the spoken form of the language. A person who says *I ain't got none* or *I already seen it* or *He done it hisself* may write those sentences that way as well. Whether spoken or written, utterances such as these trigger negative reactions from many people. Someone hearing such statements is likely to judge them as incorrect and associate them with lack of education and low social status. As we will see in our later discussions, it is largely historical accident that leads to one particular form of English being favored over another, and not any actual linguistic superiority. Nevertheless, however misguided these judgments may be, we cannot deny that they are widespread and can affect our lives in many ways. That is why we often experience a degree of linguistic insecurity and worry about whether some things we say are standard or nonstandard, correct or incorrect.

Interestingly, our reactions to nonstandard English are not always negative. In some cases, people hypercorrect—that is, in an attempt to avoid what they know to be a grammatical error, they overapply or misapply a rule. *Between you and I* is a common example of such **hypercorrection.** Hypercorrections tend to occur occasionally in otherwise standard usage, so they often go unnoticed or do not characterize a person's usage as uneducated. Furthermore, they tend to be used by people who, for reasons other than language, carry higher social status. Hypercorrections, although nonstandard, may even signal higher status, at least to those who are themselves unsure of the standard forms.

DISCUSSION EXERCISE 1.1

Each of the sentences below violates some rule of strictly formal Standard English. By the end of this book, you will understand what makes them nonstandard. For now, try to anticipate what your reactions might be to someone who said them. Would you have the same reaction in each case? Which make you think that the speaker lacks education? Do any sound fine to your ear? Do any make you think the speaker is well-educated? Why do you think your reactions might change from sentence to sentence even though they are all nonstandard? Do different people register different reactions to the same sentences?

Kathy and me arrived first.

I ain't seen 'em.

(continued)

(Whom) shall I say is calling? — *higher class / education*
It do<u>n</u>'t matter to me. — *lower class*
We been here a long time. — *LC*
That man was kind to my sister and I. — *higher class ed.*
                                        seems standard but ungrammat.
Someone left their umbrella here. — *seems standard*
We was right. — *LC*
If the weather was warmer, we could have a picnic. — *ingram, but widely used.*
They did it their<u>selves</u>. — *LC*
I'm right, aren't I? — *common*
That's me in the photograph. — *?*
Nobody gets nothing for free. — *LC*
She is smarter than him. — *seems standard but ingram.*

JUDGMENTS ABOUT ENGLISH

standard not always recognized

You might be surprised to learn that speakers of English did not always make such strong judgments about others' use of the language. Before the printing press was introduced into England, where English began, <u>there was no recognized standard</u>, nor was there any real need for one. Much of the important public writing was either in French or in Latin. <u>English was used primarily for oral and informal purposes and</u> varied quite a bit from place to place, with especially large differences between the north of England and the south. William Caxton, who introduced the printing press into England, noted in his writing in 1490:[1]

> And certainly our language now used varyeth ferre from that whiche was used and spoken whan I was borne. For we englysshe men ben borne under the domynacyon of the mone, whiche is never stedfaste, but ever waverynge, wexynge one season, and waneth & decreaseth another season. And that comyn englysshe that is spoken in one shyre varyeth from a nother.

When people did write English, they had no common spelling system, so the same word would be spelled different ways from one author to the next, and sometimes even in the work of one author. For example, in one fourteenth-century poem we see "English" spelled both "English" and "Englysch," both different from the spelling in the passage from Caxton's work.[2]

need for written standard arises

After 1476, the year the printing press was introduced into England, lack of a written standard became a practical concern. Now England had the technological capacity to spread the written language to large numbers of people throughout the country, but they could not count on a large reading audience unless there was a shared written language. What would that be? The natural choice for this standard was <u>the form of English used in Lon-</u>

don. In some ways, it represented a compromise between the north and the south, sharing some of the features of each. It also enjoyed prestige throughout England. London was a prosperous city and was generally recognized as a center of learning, with both Oxford and Cambridge Universities nearby. And so, by general consensus and without decree, London English became the model that others looked to for use as a formal standard. Of course, there were authors who used other varieties of English as well, and there was still a great deal of variation as writers and printers sorted out how they would represent English on paper.

What is not in evidence during this period of development of English is any sense of condemnation of those who did not use the standard. But with the coming of the eighteenth century, the Age of Reason, we see a dramatic shift in attitude among a small but influential group of writers and scholars. Believing that language ought to be unvarying and permanent, like Classical Latin and Greek (which were no longer spoken), and logical, they were appalled at what appeared to them as chaos in English. They thought it was wrong that people who spoke English invented new words and phrases, shortened others, borrowed words from other languages, allowed the meanings of words to change, and expressed the same grammatical idea in more than one way. For example, one source of concern to them was the fact that some people said *My brother is taller than I* while others said *My brother is taller than me.* They thought English should be "pure": without variation from one person to the next, without change over time, without irregularities, and without contamination from other languages. And they apparently believed that English *could* be pure, if not for the corrupting influence of the people who used (and abused) it. In their fervor, they sought to have an academy established in England, a governmental body that would officially regulate use of the language. Such academies were already in operation in other European countries, such as France and Italy. But the proposal, among whose greatest supporters was Jonathan Swift, the author of *Gulliver's Travels,* failed to gain the necessary support in the English parliament and eventually died.

The failure to establish an academy was a blow to its supporters, but rather than accept defeat, they responded with linguistic entrepreneurship. Individuals set out to write dictionaries and grammar books designed to achieve the same purposes. These publications, by setting down rules for the English language, would tell the English (and later the Americans) what was right and what was wrong once and for all. Among those early grammarians and dictionary makers (lexicographers) were Samuel Johnson, Robert Lowth, and Noah Webster. Noah Webster, of course, was most influential in establishing an American standard, which was somewhat different in detail from the British standard, and we still see his name associated with some of our current dictionaries.

It is interesting to consider how the eighteenth-century grammarians decided what the rules of English ought to be. Actual usage could not be their guide, since for them that was the source of the problem. They certainly were not to be swayed by the preferences of ordinary people using the language in ordinary ways. Believing that language systems were by nature logical, they relied on logic to help them make decisions among competing usages. Remember the example mentioned earlier: should we say *My brother is taller than I* or *My brother is taller than me*? In this case they reasoned that there was an implied continuation of a sentence that we do not actually say: *My brother is taller than ___ am tall.* Continuing the sentence in our heads would tell us that the correct choice is *I* rather than *me*.

In other cases they looked to Classical Latin and Greek as models for correct structure. These languages only existed in written form as of the eighteenth century. They were not used any longer by people for everyday conversation, and so they had the stability and uniformity that the English grammarians craved for English. What did they say about the choice between *This is her* and *This is she*? You might be able to guess if you knew Latin, which has a rule that says "after a copular verb use the nominative case." If you apply the rule to English, *This is she* becomes the correct choice.

The grammarians also based their judgments on English history. Since they viewed language change as the equivalent of language decay, they tended to assume that earlier forms and meanings were correct, while the more recent ones were wrong. For example, using the criterion of history, they declared that *demean* should mean "behave" (as it still does in *demeanor*), rather than its later meaning of "debase."

From this brief description, you can see that the foundations of English grammar were based on reasoning (often flawed) and on introspection, not on actual usage. What was current and popular was not necessarily considered correct by most grammarians. By the nineteenth century, views of grammar had begun to shift and more value was placed on usage and the collection of information about actual usage. The *Oxford English Dictionary*, for example, begun in 1879 and finally published in 1928, recorded the history of words based on their occurrence in writing over many centuries and gleaned the meanings of words from the contexts in which they were used.

Then in the twentieth century the developing field of linguistics clearly demonstrated that all languages change over time, that variation is natural and inevitable, and that all grammatical systems are equally capable of expressing whatever it is that people want or need to communicate. Language study began to incorporate the fundamental principle of linguistics that the structure of each language is to be described on its own terms and not forced into the mold of another language, such as Latin. The related field of sociolinguistics in particular recognizes the scholarly benefits of analyzing the grammars of different varieties of a language rather than trying to suppress them as inferior forms of the one designated as standard.

DISCUSSION EXERCISES 1.2

1. One of the better known grammar rules that emerged from the eighteenth-century deliberations on English is the rule about negatives: you may not have two negatives in the same sentence. Thus, although double negatives such as *I don't have no money* were common in earlier forms of English and occur in many other languages as well, they were banned from Standard English in the next century. Why do you think the grammarians frowned upon them? *redundancy? mathematical notion 2 neg = positive*

2. You will remember that the grammarians decided that *He is taller than I* is correct, while *He is taller than me* is not. Can you think of an equally plausible argument for choosing the second sentence as the correct one? *– usage/. comparison* *he likes it better than me*

3. Standard English grammar requires that we say *different from* and not *different than*. How do you think grammarians arrived at this conclusion? (Hint: think of the verb *differ*.) *–* *similar examples using comparatives*

4. What do you think eighteenth-century grammarians might have said about Shakespeare's *most unkindest cut of all*? *– two superlatives are redundant as double negatives*

THE LEGACY OF THE EIGHTEENTH CENTURY

Although in more recent centuries language scholars have recognized the realities of language usage, we are still left with some of the attitudes about English that dominated the thinking of the eighteenth-century grammarians. We still assign particular value to standard English and see it as better than other varieties of English. We devote a considerable portion of our educational resources to teaching people how to read and write it. We regard knowledge of it as a prerequisite to many professions and question the abilities of people who have not mastered it. As a society, we are not especially accepting of variation in usage and tend to assume that one way is the "right" way while the others are "wrong." How many times have you asked yourself questions like: which is right, *This is the man who I met* or *This is the man whom I met*? It is rare for someone to assume that they are both right. We voice similar questions about pronunciation. Which is it, *harássment* or *hárassment*? To reinforce this notion of "one right answer," we have the writings of grammatical purists, such as John Simon and Edwin Newman, authors of best-selling books telling us grammatical right from wrong.[3]

We also tend to assume that somewhere "out there" lie the answers to all our questions, just as the eighteenth-century grammarians assumed that all grammatical differences could be explained away by some principle of logic or an appeal to an older language. It is just a matter of finding the answer that we need. Sometimes we will consult someone whom we view as an authority on the language (an English teacher, for example) or enroll in a course in English grammar. In other cases we may consult a grammar book in the library or even look something up in the dictionary. As we will see in the next chapter and all the chapters after that, getting satisfying answers to our grammar questions is never that simple because English is not Classical Latin or Greek; rather, it is a dynamic, living language, and the creation of the many millions of people who use it.

Before we turn to questions about how we study grammar, we might ask one more question about English usage. If, as a society, we generally recognize that standard English is highly valued by us, why doesn't everyone speak it and write it? In other words, why does variation in English persist? As you might guess, this too is a complex question with no easy answer. But we can suggest some ways of approaching an answer. In some cases, people are simply not presented with a ready model of standard English and might not be fully aware of the extent to which it is valued, or if they do know, they might not have enough exposure to it to model their own language after it. In other cases, people might recognize that other people use standard English but might not see it as appropriate to their own circumstances. For many, standard English carries with it an aura of formality, even stiffness, that makes it inappropriate in intimate or casual settings or in some work settings. In those instances, the less formal nonstandard variety is more valued and signals a person as part of the group, an insider. Think about the lyrics of popular songs, for example. How often do you hear *ain't* or double negatives? Often people need to choose between grammatical correctness and appropriateness. If you see your best friend lingering after class, would you ask *For whom are you waiting*? or *Who are you waiting for*? (Ignore the question if your best friend is a grammatical purist.) Like forms of dress, different forms of English are appropriate for different circumstances.

In the next chapter we will talk about how we approach the study of English. Our goal is to focus our sights so that we come away with a coherent picture of how the language works despite the complexity that naturally accompanies any discussion of human behavior.

REFLECTIONS

1. One eighteenth-century grammarian defines grammar as "the art of speaking and writing any language with propriety. An art is a rational method, a system of rules, digested into convenient order, for the teaching and learning of something." Is this how you would define grammar? Is this how you would define an art?

2. Show the sentences of Discussion Exercise 1.1 to several different people whose grammar usage you respect. Ask them to tell you which are not standard English. Did you get some disagreement among them? Did anyone say they are *all* not standard English? Why do you think there are differences of opinion about these sentences (assuming that there are) even among speakers of standard English? (A word of caution: educated people can be *very* touchy about grammar!)

3. Can you think of a situation in which you had a grammar disagreement with someone? How did you resolve it?

4. The French academy periodically tries to purge French of its English borrowings, such as *le weekend*. How successful do you think it has been in keeping French "pure"?

NOTES

1. From Caxton's preface to his *Eneydos*, as quoted in A. C. Baugh and T. Cable, *A History of the English Language*, 4th ed. (Englewood Cliffs, NJ: Prentice Hall, 1993, p. 191). Here is a translation:

> And certainly our language now used varies far from that which was used and spoken when I was born. For we Englishmen are born under the domination of the moon, which is never steadfast, but ever wavering, waxing one season, and wanes and decreases another season. And that common English that is spoken in one shire varies from another.

2. William of Nassyngton's *Speculum Vitae* or *Mirror of Life* (c. 1325) as quoted in Baugh and Cable, p. 141.

3. See, for example, Edwin Newman's *Strictly Speaking* or *A Civil Tongue;* or John Simon's *Paradigms Lost*.

TWO

HOW DO WE STUDY ENGLISH GRAMMAR?

WHY DO PEOPLE DISAGREE ABOUT GRAMMAR?

Who Is the Authority?

In the preceding chapter we discussed how many of our rules of English grammar were handed down to us from the eighteenth-century grammarians, who based their decisions about right and wrong largely on logic, history, or comparison to Classical Latin and Greek. For some people today, those rules are the final word about correct English. But most of us do not rely heavily on books that were written two hundred years ago to tell us about English today. Rather, we take a more practical view of language use and look for cues in our contemporary lives to guide us in the use of standard English. We look for models of what we regard as standard usage, and we consult contemporary sources, including teachers, editors, dictionaries, and grammar handbooks. But we still find that getting answers is not so easy as it might seem at first. If we had an academy, perhaps the problem would be less troublesome. At least there would be a unique authority that everyone could consult, and differences of usage and opinions about usage might be resolved in a fixed and predictable way. But we do not have an academy, nor do we have any other special authority recognized by everyone as the last word on English usage. Instead, we have lots of different sources, and by *sources,* we mean real people who are faced with decisions just as the eighteenth-century grammarians were.

What Role Do Dictionaries Play?

Let's take a closer look, for example, at the task of publishing a dictionary of English. Suppose you decided to publish one. How would you decide what meanings and pronunciations of words to include? Would you rely on older uses? Would you rely on the judgments of a few well-educated and influential scholars? Would you try to sample a wide range of people in different walks of life and list the most common usage? Would you rely only on written documents as sources of information? There are no right answers to these questions and, in fact, different dictionary makers have different answers to them, so that dictionaries themselves may differ in their purposes and their methods of making decisions. *Webster's Third New International Dictionary*, for example, attempts to reflect actual usage in neutral, descriptive terms, omitting designations such as *illiterate*. These values are articulated in the preface to the dictionary. In the words of the editor-in-chief, Philip Gove

> Accuracy in addition to requiring freedom from error and conformity to truth requires a dictionary to state meanings in which words are in fact used, not to give editorial opinion on what their meanings should be.[1]

About pronunciation, he says

> This edition shows as far as possible the pronunciations prevailing in general cultivated conversational usage, both informal and formal, throughout the English-speaking world. It does not attempt to dictate what that usage should be.[2]

Another widely used dictionary, *The American Heritage Dictionary of the English Language*, Third Edition, leans more toward representing educated speech only and relies on the judgments of a usage panel made up of writers, editors, and scholars, including professors of English and linguistics, and others who "occupy distinguished positions in law, diplomacy, government, business, science and technology, medicine, and the arts."[3]

Suppose you wanted to check the status of the word *ain't*. *Webster's Third International* tells us

> though disapproved by many and more common in less educated speech, used orally in most parts of the U.S. by many cultivated speakers esp. in the phrase *ain't I*." (p. 45)

The American Heritage Dictionary, on the other hand, says

> The use of *ain't* . . . has a long history, but *ain't* has come to be regarded as a mark of illiteracy and has by now acquired such a stigma that it is beyond any possibility of rehabilitation. (p. 37, 3rd ed.)

If you want to use a dictionary as a guide to your own usage of *ain't*, or as a means of judging the usage of others, then you will have to decide which of these accounts to rely on. And, of course, there are other dictionaries on the market as well, each with its own approach to representing English. A recent addition to the market is the *Encarta World English Dictionary*, associated with the Microsoft Corporation. Reflecting current technology, the editors gathered their data via e-mail from consultants in twenty countries. Among the words it defines are *nose stud* and *yadda yadda yadda;* it labels some words, such as *butch,* as offensive without defining them at all. As discouraging as it might be to those of us who want definitive answers, the reality is that there is no unique authority on our language, and looking up a word in "the dictionary" is a comfortable fiction. In reality, we are looking up a word in "a dictionary."

▄▐█▐█▐█▐█▐█

DISCUSSION EXERCISES 2.1

1. Before 1961, Webster's dictionaries were more prescriptive in their approach to English usage, that is, more inclined to dictate correct usage. When the *Third International* announced its new policies in 1961, many people reacted with outrage. What do you think prompted this reaction? What do you think your own reaction might have been?

2. Which is standard English, *He has swam a mile* or *He has swum a mile?* What do you think the difference is in the way *Webster's* and *American Heritage* convey information about their use?

3. The *Encarta Dictionary* has been criticized by other dictionary makers for labeling words as offensive but not defining them. Do you agree with this practice?

Why Is There No One Standard?

Another reason we have difficulty fixing on just one "correct" English is that modern English is spoken all over the world by hundreds of millions of people, and so perceptions of correctness will vary, even among the most educated and influential. As English spreads, it develops different standards. As we noted in the first chapter, Noah Webster succeeded in distinguishing an American standard from a British standard, an important step in the development of an American national identity. So now we recognize that there may be two acceptable ways to spell a word—*check* or *cheque, center* or *centre,* for example. Similarly, there are two standard pronunciations for some words, such as *schedule* and *lieutenant.* Or it might be equally correct to say *the team is playing* (American English) or *the team are playing* (British English). British and American English are the two most influential standards around the world, but we must remember that each English-speaking country develops its own, so we should expect to find standard forms of English specific to Canada, Australia, and New Zealand. English is now also used as one of the major languages in many countries of Africa and Asia and is developing standards specific to those areas as well. What was originally a language spoken by a few million people on one small island in Europe has now become a world language with many different varieties and with identities separate from either British or American English.

Why Do Languages Change?

To complicate the picture still further, we have to keep in mind that languages change over time, and along with changes in language come changes in judgments about language. That is, "correct English" is a moving target. What was considered correct a hundred years ago is not necessarily what is considered correct today. The eighteenth-century grammarians argued that English could *I views* be perfect and permanent if not for the laziness and carelessness of its users. *of* For them, change was the equivalent of language decay. But modern linguists *change* argue that change is inherent to all languages; without the flexibility to change, languages would not be able to serve the continuously evolving needs of the people who use them. If English had not been able to change, you would not have the words to talk about your hard drive or your floppy disk or even your carburetor! Language users are receptive to the enrichment of added vocabulary, while they shed words that are no longer of use to them. When was the last time you heard someone talk about their *trousers* or *breeches* or their *icebox* and *phonograph*? Do you still sit on a *davenport* or keep your clothes in a *bureau*?

In addition to shifts in vocabulary, there is an even more important facet of language change that we are all particularly sensitive to, and that is changes in our grammatical system. Grammatical systems are based on rules, or patterns. As people learn their language as children, they learn these patterns. For example, children learning English figure out that to make a noun plural, you have to add the suffix -*s,* or to express a past action, you must add the suffix -*ed* to a verb. But it is also true that there are exceptions to these patterns, sometimes because words remain unchanged from earlier times, when other patterns held, or sometimes because we borrow words into English from languages with different patterns. So, for example, *boy* fits the regular pattern for noun plurals (*boys*), while *man* and *crisis* do not (*men*, not *mans* and *crises,* not *crisises*). *Talk* fits the regular pattern for the past tense (*talked*), but *buy* does not (*bought,* not *buyed*). Unlike words that fit the regular patterns, exceptions are hard to learn. We have to learn them one by one and we have to remember each one separately. We need to hear them frequently for the irregularity to become fixed in our memories. When we look at how English has evolved since its beginnings, we see that collectively in our use of the language we strive to eliminate the irregularities by changing them to fit the normal pattern. If you look at earlier forms of English, you will find that *shoes,* for example, used to be *shoon,* and *eyes* used to be *eyen; climbed* used to be *clomb,* and *helped* used to be *holp.* Although no one person decides to make a change, together over the years we have changed English a great deal, so that many more nouns and verbs now fit the regular pattern. What this tells us is that language users can detect patterns easily and, from a broad historical perspective, prefer to have words fall within the patterns rather than outside them.

Clearly then, some words that are considered standard at some point in the history of English will drop out and be replaced by their regularized counterparts. Most of us can accept that without difficulty; we don't expect even the most educated among us to sound like Chaucer or Shakespeare. But what some of us find hard to accept is that English continues to change. It is a dynamic, living system forever being shaped by the people who use it. The preference for regularity is no less compelling now than it was two hundred or more years ago, and people's linguistic behavior is no different from the way it has always been. Nevertheless, it is one thing to observe language change from a comfortable distance; it is quite another to experience it yourself. The first is often an interesting academic exercise, while the second can be disconcerting or even disturbing. Consider, for example, your reaction to someone who says *I knowed it.* Intellectually, we can register this as merely another example of regularization of the past tense. At the same time, for many of us it also signals lack of education. But as we know from observing the history of English, many regularized forms do take hold over time and come to be regarded as standard and educated.

How does that transition take place? How do we know when a newer form has replaced an older form? How do we know when it is no longer a stigma to use the newer form? Where's that academy when we need it? This is the source of grammar anxiety for many speakers of English. When a newer form is replacing an older form, they may both be used for a long time. It is only gradually that the older one will drop out. Meanwhile, we hear both being used. The ghosts of the eighteenth-century grammarians whisper to us that if there are two forms, one must be wrong. Our own experience tells us that regularized forms are stigmatized when they are first introduced. So we want to know when a word has achieved acceptability. (This could apply to grammatical constructions as well, as we will see later in the book.) But only our collective judgment determines that, so individually we often cannot get the immediate answers we seek. Should we say *dreamt* or *dreamed, lit* or *lighted, I have proven the theorem* or *I have proved the theorem?*

WHAT ARE THE COMMON ELEMENTS OF ENGLISH?

When we study the grammar of English, we have to take all of this into account: the absence of a unique authority, the variety of standards that exist around the world today, and the fact that English is continuously evolving and so are judgments about usage. This makes the study of English grammar an exciting challenge, but not impossible. As we said in Chapter 1, we need to focus our efforts so that we aren't trying to do everything at once. In this book, we focus on standard American English. Even that, as we now know, is no simple exercise. We have to be flexible in our approach, attentive to the fact that we are talking about real people and not abstractions, and accepting of the idea that the answers to our questions may come in the form of thoughtful discussion rather than labels of "correct" and "incorrect."

Most importantly, however, we need to recognize that for all its variation and for all the indeterminacy in defining it, English is still English. People who speak it in all its varieties can understand one another, more or less, and share the same written language. English, like all languages, must meet the communication needs of the people who use it. That means no matter what variety of English we speak it at least must allow us to identify and make reference to things, to people, and to ideas. It must be able to describe actions and tell when they happened. It must allow us to give descriptions of things, people, and ideas. It must allow us to give information and to get information; to give orders; to express our feelings; to indicate relationships among things, people, and ideas; and to combine simpler ideas into more complex ideas. All forms of English meet these expectations and do so in similar ways. The rest of this book will concentrate on the common elements, using standard American English as the focus of attention and the basis for comparison to other varieties.

Constituent Structure — *common to all forms of Eng.*

One feature common to all forms of English is that they have *constituent structure*. When we hear English, it seems to us that words just come out one after the other, like beads on a string. But, as we will see when we begin to examine the language, sentences are organized so that some elements bear a special relationship to each other that excludes others. For example, if you look at the sentence in (1) you will see that it consists of ten words.

(1) The excited child chased the new puppy around the garden.

But you will notice that some of these words seem to group together and may stand alone in conversation as an answer to a question about this event. For example

> Who did it? *the excited child*
> What did she chase? *the new puppy*
> Where? *around the garden*
> Around where? *the garden*
> Did what? *chased the new puppy around the garden*

If you were asked to draw lines separating the parts of the sentence, you would probably insert them after *child, puppy,* and *garden.* Our mind simply tells us that certain words group together. Notice that there are other words that appear in sequence also, but they do not constitute a grouping. There is no question that could be answered *child chased the* or *excited puppy around.* Nor would we separate off those words together as groupings according to our intuitions. The groupings that hold together are called **constituents.** Constituents can be very short, like *rice* in sentence (2) or very long, like *because she knew that her life would be in danger if she revealed her sources to the FBI* in sentence (3).

(2) *Rice* is high in carbohydrates.
(3) The reporter refused to speak *because she knew that her life would be in danger if she revealed her sources to the FBI.*

Furthermore, you have already seen in sentence (1) that constituents can nest inside other constituents. In other words, constituents are arranged hierarchically as well as linearly. For example, the constituent we have identified in (3) contains constituents within it: *her life, in danger, her sources, to the FBI.* And *to the FBI* itself contains the constituent *the FBI.*

DISCUSSION EXERCISES 2.2

1. Identify some constituents in each of the following sentences. Judge what feels like a group to you and then see whether it could stand alone as an answer to a question in a conversation. Remember that constituents can nest inside larger ones.

   The bored students ignored the teacher's questions.
   She sobbed uncontrollably when the jury announced the verdict.
   The fact that the speaker showed up late annoyed many members of the club.
   Skiing in the Alps is my favorite vacation.
   The baby crawled into the closet and fell asleep.

2. We might show how one constituent is included within another by using brackets, as in the following: [to[the FBI]]. Place brackets around the constituents of *the man in the white coat.*

Constituents, or groupings, occur at many different levels of English, from the lowest level of the **root** and the **affix,** to the **word,** the **phrase,** the **clause,** and the **sentence.** In this book we will work our way from the lowest to the highest constituents. *Roots* and *affixes* (the more general term for prefixes and suffixes) are the components of words. For example, the word *cats* consists of the root *cat* and the suffix *-s;* the word *talked* consists of the root *talk* and the suffix *-ed; redo* consists of the root *do* and the prefix *re-.* Affixes are of two types: **inflectional** and **derivational.** *Inflectional affixes* express some grammatical information, like plural, or past tense, and do not change the basic category of the root. English has a small number of these and, when they occur, they help us to identify the category of the root. We know *talked* is a verb, for example, because it has the inflectional affix *-ed,* which gets attached only to verb roots, either as a past tense (*we talked yesterday*) or as a past participle (*we have talked often*). *Derivational affixes,* on the other hand, usually change one category into another. *Educate* is a verb; if I add the suffix *-tion,* it turns into the noun *education.* The suffix *-tion* is an example of a derivational affix in English and, as you might guess, there are many more derivational than inflectional affixes.

DISCUSSION EXERCISES 2.3

1. All the inflectional affixes in English are suffixes. The most common ones signal

   the plural *-s*
   the possessive *-s*
   the third person singular present tense *-s*
   the past tense *-ed*
   the past participle *-ed*
   the present participle *-ing*
   the comparative *-er*
   the superlative *-est*

   You might not be familiar with all this terminology yet, but try to pick out one example of each of these in the following sentence:

   > The man's son decided that he was leaving home because he had wasted all his time shoveling sidewalks and now he wants to live in a warmer climate where the lowest temperature is 50°.

2. All affixes that aren't inflectional are derivational. English has many derivational prefixes and suffixes. For each one given, list several more words that use the same affix. Notice that the suffixes typically change the grammatical category of the word, while the prefixes do not. Instead, they alter the meaning of the root.

*un*happy	govern*ment*	*membership*
*dis*connect	seren*ity*	
*re*read	equal*ize*	

The next level of grammatical structure, as we have already implied, is the *word,* the result of putting roots and affixes together. Some words are just roots; others are combinations of roots and affixes. Words fall into different categories depending on their meanings, their functions, and the kinds of affixes they have. We sometimes refer to these categories as **lexical categories, word-classes,** or **parts of speech.** They have names that are familiar to most people: *noun, verb, adjective, adverb, pronoun, preposition, conjunction,* and *article* are some of the most common. Many of these word classes also have subcategories. You probably know the difference between a *common* noun like *boy* and a *proper* noun like *Bill.* You might also know the distinction between a *transitive* verb like *buy* and an *intransitive* verb like *laugh.* Do you know the difference between a relative and a reflexive pronoun? A gradable or nongradable adjective? If not, you soon will.

✳ Words group together at the level of the **phrase.** A phrase has one part of speech at its core, called the **head** of the phrase. It gives the phrase its name, such as *noun phrase* or *verb phrase*. The phrase also includes all the other things that go with the head to form a group. These additional elements are called **modifiers.** If you look again at sentence (1) shown previously, you will see that all the constituents we identified happened to be phrases.

DISCUSSION EXERCISES 2.4

Look again at sentence (1): The excited child chased the new puppy around the garden.

1. Find

    three noun phrases
    one prepositional phrase
    one verb phrase

2. What are the head and modifiers of each phrase you identified?

Phrases may occur together to make larger groupings, of course. The combination of a noun phrase followed by a verb phrase has special status: it is called a *clause.* The noun phrase and the verb phrase of the clause are also referred to as the **subject** and the **predicate** of the clause. Some clauses can stand all by themselves and are called **independent clauses;** others must attach to another clause and are called **dependent clauses.** Clauses may then combine into a larger constituent called a *sentence.*

All forms of English operate at all of these levels simultaneously, which sometimes makes it difficult to talk about one level without talking about the others. The following diagram may help you to visualize the hierarchical structure of English that we have just described.

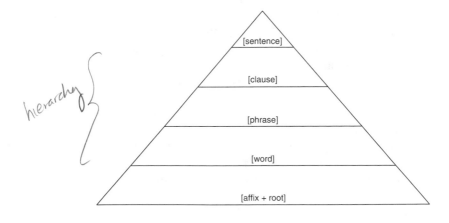

Rules and Regularities

Also common to all forms of English are rules that express patterns in the language. Rules may vary somewhat from one variety of English to the next, but most of them are the same, which is what gives the language its continuity. One kind of rule expresses the linear order in which elements must occur within their constituents. An example of such a rule is: "adjectives precede the nouns *ex* they modify." We all know that no one would say *I caught the ball red*, for example. We take that for granted, but we must keep in mind that this rule is one of the things that makes English different from, say, Spanish or French. Another kind of rule in English grammar expresses what elements can occupy the same constituent, that is, what elements are allowed to group together. Shared knowledge of the rules of acceptable grouping is what allows us to make the same judgments about what does and does not make up a constituent. Finally, there are rules for English that express relationships between elements, sometimes within one constituent, sometimes across constituents. We call these **cross-referencing** rules. One such cross-referencing rule for English is: "pronouns must agree in gender and number with their antecedents." You may not be familiar with the terminology, but if someone says *the girls hurt himself,* you know something is wrong!

① ③ ③

DISCUSSION EXERCISE 2.5   *→ the 3 rules*

What type of rule is each of the following: linear order, grouping, or cross-referencing? Can you translate them into ordinary English by explaining what we *don't* say?

Verbs agree with their subjects in person and number. *CR*
Single-word modifiers precede the head noun in a noun phrase. *LO*
Transitive verbs require an object noun phrase. *(G)*
Prepositional phrases are made up of a preposition and a noun phrase. *LO*

---

exceptions

English also has exceptions to its rules. There are parts of English that do not conform to regular patterns and do not lend themselves to generalization. We have already seen some examples of those: nouns that do not add the suffix -*s* to form the plural, verbs that do not add the suffix -*ed* to form the past tense. As we said earlier, sometimes these irregularities are holdovers from older patterns, and sometimes they are borrowed from other languages. They tend to be the least stable part of the language because people prefer regularity in their grammatical systems. They are the most interesting part of the language as well, because individuals approach the problems they present in different ways, giving rise to variation in usage.

In the chapters to come, we will embark on a careful examination of English, from the lowest to the highest levels of grammatical organization. We will talk about the categories that make up each level and describe the rules for organizing them into acceptable patterns. We will also talk about the people behind the rules: how do we react to the irregularities in our grammatical system? what happens when standard English is inefficient or doesn't allow us to express what we need to express? Observing people's language behavior gives us insight into how people organize a complex system of information in their minds and apply it in their everyday lives to communicate with others.

DISCUSSION EXERCISE 2.6

You have just been presented with much of the grammatical terminology that we will use to describe English in the rest of this book. At this point, it is certainly not expected that you will understand exactly what each means nor how it is applied in grammatical description. But we can use these terms for a "warm-up." As native speakers of English, we all have intuitions about the structure of the language. We know what sounds right or complete; we know what makes sense and what doesn't. What we need to begin to do now, as students of grammar, is couch our descriptions in grammatical rather than subjective terms. Imagine, for example, that someone who doesn't know English very well has made the following statements. Describe what is non-English about these, using as much as possible the grammatical terminology we have introduced and avoiding impressionistic judgments like "it just sounds funny."

What your name is? *violates linear order rule*

The Mr. Smith wrote this letter. *violates grouping rule*

My friend taked the train to work. *Irregular verb*

These book is difficult. *violates crossreferencing rule - # agr.*

They laughed the girl. *violates grouping rule - prep phr.*

? — When I get to school.

Little boy caught ball. *linear ord / missing article*

— The woman in the courtyard.

This is the most biggest package.

He a hat bought. *linear order*

REFLECTIONS

1. If you would like to know more about dictionaries and dictionary-making, here are some suggested readings:

Bryson, Bill, "Order Out of Chaos," *About Language: A Reader for Writers,* 3rd ed., William H. Roberts and Gregoire Turgeon, eds. Houghton Mifflin (1992), pp. 184–196.

Gove, Philip B., "The Dictionary's Function," in *Dartmouth Alumni Magazine* (May 1962 pp. 10–11). Reprinted in *Focusing on Language: A Reader,* Harold B. Allen, Enola Borgh, and Verna L. Newsome, eds. Thomas Y. Crowell (1975), pp. 239–244.

Marquardt, Albert H., "The New Webster Dictionary: A Critical Appraisal," in *Readings in Applied Linguistics,* 3rd ed., Harold B. Allen and Michael D. Linn, eds. Alfred A. Knopf (1964). Reprinted in *About Language: A Reader for Writers,* William H. Roberts and Gregoire Turgeon, eds. Houghton Mifflin (1986), pp. 127–139.

Soukhanov, Anne H., "Welcome to the Web of Words: The Lexicographer's Role in Observing and Recording the Changing Language," in *About Language: A Reader for Writers,* 2nd ed., William H. Roberts and Gregoire Turgeon, eds. Houghton Mifflin (1989), pp. 121–133.

2. What do you think people generally see as the purpose of a dictionary? Ask five or six people. Are their responses all the same?

3. One response to the lack of a unique authority has been the emergence of various public forums through which people can exchange ideas about grammatical correctness. Sometimes people write to general advice columnists with their grammatical complaints, where they may get sympathy in place of linguistic enlightenment. For example, in response to a reader who complains about the rampant misuse of the apostrophe in current English spelling, Ann Landers says, "You are a 'purist,' a dying breed, and I share your pain." (The *Flint Journal,* February 14, 2000). Other sources that respond more directly to grammar issues are the bimonthly feature of the *Atlantic Monthly* called "Word Court," edited by Barbara Wallraff, and the online newsletter *TipWorld* (http://www.tipworld.com), which has a section on Grammar and Usage. These resources offer the public an opportunity to become active participants in a conversation about their language. If you have an unresolved grammar question, you might want to send it to one of these sources.

4. If your child said *I gived it to her* would you offer a correction? What about if your child said *I dreamed I was a clown?* Do you give different feedback on *gived* and *dreamed?* If you do, what does that tell you about how the next generation of English speakers will view these two past tense verbs?

5. The verb *be* is highly irregular, yet it isn't particularly susceptible to regularization. Why do you think this is so?

6. Occasionally a regular verb becomes irregular. For example, it is thought that *dived* preceded *dove* and *pleaded* preceded *pled.* What explanation can you give for these occasional irregularizations?

NOTES

1. *Webster's Third New International Dictionary* (unabridged) (Springfield, MA: Merriam Webster 1986), p. 4a.

2. Ibid.

3. *The American Heritage Dictionary of the English Language,* 3rd ed. (Boston: Houghton Mifflin 1992), p. vi.

THREE

NOUNS AND NOUN PHRASES

WHAT ARE NOUNS?

We will begin our discussion of English grammar with a close look at the lexical category **noun.** As with all other parts of speech, we will fold together our discussion of the two lowest levels of grammatical structure and discuss roots and affixes as part of our discussion of the word. Most of us recognize nouns by the traditional definition of their function: they name a person, place, thing, or idea. This is a reasonably useful definition, but it is not always sufficient to help us distinguish a noun from other parts of speech. It is additionally helpful to keep in mind that nouns have two inflectional markings: they are marked for **number** and **possession.**

inflectis marking →

When we talk about the number of a noun, we mean that it is either singular (one) or plural (more than one). Singular nouns in English have no special marking, but plural nouns are typically marked with the inflectional suffix -*s* (or -*es*): *pencils, jars, glasses.* We know, of course, that not every noun fits this pattern. There is a group of nouns that changes the vowel sound of the root to make the plural: *foot-feet, mouse-mice, woman-women.* Other irregular plurals do not fit any pattern, such as *oxen, children, deer.* All of these are holdovers from earlier forms of English that we now learn one by one. Another important category of irregular plurals contains those borrowed from other languages. Most of them are taken from Latin or Greek and tend to be more formal and less common than the Old English holdovers, such as *alumnus-alumni, criterion-criteria, phenomenon-phenomena, formula-formulae.* You are probably thinking that not everyone uses such singular and plural forms exactly the way we have described them. There is a lot of evidence that people are trying to bring them into the fold of the regular noun pattern. *Formulas* is fully standard and exists side-by-side with *formulae. Syllabuses* and *hippopotamuses* are already within the range of acceptability for most people. Others speak of *one criteria* and *one phe-*

nomena. These are not considered to be standard English, but they are very common and they are showing up more and more often in respectable written sources such as newspapers and textbooks. (See Reflections 12.) If we say *one umbrella* and *one sofa,* why not *one criteria?* It is certainly likely that they will one day be considered the standard singulars, and when they are, *criterias* and *phenomenas* will probably follow. Meanwhile, if we want to stay within fully acceptable standard English, we need to overcome our instincts to think of them as singulars when we say them.

DISCUSSION EXERCISES 3.1

1. *Agenda* and *media* are historically plural forms, with singulars *agendum* and *medium.* What is the evidence that the plural forms have become accepted as singulars? *agendas + Medias used*

2. The plural of *fish* is historically *fish,* yet the regularized plural *fishes* has come into usage in recent times. Some people assign different meanings to the two plural forms: do you know what those two meanings are?

3. The use of *alumnus-alumni* has one other interesting complication. The words are derived from the Latin word meaning "student," and in Latin referred to male students. The corresponding female forms were *alumna* and *alumnae.* Would you object to naming the magazine for graduates of your college *The Alumnus?* That objection has been raised about the University of Michigan's *Michigan Alumnus.*

4. Why do you think the irregular plural *feet* has been more resistant to change than the irregular plural *syllabi?*

The other inflectional affix associated with nouns is the possessive. It also adds the suffix -*s,* separated from the noun root in writing with an apostrophe: *boy's, cat's, judge's.* Unlike the plural, the possessive form of nouns is completely regular. Even if the plural of the noun is irregular, its possessive fits the regular pattern: *men* for plural, but *man's* for possessive, for example. That is why we never hear any fluctuation in the use of the possessives and also why they are not very interesting as a subject of conversation. We do need to remember certain rules of spelling for possessives, and we must also keep in mind that the possessive and the plural can occur together in one word. Although there is some variation from one handbook to another, the general spelling rule is that we add -*'s* to make a noun possessive, regardless of whether it is singular or plural: *car's, man's, men's, children's, Charles's.* But if the plural noun ends in *-s,* you simply add an apostrophe to make it possessive: *the Smiths' garage, the boys' uniforms.*

In addition to these telltale inflectional suffixes, nouns in English may also be marked by certain derivational suffixes, that is, suffixes that turn a root into a noun. Some common examples are *-er,* as in *dancer, singer, printer; -ment,* as in *government, filament, sediment* (notice that the noun root isn't always capable of standing on its own); *-ion,* as in *election.* Inflectional suffixes can occur together with the derivational ones and always appear at the end of the word: *dancers, dancer's, dancers'.*

[handwritten left margin: derivational suffixes]

DISCUSSION EXERCISES 3.2

[handwritten: sincerity, action, fearless]

1. Give some other derivational suffixes that turn roots into nouns.

2. Which of the following words are nouns? *visualize, national, realization, sincerity, fruity, engineer, dentist, happy, fearless, fearlessness, truthful, occurrence*

3. Some noun roots can add derivational suffixes that do not change the part of speech. That is, the resulting word is still a noun, but with a somewhat altered meaning. What alteration in meaning is made by the suffix *-ette,* as in *kitchenette* and *cigarette?* What about the suffix *-ess,* as in *princess* and *actress?* *[handwritten: → small]* *[handwritten: → fem.]*

WHAT ARE SOME COMMON SUBCATEGORIES OF NOUNS?

We can use the various criteria we have already mentioned as guidelines for identifying a noun as distinct from some other part of speech, but we also know that the criteria do not constitute an absolute definition that we can apply to any noun. Nouns fall into subcategories with their own special characteristics and do not all fit exactly the same mold. For example, we are familiar with the distinction between **common nouns** and **proper nouns.** Common nouns are written with lower case letters and refer to general categories: *girl, teacher, ball.* Proper nouns begin with capital letters and designate a specific noun: *Mary, California, Fifth Avenue.* There are many differences in how these two subclasses of nouns behave, but an obvious one is that common nouns occur often in their plural forms, while the use of the plural for proper nouns is highly restricted. Other subclasses of nouns are **concrete nouns** and **abstract nouns.** Concrete nouns are the ones we can visualize: *table, chair, flag, hairdresser.* Abstract ones are usually ideas or concepts with no clear visual image associated with them: *sincerity, construction, foolhardiness.* Again, the concrete nouns are more typical, in that they can be plural or possessive, and the abstract nouns are more limited in that respect. Nouns can also be divided into subclasses of **animate nouns** and **inanimate nouns.** Humans and animals fall into the first subcategory, while things fall into the second. Within the category of animate, we further divide nouns into **human nouns** and **nonhuman nouns.** It may be useful to know this terminology when talking about the different kinds of nouns, but for the most part the difference in the behavior of these subcategories is based on meaning, so we have no trouble using them appropriately. For example, we wouldn't ordinarily have occasion to say "the rock smiled," and if we did, it would be recognized as a metaphorical use of language. Sometimes, though, certain grammatical choices depend on which subcategory a noun belongs to; if a noun is human, we refer to it as *he* or *she;* if it is nonhuman or inanimate, we refer to it as *it.* If we hear a noise and think a human is making it, we ask *who is making that noise?* If we think it is nonhuman, or inanimate, we ask *what is making that noise?*

DISCUSSION EXERCISES 3.3

1. Suppose your neighbors arrive with their brand new baby wrapped in a yellow blanket. What difficulty might you have, grammatically speaking, finding out from them the baby's name or age?
2. Can you think of any circumstances in which people treat inanimate nouns as if they were grammatically human? Why do you think they do that?
3. How do you treat your family pet grammatically, as human or nonhuman? Do you differentiate grammatically between animals in your home and those in the zoo or the jungle? What about insects?

An especially good example of subcategories, or subclasses, of nouns that have grammatical consequences are **count nouns** and **noncount nouns** (or **mass nouns**). Let's compare the noun *bean* to the noun *rice.* There are similarities in the things they refer to: both are foods, and both occur in small, cylindrical pellets. Yet grammatically, we don't treat them alike at all. Suppose you want to count beans. One bean, two beans, three beans. . . . But if you want to count rice, you can't do it directly. You must provide some linguistic boundary for rice, like *grain* or *piece.* Then you can count one grain of rice, two grains of rice. . . . Or you can put the rice in something and count that: one cup of rice, two cups of rice. . . . That is why we call *bean* a count noun and *rice* a noncount noun. What are the other differences between count and noncount nouns? (we use the conventional * to indicate something that is generally considered to be "un-English.")

Count Nouns	Noncount Nouns
have plural forms: *beans*	do not have plural forms: **rices*
may not stand alone in the singular:	may stand alone in the singular:
*Bean is good for you	*Rice is good for you*
can occur with *a* or *an*	cannot occur with *a* or *an*
a bean	**a rice*

Standard English also requires some very interesting differences in expressing quantities:

(too) many beans	*(too) much rice*
(too) few beans	*(too) little rice*
more beans	*more rice*
fewer beans	*less rice*

If we look at the patterns for expressing quantities, we can understand why people stray from the standard English pattern. We have two nouns that are not essentially different in meaning, yet standard English requires that we learn whether each is count or noncount and then make the appropriate grammatical distinctions. From the point of view of the speaker, this is an un- necessary complication of the grammar. We do not gain any meaning distinc- tion; we just have to do more work. If you observe people's usage of count and noncount nouns, you will see attempts to avoid unnecessary work. Instead of distinguishing between *many* and *few,* people will say *a lot of beans, a lot of rice.* This is considered standard (as long as you spell *a lot* as two words) but infor- mal. Or people might use *much* and *little* for both: **too much beans, *too little beans.* Although these have not achieved standard acceptability, we can see the reason for their use: with no loss of meaning and no loss of a valuable distinc- tion, people manage to make the overall system more predictable and less complicated, with *much* indicating a large quantity, and *little* indicating a small quantity. The situation is even more interesting when we are comparing quan- tities. Notice here that they are the same for the greater amount: *more beans, more rice.* But once again, for the lesser amount, we have to choose different words according to the rules of standard English: *fewer* for count nouns, *less* for noncount. What would be wrong with a simpler pattern that uses the same word for both, comparable to *more?* That is exactly what speakers of English seem to be asking every time someone says *less calories* or *less restrictions* or *less any-other-count-noun.* How we treat the subcategories of count and noncount nouns is a very good example of how people collectively react to unnecessary burdens in their grammatical system. Without conscious agreement, there is movement towards a simpler, more regular pattern.

DISCUSSION EXERCISES 3.4

1. Which of the following nouns are count? Which are noncount? Use various grammatical tests to justify your decisions: *furniture, table, peace, student, sugar, university, greed.*

2. Some nouns in English can be both count and non-count, depending upon how they are used in a sentence. *Beer* is an example of such a noun: *two beers, beer is a beverage.* Show how each of these nouns can be either count or non-count: *space, coffee, chocolate, time.*

3. You might have noticed that we used the word *amount* in the paragraph before the Discussion Exercises to refer to both count and noncount nouns. If you are a grammatical purist, you might raise an objection to this usage. Traditionally, standard English has required that we speak of *amounts* of noncount nouns but *numbers* of count nouns: *the number of beans, the amount of rice.* What would you say is the status of this distinction? Is it nonstandard to use *amount* for both?

WHAT MAKES UP A NOUN PHRASE?

As we mentioned in Chapter 2, nouns often occur with modifiers to form the constituent type known as a **noun phrase.** The noun is the core, or the head, of the phrase, and everything else in the constituent describes or identifies the noun in some way. For example, the phrase in (1) is a noun phrase; *errors* is the head and *serious* and *in translation* are modifiers of the head. Together they form a constituent.

(1) serious errors in translation

The descriptive modifiers of a noun are ordinarily adjectives, prepositional phrases, or relative clauses, all of which we will discuss in later chapters. Another type of modifier serves to identify rather than describe a noun. These modifiers are part of what we call the **determiner system.** The noun phrases in (2) illustrate the determiner system:

(2) my second marriage
    both his wives
    the divorce
    all her many stepchildren

You can see three different elements of the determiner system in these examples: **determiners,** such as *my, his, the, her;* **predeterminers,** such as *both* and *all,* which precede determiners; and **postdeterminers,** such as *second* and *many,* which follow determiners. A noun phrase with all elements of the determiner system present, such as the last example in (2) looks like this schematically:

Noun Phrase = Predeterminer + Determiner + Postdeterminer + Noun

Of course, as we have already seen, it is not required that all the elements of the determiner system be present at the same time in a noun phrase. As you read further, you will recognize that the first noun phrase in (2) has no predeterminer, the second has no postdeterminer, and the third has only a determiner. In fact, nouns often appear as the sole element of their noun phrase, with no modifiers at all, such as *rice* in *Rice is a staple in China.* It may seem counterintuitive to call a single noun a noun phrase, but as we will see shortly, many nouns standing alone (mainly noncount and proper nouns and most plural nouns) behave grammatically just like larger groupings of nouns and modifiers.

DETERMINERS

One way to judge what to call a determiner is to ask what occurs right before the noun. By virtue of its location alone, we can call that element a determiner. The most common determiners are **articles, demonstratives, possessive pronouns, quantities,** and **possessive noun phrases.**

There are two articles in English, the **definite article** and the **indefinite article.** The definite article is *the.* The indefinite article in standard English has two forms in the singular, *a* before a consonant sound and *an* before a vowel sound. *Some* can be considered the plural indefinite article, although it may also be considered a quantity. Some examples of noun phrases with articles are *the boy, a girl, an olive, some books.* Native speakers of English have no difficulty deciding how to choose between a definite and an indefinite article, but it is not easy to explain how we make that decision. Their traditional grammatical labels are misleading. For example, if I tell you *There is a book on the table. Please pick it up,* "a book" is just as "definite" as if I had said *Pick up the book on the table.* Perhaps a better way to look at the use of the articles is to imagine a speaker trying to communicate with a listener. If the speaker assumes that the listener already has a certain noun in mind, the speaker uses *the.* But if the speaker thinks the listener does not have the noun in mind, *a* (or *an,* or *some*) can be used to introduce the noun. Once it is placed in the mind of the listener, then the speaker can use *the.* I can say *the book* if I think you have already identified it in your mind; if not, I will introduce it by saying *a book* first.

DISCUSSION EXERCISES 3.5

1. Are *an honor* and *a use* exceptions to the rule governing the choice of indefinite article?

2. Why do you think there is fluctuation in standard English between *a* and *an* before a noun that begins with the sound *h* in an unstressed syllable: *a/an historical event, a/an hysterical patient, a/an hypothesis?*

3. Why do you think it works to start a conversation with a stranger by referring to "the president," or "the sun" or "the moon." How is that different from starting a conversation about "the secretary" or "the star"? *[handwritten: — might]* *[handwritten: 2, there are many]*

Demonstratives are like the definite article in function, with two differences: they also indicate the location of the noun relative to the speaker, and there is a cross-referencing rule that requires number agreement with the noun they modify. Two indicate that the noun is near the speaker, and two indicate that the noun is far from the speaker. You have probably figured out what they are:

> *this hat:* (singular, near the speaker)
> *these hats:* (plural, near the speaker)
> *that hat:* (singular, far from the speaker)
> *those hats:* (plural, far from the speaker)

Possessive pronouns make up another category of determiner: *my life, your idea, his ring, their reason. Quantities* are the fourth major kind of determiner: *many, several, enough, few, little, much, any, some, no, two,* for example. One other kind of determiner is a *possessive noun phrase.* You may wonder how we can use a noun phrase as part of a noun phrase, but that is typical of the nesting, hierarchical nature of language. Consider the noun phrases in (3):

(3) The mechanic's advice
     My mechanic's advice
     That mechanic's advice
     Those mechanics' advice

You'll notice that in each case, *advice* is the head noun of the noun phrase, but the determiner is also a noun phrase, with its own head noun, *mechanic's* (or *mechanics'*). We might visualize this as :

> **[[the mechanic's] advice]**
>   **NP   NP**

In other words, a possessive noun can be the head of a noun phrase, and the noun phrase it heads can serve as a determiner. Suppose you wanted to construct a noun phrase with a determiner and the head noun *wish*. Here are some possibilities:

Determiner	Head Noun
my	
a	
the	
that	wish
his	
Ben's	
the child's	
the happy child's	

You'll notice that the last three determiners on this list are noun phrases with their own heads and their own modifiers, but they can work as determiners themselves, modifying the noun *wish*.

DISCUSSION EXERCISES 3.6

1. Find all the determiners in the previous sentence and tell what kind each one is. Can you find any noun phrases that have no determiners?

2. Make up noun phrases using all of the quantities listed in the previous paragraph as determiners. What determines whether you use *few* or *little*? *many* or *much*? Does the same restriction hold for *enough*?

3. Think of sentences in which we use *any* as a determiner. Do you notice any restriction on its use? (Hint: we don't say **I have any books*)

4. What is the head of each of the following noun phrases? What kind of determiner does each have?

   POS. *your insecurity*   artcl NP *a fool's mission*

   Demonst. *this explanation*   Dem. *that woman's child*

   quant *the very important package*   POS *Sue's business*

PREDETERMINERS AND POSTDETERMINERS

As their names suggest, these occur surrounding the determiner, either before or after, and only occur if there is also a determiner present. Some common **predeterminers** are *all, half,* and *both*. These may be followed by the preposition *of*: *all (of) the people, half (of) the class, both (of) the students. What* and *such* are also considered predeterminers: *what a party, such a fool,* although their use is restricted to the indefinite article determiner. We can't say *what the party* or *such my fool.*

Postdeterminers express quantities as well, and are called postdeterminers when they follow a determiner. Some common ones are cardinal numbers (*one, two, three* . . .), ordinal numbers (*first, second, third* . . .), and indefinite quantities like *several, many, few.* Some examples of noun phrases with postdeterminers are *my few friends, the first call, those many years, his six children.*

It should not trouble you that some words that express quantity can be used as predeterminers, determiners, or postdeterminers. It is often the case that a word's label is not inherent to the word, but rather is derived from the way the word functions in a particular context. If you want to know what a word is in a noun phrase, look to see what else is in that noun phrase.

DISCUSSION EXERCISES 3.7

1. Label all the parts of the following noun phrases. Give all the information you can about each part.

   her bike

   the two children

   all my sister's many friends

   several questions

   both of his first choices

   half that pie

2. Show how the word *many* can be used as a determiner or a postdeterminer. Show how *all* can be a predeterminer or a determiner.

WHAT ARE THE FUNCTIONS OF NOUN PHRASES?

Now that we know how to identify noun phrases and label their parts, the next step is to understand how they function in sentences. You can think of each sentence as a mini-drama in which noun phrases play different roles. The most common roles, or functions, of noun phrases are **subject, direct object, indirect object, object of a preposition,** and **complement.** You will come to understand more about these functions as we discuss the other parts of the sentence, because they are primarily relational terms; that is, they describe how noun phrases interact with other parts of the sentence. Our goal at this point is to learn to identify them in sentences.

Subject

Although *subject* is a common grammatical term, and most of us have some intuition about what it is, it is surprisingly hard to define. When we refer to the *subject noun phrase* of a sentence we often mean the doer of the action. In the sentences in (4), the subject noun phrase is underlined.

(4) Mary left early.
The dog jumped over the fence.
My children caught the balloons.

But the doer of the action might *not* be the subject, as in (5):

(5) The house was built by the contractor.
The exam was graded by the professor.

And often there is no "doer" expressed at all, as in (6):

(6) This old house is a mess.
My many attempts at learning to play chess all failed.
The doctor's bill was astounding.

Probably a more reliable way for us to identify the subject noun phrase of a sentence is by its location. It is almost always the first noun phrase in the sentence and the one that immediately precedes the verb. By those criteria, you can identify the subject noun phrases in all of the above sentences.

We also need to keep in mind that, except for commands, all English sentences must have a subject, grammatically speaking. That is, there must be a noun phrase (or its equivalent) preceding the verb. For example, if we look out the window and see water falling from the sky, we must express this event by using a subject. Since there is no real subject, we use a "dummy" or "placeholder": *It's raining.* All speakers of English know that this subject is just a "dummy," so no one ever asks *What's raining?* Similarly, we use the word *there* as a dummy in sentences like *There are too many people on this bus.* Some grammarians call these placeholder words *expletives.*

DISCUSSION EXERCISES 3.8

1. Sometimes grammar books define the subject of the sentence as "what the sentence is about." What are the inadequacies of such a definition? To discuss this, use the sentence *The librarian found the book the student was looking for.* Say it aloud in different ways by moving the stress from one noun phrase to another. What is this sentence about?

2. Remember that whatever is not the *subject* of the sentence is the *predicate.* Identify the subject and the predicate of each of the following sentences. (Remember too that subjects are noun phrases, not just nouns!)

The playful child frightened the pony.
My cat hid in the cupboard.

(continued)

Mrs. Waters just left.

The telephone in the living room is portable.

A small bird flew into the chimney.

His computer is obsolete.

The book that you just finished is a best-seller.

Those three packages are for you.

Both her parents attended her wedding.

Love makes us happy.

3. Which of the following have placeholder subjects? How do you know? Can any be interpreted in two different ways?

There is where I left my purse. *PH*

It is snowing. *PH*

There is an excuse for his tardiness. *PH*

It is in the closet.

It is too hot to eat. *PH*

4. Some grammar books make a distinction between *simple subjects* and *complete subjects*. In a noun phrase like *the little red house, house* would be the simple subject and the whole noun phrase would be the complete subject. What term is used in this book for the simple subject? *Noun*

5. It is very common in casual conversation for people to say things like "My sister, she gets all the breaks." This is called the *double subject* and is considered nonstandard in formal writing. Can you think of any useful purpose it might serve in conversation? It might interest you to know that such constructions are considered standard in many other languages.

Direct Object

Direct object eludes definition much the way *subject* does. It is often thought of as the "receiver of the action," which is helpful sometimes, as in the sentences in (7), where the underlined noun phrases are direct objects:

(7) The girl hit the ball.
The clown entertained his children.
My aunt tossed the salad.

But again, the receiver of the action might *not* be the direct object, as in (8):

(8) Mary received a blow.
The ball was hit by the girl.

Or the direct object might not be the receiver of the action, but might come into being as a result of the action, as in (9):

(9) My friend wrote <u>a letter.</u>
She invented <u>the wheel.</u>
They built <u>a bridge.</u>

Although meaning criteria are sometimes helpful in identifying direct objects, once again <u>location is probably a more reliable gauge of whether a noun phrase is a direct object. Direct objects usually come immediately after the verb.</u> An additional important test for direct objects is the **passive** test. We will learn about passives in a later chapter, but for now you can see how the test works by comparing the two sentences in (10).

(10) (a) The pitcher threw <u>the</u> *ball.*
(b) <u>The ball</u> was thrown by the pitcher.

A noun phrase following a verb is likely to be a direct object, as in (a), <u>if you can make a corresponding passive sentence just like (b) without changing the basic meaning.</u>

DISCUSSION EXERCISES 3.9

1. Use meaning, location, and the passive test to identify the direct object noun phrase in each of the following sentences:

Mary found Tom's <u>keys.</u>
The engineer designed <u>that building.</u>
He invited all <u>my dearest friends.</u>
Everyone loved <u>the charming little puppy.</u>
The clerk stamped <u>the package.</u>

2. Do both the following sentences have direct object noun phrases? What is your reasoning?

Jane saw <u>the president.</u> D/o
Jane was the president. x

Indirect Object

Indirect object is also not easy to define. <u>Indirect objects almost always refer to the people who are,</u> in some way, indirectly affected by the action, although pinning it down more precisely can be a problem. Sometimes this person is a recipient of the direct object. In the sentences in (11), for example, *the teacher* and *Hannah* would be considered indirect objects.

(11) Jimmy gave an apple to the teacher.
　　 Rachel bought a sweater for Hannah.

Sometimes the indirect object is the beneficiary of the action, as illustrated in (12), in which *Ben* is an indirect object.

(12) Mike read a bedtime story to Ben.

But again, location in the sentence is probably a more reliable indicator of indirect objects. One place to look for indirect objects is immediately following the prepositions *to* and *for*. Another location for indirect objects is between the verb and the direct object, as illustrated in the sentences in (13).

(13) Jimmy gave the teacher an apple.
　　 Rachel bought Hannah a sweater.
　　 Mike read Ben a bedtime story.

You will notice that the meanings of the sentences in (13) are exactly the same as their counterparts in (11) and (12), as are the relationships among the various noun phrases. To recognize the connection between sentences like those in (11) and (12) and those in (13), we say that there is a rule in English grammar called **indirect object inversion,** which operates as follows:

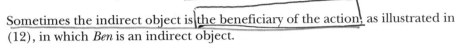

[Verb + Direct Object + {to,for} + Indirect Object] → **[Verb + Indirect Object + Direct Object]**

In other words, indirect objects can sometimes be moved in front of direct objects, and when they do they lose their prepositions. They are now called **inverted indirect objects.** The formula is not foolproof and tends to work better with indirect objects preceded by *to* rather than *for*. But it is one more criterion to use in deciding whether to call a noun phrase an indirect object.

You need to be aware that the designation *indirect object* is controversial. Many linguists disagree with this traditional definition. For some, only the inverted version is called an indirect object, whereas the noun phrase following *to* or *for* is merely an object of a preposition (described in the next section). The description presented here has the advantage of connecting in a systematic way sentences that mean the same thing. We will continue to do this throughout this book, because it is often the case that we can gain insights about what to call something by thinking about how it behaves in related sentences.

DISCUSSION EXERCISES 3.10

1. Consider the sentence *Peter mowed the lawn for a dollar.* Is *a dollar* an indirect object? What is your reasoning? Is *the elevator* an indirect object in *She walked her father to the elevator?*

2. Which of the following sentences have indirect objects? Which are inverted indirect objects?

   Keith gave Mary a present for her birthday.
   The professor taught those students linguistics.
   Kathy gave Sam a second chance.
   John cooked dinner for his folks.
   Jack read this book to Mildred.
   My daughter wrote this poem.
   The fabric is torn.
   Mary feels tired.
   The salesperson sold Maxine this radio.
   Sue sent flowers to Chuck.

3. How does indirect-object inversion affect our definition of direct object noun phrases? Are the noun phrases immediately following the verb always direct objects?

Object of a Preposition

Noun phrases that are **objects of prepositions** are easy to recognize if you know what a preposition is. We will have much more to say about prepositions in a later chapter, but for now we can say they are words that indicate the relationship of the following noun phrase to the rest of the sentence. Those relationships are many, including location, direction, accompaniment, and purpose. Prepositions link with a following noun phrase to form a constituent called a **prepositional phrase.** All the phrases in (14) are prepositional phrases, and the underlined noun phrases are objects of prepositions. Notice that once again we see a phrase nested inside another phrase.

(14) in the barn (location)
  towards the fire (direction)
  with an escort (accompaniment)
  for a good reason (purpose)

You may be wondering why we don't call indirect objects "objects of prepositions" instead. After all, *to* and *for* are prepositions. You would not be wrong to call them objects of prepositions, as long as you also recognize that some objects of prepositions are able to move to another location in the sentence and drop their prepositions. This is called the capacity for "inversion." Only indirect objects can do this, as evidenced by the ungrammaticality of sentences like those in (15).

(15) Al studied algebra for a reason. → *Al studied a reason algebra.
   Ted drove his car to the reunion. → *Ted drove the reunion his car.

Complement

Some noun phrases do not designate independent entities in a sentence. Rather, they serve to describe another noun phrase of that sentence. These noun phrases are called *complements*. Consider again the two sentences you were asked to compare in Discussion Exercise 3.9, question 2:

(16) Jane saw the president.
   Jane was the president.

You undoubtedly discovered that in the first one *the president* is a direct object. It receives the action (to the extent that seeing is an action), and it works in the passive test: *The president was seen by Jane. The president* in the second sentence fails the passive test and is not the receiver of an action. In fact, it is not a separate person at all, but a way of describing Jane. *The president* in this sentence is called a complement, and since it describes the subject of the sentence, it is called a **subject complement.** Now consider the underlined noun phrases in (17):

(17) They considered the child a genius.
   She declared her brother a liar. → *obj. comp.*

In these sentences, the underlined noun phrase describes the direct object, and so it is called an **object complement.**

DISCUSSION EXERCISES 3.11

1. Pick out the objects of prepositions in the following sentences.

   I'll meet you near the fence after school.
   Larry cut the bread with a knife.
   Put the box in the drawer under the sink.
   She delivered the prescription to the pharmacy in the mall.
   Ben went to the dance with Flo.

2. Identify the complements in the following sentences. Tell whether they are subject complements or object complements.

   The earthquake was a frightening experience. *Subj comp*
   You are my best friend.
   → *subj. comp*

(continued)

Everyone considered James an honest person. *obj comp*

The main dishes were beans and rice. *sub comp*

We declared Judy the designated driver. *obj comp*

I appointed him executor of my will. *obj comp*

(Note: sometimes object complements sound better if you insert "*to be*" in front of them)

3. Are the following sentences identical in structure?

     S   *DO*   *IO*
     The teacher taught Sam a lesson.
     S   *DO*   *obj comp*
     The teacher considered Sam a fool.

     What is the grammatical function of each noun phrase in these sentences?

VERBAL NOUNS AND NOUN PHRASES

There is one kind of noun that deserves special attention, a **verbal noun.** You might not recognize verbal nouns as nouns at first because their meanings tend to be actions rather than things. These are words that are built from verbs, but they exhibit many of the properties of nouns. There are two kinds of verbal nouns: **gerunds** and **infinitives.**

Gerunds are constructed from verb roots by adding the suffix *-ing: laughing, coughing, playing,* for example. What makes them nouns? One reason we call them nouns is that they can be heads of noun phrases, with many of the usual modifiers that occur with nouns. Look at the noun phrases in (18):

(18) His laughing annoyed her.
      All that coughing disturbed the musicians.
      The child's crying made me nervous.

In these, we see that gerunds can occur with determiners such as possessive pronouns, demonstratives, and possessive noun phrases, as well as with predeterminers. Verbal nouns are abstract nouns, so the determiner system is somewhat limited, as is the case with all abstract nouns. Nevertheless, we can see that the gerunds in the above examples are clearly the heads of noun phrases. Noun phrases with gerunds as their head are called **gerundive phrases.** Gerundive phrases may be further expanded with modifiers, like manner, place, or time, as in the sentences in (19).

(19) His laughing like a hyena annoyed her.
      All that coughing in the audience disturbed the musicians.
      The child's crying all night made me nervous.

Gerundive phrases also perform the typical grammatical functions of noun phrases. They may be the subject of the sentence, as we see in the sentences in (19), or they can be direct objects, as in the sentences in (20).

(20) She resented his laughing like a hyena.
The musicians don't like all that coughing in the audience.
I couldn't bear the child's crying.

They can be objects of prepositions, as in the sentences in (21).

(21) She teases him about his laughing like a hyena.
The musicians are upset over all that coughing in the audience.
I was disturbed by the child's crying.

Gerundive phrases can also be complements:

(22) The thing that bothers me most is his laughing like a hyena.
The cause of the noise is all that coughing in the audience.
The reason for my irritation was the child's crying.

So we see that gerundive phrases behave more or less the way other noun phrases do.

The other type of verbal noun is called an **infinitive.** Infinitives are verbs with the word *to* in front of them: *to talk, to love, to run,* for example. These may serve as the heads of noun phrases called **infinitival phrases.** These too exhibit many of the properties of noun phrases. Although they are not as versatile as gerundive phrases, they may be subjects, direct objects, and complements, as can be seen in the sentences in (23).

(23) subject: To give up now would be foolish.
direct object: Everyone desires to live in peace.
complement: His first instinct was to run away.

DISCUSSION EXERCISES 3.12

1. You probably noticed that we didn't give any examples of gerundive and infinitival phrases as indirect objects. Why do you think they can't be indirect objects?

2. Find the gerundive phrase in each of the following sentences. Tell what its grammatical function is in the sentence.

   You learn by studying every day. DO

   S Hiking in the woods is fun.

   We don't mind leaving early. DO

   Thank you for not smoking in my car. —— ?

   The most exciting activity at camp is swimming in the lake.
   DO

   (continued)

3. Even though we haven't talked in depth about verbs yet, it is important to note here that gerunds and present participles (see Chapter 2) are different lexical categories even though they look exactly the same. Use these two sentences to show that *playing* in the first (a present participle) is grammatically different from *playing* in the second (a gerund):

The pianist (is playing) the piano. ——helping verb present progressive

My hobby is playing the piano. gerund /DO

4. Present participles are also used descriptively, as in

Sliding down a rope, Jill scraped her leg.

Compare that to the gerund in

Sliding down a rope can be challenging.

How are they different grammatically?

5. Find the infinitival phrase in each of the following sentences. Tell what its grammatical function is in the sentence.

The important thing is [to print] your name legibly. DO

She prefers [to work] alone. DO

His goal in life is [to make] a lot of money. DO

[To bail out] now would be a mistake.

Rose liked [to bask] in the sun. DO

COMPOUNDS

Throughout this chapter we have been looking at nouns and noun phrases one at a time. But we can also make larger constituents of the same type by putting more than one together. We do this using the process of **conjoining** (or **co-ordination**), and the resulting structure is called a **compound.** Let's look first at compound noun phrases. We see some examples of compound noun phrases in (24).

(24) The man and the woman met at the baseball game.
      I will contact the plumber or the electrician.
      I planted both a clematis and a trumpet vine.
      You can use either celery or snow peas in the recipe.
      Neither Lauren nor Wendy will come to my party.
      I lost not only my house but my car.

Compounds are created by connecting two like constituents, in this case noun phrases, with a **coordinating conjunction.** Coordinating conjunctions can be **simple** (*and, or*) or **correlative** (*both . . . and, either . . . or, neither . . . nor., not only . . . but*). When we conjoin one noun phrase to another, we create a new noun phrase that can be represented schematically like this (where NP = noun phrase and cc = coordinating conjunction):

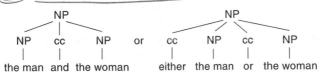

The compound performs all the typical functions of single noun phrases. So, for example, in the first sentence of (24) *The man and the woman* is the subject, and in the second sentence *the plumber or the electrician* is the direct object. There is no fixed limit to the number of noun phrases that can be conjoined together; the number in any given circumstance is a function of the purpose and the style of the communication. The standard requirement is that the co-ordinating conjunction appear before the last element only, with commas separating the others and an optional comma before the conjunction:

(25) The house smelled of old shoes, candle wax, cats, cheap perfume, and beer.

Nouns themselves can also form compounds, as in (26):

(26) She is my *friend and colleague.*

Structurally, the subject complement noun phrase in (26) looks like this, where DET = determiner, N = noun):

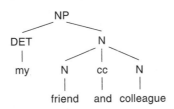

DISCUSSION EXERCISES 3.13

1. Give examples of compound noun phrases with the following functions:

   subject complement *He wrote Sarah + John a letter*
   indirect object *He made a cake for Sarah + John*
   object of a preposition *He gave the cake at Sarah's + John's request*

2. There are other simple coordinating conjunctions in English, but they are not used with nouns and noun phrases: *but, nor, yet, so,* and *for.* Can you think of examples where they serve to make compounds of other lexical categories?

(continued)

3. Traditionally, nouns such as *underwear, doghouse, blackboard,* and *drag-onfly* are also called compounds. How are they different from the noun compound illustrated in (26)? Compound nouns

4. Usually, the correlative coordinating conjunctions carry the same meaning as their simple counterparts, but there is at least one situation in which they are different. What is the difference in meaning conveyed by the coordinating conjunctions in each of the sentences below?

Mark and Cindy are married.
Both Mark and Cindy are married.

We have now examined the roles of all the players in the sentence mini-drama. In the next chapter we examine what they are doing or what is being said about them. The constituents that express this part of the drama are verbs and verb phrases.

REFLECTIONS

1. There seems to be an increasing use of the apostrophe in the plural. You might see an apartment building that advertises "studio's for rent," a campus flier that offers information on cold's and the flu," or a fast food restaurant that advertises "taco's" and "burrito's." A real estate ad in a Michigan newspaper advertises "3 condo's to choose from with 1st floor laundry's." What might be the explanation for this widespread deviation from conventional spelling?

2. *Data* is another example of a noun that is historically plural. Its Latin singular is *datum. Data* is still used in English as a plural noun, but it also occurs as a singular noncount noun. What would be an example of this usage? What does your dictionary say about the status of *data* as a singular noun?

3. Some language change is motivated by political or social change. For example, many women have objected to the use of the feminine suffix *-ess* as an add-on to an occupation, and prefer to be called a *poet,* not a *poetess,* an *author,* not an *authoress.* Can you think of any other nouns with *-ess* that have fallen into relative disuse?

4. A related change is the replacement of occupations that have traditionally ended in the suffix *-man* with gender-neutral terms: *postal carrier, fire fighter.* Can you think of others?

5. Visit your local supermarket and see how many product labels advertise products as having "*less calories.*" At this point, could we consider *less calories* standard English? You might be interested to know that the following appeared recently in one Michigan newspaper:

> "Sample has noticed less children at the center since the strikes began."

"Study finds patients who were prayed for recovered quicker with less complications."

"Nationally, women are known to receive less clot-busting medications, less interventions . . ." (quoted from a physician's comments)

And this appeared in an Aetna ad:

"Because we believe a good investment plan should give you more choices, not less."

What does the following student comment tell you about grammar in transition?

"Fewer loopholes would allow for less criminals to go free."

6. Some people do not use *an* in casual speech. Instead, when the noun begins with a vowel sound they insert a sound called a "glottal stop," which sounds like a catch in the throat. Listen for it the next time you hear someone say "*a apple*" or "*a orange.*"

7. Notice that if we do indirect-object inversion on a sentence, the indirect object ends up in the position where we expect to find the direct object, right after the verb:

Kathy gave Sam a second chance.

As suggested in Discussion Exercise 3.10, question 3, that means we can't say that the noun phrase after the verb is *always* the direct object. How does indirect-object inversion affect the passive test? Is it a totally reliable test for the direct object?

8. One common nonstandard usage appears in the following sentence:

We appreciate you not smoking.

What makes this nonstandard?

9. Another rule passed down from the eighteenth century is a prohibition against splitting an infinitive. This means nothing should come between *to* and the verb. *To never see daylight* is an example of a split infinitive. What do you think the status of this rule is in modern English usage? One current dictionary, the *New Oxford Dictionary of English,* gives its official approval to split infinitives, but the patron of the Queen's English Society, based in London, says "Approving of split infinitives is like abolishing history."

10. New nouns are added regularly to English. Dictionaries update their listings periodically to reflect these changes in the language. For example, *Webster's* has recently added *wannabe, homeboy, liposuction,* and *cash cow,* to name a few. What are some new words you would include if you were publishing a dictionary?

11. We said that nouns are normally made possessive by adding an apostrophe -*s* to their ends: *woman's, dog's.* But suppose a modifier follows the noun we want to make possessive: *the Queen of England, the man in the red sweater.* To what do we attach the possessive suffix? In the fourteenth century Chaucer called his tale *The Tale of the Wife of Bathe*. What do we call it now? This more recent construction is called the "group possessive."

12. The following quotes are taken from newspapers and textbooks. What is the common element among them? What conclusions do you draw from them? Ask some other people what they think about them.

> "Two years ago, when the phenomena was relatively unknown, the Michigan Public Service Commission had 391 complaints of billing errors. . . ."
>
> "Williams said the criteria for acceptance was exacting."
>
> "As we shall see momentarily, this is an intricate phenomena. . . ."
>
> "At this stage let it suffice to say that Chicano English is a more complex phenomena. . . ."
>
> "Writing for the court, Justice Sandra Day O'Connor determined that the law using a decency standard as a criteria for grants. . . ."
>
> "The criteria for their selection includes having a connection to the state and making a lasting contribution as a role model."

PRACTICE EXERCISES FOR CHAPTER 3 (Answers on p. 223)

1. Underline all the nouns in the following sentences.

   Example: Mike bought some candy for his girlfriend.

   1. Calcium is an element necessary for strong bones.
   2. The instructor asked the students to review the exercises.
   3. A worker in the factory sensed the dissatisfaction among his colleagues.
   4. Cats and dogs provide friendship and love for lonely people.
   5. The state animal of Minnesota is the gopher.

2. Identify all the nouns in the following sentences and tell whether they are count or noncount.

   1. The wind tore a hole in the tent.
   2. Too much sugar in your diet leads to poor health.
   3. My mother enjoys wine with her meals.
   4. Dinner is the most important meal of the day.
   5. The babysitter fed the baby milk with his cereal.

3. Label all the predeterminers, determiners, postdeterminers, and heads of the following noun phrases.

   1. both my older sisters
   2. half of his geometry class
   3. what an exciting event
   4. the girl's third attempt
   5. three boats

(continued)

6. my seven cousins

7. such a shame

8. all the children

4. What specific kind of determiner appears in each of the noun phrases above?

5. Identify all the noun phrases in the following sentences. Tell the grammatical function of each noun phrase you identify.

1. The weekend is my favorite part of the week.

2. Martha's boss gave her a bonus.

3. Bob considered the doctor the answer to his prayers.

4. A quaint old boat drifted down the river near Sally's farm.

5. The cashier gave the receipt to the woman in the fur coat.

6. Give the noun phrases in these sentences that play the indicated grammatical roles:

1. The child gave a present to her mother on Mother's Day.

subject: _____

direct object: _____

indirect object: _____

object of a preposition:_____

2. The first day of April is my favorite time of the year.

subject: _____

subject complement: _____

object of a preposition: _____

object of a preposition: _____

7. Which of the following sentences have indirect objects? Which of the indirect objects are inverted?

1. The grateful student sent the teacher a note.

2. My father cooked dinner for the whole family.

3. Randi bought a toy for her child for Christmas.

4. Pam read Jim the instructions.

5 The trainer fed the lions raw meat.

8. Label the roles of all the noun phrases in:

1. Mr. Allen taught the boy geometry.

2. Mr. Allen considered the boy an idiot.

9. Underline the verbal noun phrase in each of the following sentences. Is it a gerundive or an infinitival phrase? What is its grammatical function in the sentence?

1. Winning a race is exhilarating.

2. You achieve success by working hard.

3. I've always liked to hike in the woods.

(continued)

    4. To live honestly is my main goal in life.

    5. You can't accuse him of not trying.

    6. The most important thing is to remain calm.

    7. I can't tolerate all this whining.

    8. She appreciated learning a new skill.

    9. The hardest part is waiting for the results.

    10. They expect to arrive tomorrow.

10. Which noun phrases in the following sentence are nested inside another phrase?

The young woman's father purchased the farm at the foot of the hill.

11. From the following list of noun phrases, create sentences that contain the following:

a compound subject

a compound direct object

a compound indirect object

> a cat
>
> my two best friends
>
> the dead goldfish
>
> Barry
>
> both screaming monkeys
>
> all his relatives

12. Why might the following statement in a will cause problems?

"I bequeath all my worldly goods to my husband and lover."

13. Find an example of each of the following in the *Believers* selection below:

a subject complement

an object of a preposition

a compound noun phrase

a noun phrase with an indefinite article for its determiner

a noun phrase with a demonstrative determiner

"The house had an upstairs sleeping porch, and she first saw the young man from up there, limping through the alley and carrying a torn orange and yellow Chinese kite. He had a dog with him, and both the dog and the man had an air of scruffy unseriousness. From the look of it, no project these two got involved with could last longer than ten minutes. That was the first thing she liked about them." (Baxter: "Kiss Away" p. 3)

14. Identify the violations of formal standard English in the following letter.

Dear Chris,

I am so glad that you have decided to take a trip to Paris with me and my family. I have been thinking about our preparations and would like to give you some word's of advice. You said you would take four bags, but I think less bags would

(continued)

be more convenient. Them customs official's suspicions get aroused if you pack too much. Another criteria to keep in mind is the weight. Try to travel with as little inconveniences as possible. I always like to pack a umbrella and a overcoat this time of year. Rain is a common phenomena in the afternoon. My travel agent, he says folding umbrella's are lightweight and practical.

I am so excited at the prospect of you coming with us to Paris!

Cordially,
Pat

FOUR

VERBS AND VERB PHRASES

WHAT ARE VERBS?

Verbs are often considered to be the lexical category that indicates the action of the sentence, but you can probably imagine some of the shortcomings of this definition. We know that sometimes actions are expressed by nouns, as in

(1) The appointment of a new dean

Similarly, we know that not all verbs express actions. They may express, among other things, a sense, as in (2), a perception of another person (3), a mental state (4), or they may merely serve a connecting function, as in (5).

(2) Lora feels inspired.
(3) Lani seems contented.
(4) Jim expects a package in the mail.
(5) Steve is the youngest member of the club.

Sometimes we can recognize verbs by their derivational suffixes. There are several such derivational suffixes, that is, suffixes that turn a root into a verb. Some common ones are -ize (nationalize, subsidize), -ate (educate, motivate), and -ify (solidify, verify).

DISCUSSION EXERCISES 4.1

1. Give some other verbs formed by adding the suffixes listed above.
2. A less common derivational suffix for verbs is -esce. How many verbs can you think of that end in it?

Verbs often do not have any derivational suffix and are better recognized by the various inflectional forms they may take. For example, we have already talked about the *infinitive* of the verb. Verbs may appear with the word *to* in front of them: this combination is called "the infinitive of the verb." As we saw in the last chapter, infinitives are usually verbal nouns and serve the function of a noun in a sentence, but they are formed from verbs and are a convenient way to refer to the verb when you want to talk about it. You may also see the verb used without *to* in front, which is sometimes referred to as the **bare infinitive** or the **base form.** The bare infinitive is commonly used with what is known as a helping verb, as in the following sentences:

(6) He can type fifty words a minute.
     You may not leave yet.

Another form that all verbs take is the **present participle,** which is formed by adding the suffix *-ing* to the base form: *laughing, singing, being, feeling.* The present participle is frequently used together with another verb, as in (7):

(7) She was pretending to sleep.

It may also be used in descriptive phrases, such as in (8):

(8) Crossing the street, Marilyn found a diamond ring.

We follow traditional grammar in using the term *present participle,* but it is misleading because it is not present; in fact, it carries no time by itself. Notice how the time of the action changes in each of the sentences below while the present participle *studying* stays the same.

(9) I am studying. (now)
     I was studying. (yesterday)
     I will be studying. (next weekend)

A third form that verbs take is the **past participle.** Also misnamed because it carries no time by itself, the past participle is the form of the verb that occurs in the blank space after *have_____* or *had_____* . Often the past participle is formed by adding the suffix *-ed* to the base form, as in *talked, laughed, danced.* In other cases, we add *-en* to the base form: *eaten, beaten, taken.* But for a very large number of verbs, the form of the past participle is unpredictable and must be learned on a case-by-case basis. Sometimes the vowel of the base form changes, as in *written, spoken, driven.* Sometimes the vowel changes but no suffix is added: *run, sung, drunk.* Sometimes the past participle seems unrelated in form to the base form, as in *I have bought, gone, taught.* We will have more to say about the irregularity of past participles and its effect on people's usage. For now, our goal is to recognize the past participle in a sentence and realize that, just like the present participle, it carries no time of its own. The sentences below illustrate how the time frame may change even though the past participle *studied* remains the same.

(10) She has often studied hard. (in the recent past)
      She had often studied hard. (before something happened in the past)
      She will have studied hard. (by some time in the future)

Because the infinitive, the present participle, and the past participle carry no time of their own, they are known as **nonfinite verb forms.**

DISCUSSION EXERCISES 4.2

1. Give the present and past participles of each of these verbs: *walk, run, do, catch, fight.*

2. Identify the nonfinite verbs in the following sentences:

   Are you speaking to me?
   He needs to see a doctor.
   Sam has already locked the door.
   Did you make this mess?
   Why hasn't she consulted a specialist?
   They aren't listening to the lecture.

3. Remember that there are two different lexical categories formed by adding the suffix *-ing* to the base form of a verb. They are the present participle and the gerund. (See Discussion Exercise 3.12, questions 3 and 4.) Unlike present participles, gerunds are nouns and form part of a noun phrase. Which of the following *-ing* words are gerunds and which are present participles? How do you know?

   Spelling has always come easy to me.
   I heard that you were leaving.
   She is expecting us in an hour.
   You learn by studying.
   I heard laughing in the audience.

Verbs also have two inflectional forms that do carry time: the present and the past. Typically, verbs will add the suffix *-s* or *-es* to the base form to mark the present tense, but only if the subject is a singular noun phrase or the pronoun *he, she,* or *it.* These are known as *third-person-singular subjects.* You can see that the suffix appears when a third person singular subject is used, as in the sentences of (11), but with any other subject we simply use the base form, as in the sentences of (12).

(11)   This child look*s* hungry.
       She smile*s* too much.
       It need*s* to be proofread.

(12)   These children look hungry.
       They smile too much.
       They need to be proofread.

The past tense is typically marked by adding the suffix *-ed* to the base form. Unlike the present tense suffix, it is used for all subjects and not restricted to third person singular.

(13) The children looked hungry.
I saved the whale.
We laughed about the misunderstanding.

The past tense, like the past participle, is subject to many irregularities. There is no pattern to the irregularities; they are remnants of older patterns in English and now must be learned one-by-one. Like the past participle, sometimes the past tense is marked by a vowel change, as in *ran* and *sang*. In other instances the past tense seems to bear no relation to the base form, as in *went* and *bought*.

We will talk more about verb irregularities in the next section. Our purpose here is to lay out the different forms that any one verb can appear in. We have already identified the three **nonfinite** forms: the infinitive, the present participle, and the past participle. The third-person-singular present tense and the past tense are known as **finite** verb forms because they are identified with a particular time. If we can recognize and identify these five forms of a verb, we have all the basic tools we need for talking about verbs and how people use them.

DISCUSSION EXERCISES 4.3

1. For each bare infinitive, give the corresponding present participle, past participle, third-person-singular present tense and past tense: *talk, laugh, dance, educate, synthesize, qualify.*

2. Which of the following words are verbs and which aren't? How do you know? *special, character, invent, compute, mechanic, sadly, refer, equate.*

3. In many cases, a word can be either a noun or a verb. Can you demonstrate this for *smell, pit, laugh, part?*

4. In other cases, there are two words that differ only by the placement of stress, one a noun and the other a verb. *Subject* is one example. Can you think of others? Does the word *influence* fall into this pattern for you?

5. English has had a tendency over the years to create verbs out of nouns, a process known as *conversion. Market* and *audition* are two such examples. Can *eyeball* be a verb? What about *input* and *output?* Can *parent* be a verb?

WHAT ABOUT THE EXCEPTIONS?

Verbs present problems for speakers of English because the patterns are not reliable, as we have already seen. There are no problems associated with the infinitive and the present participle. These are always regular: the infinitive is always *to* + the base form, and the present participle is always the base form *+-ing*. The third-person-singular present tense has a few irregularities, but not enough to cause major concern. The real problem for us is the past tense and the past participle. These are the forms that have many exceptions and require us to memorize them rather than apply a rule.

Let's look again at the regular pattern for verbs. The verb *to laugh* is a good illustration:

> base form: *laugh*
> past tense: *laughed* (*I laughed all day yesterday*)
> past participle: *laughed* (*I have never laughed so much*)

In the regular pattern, the past tense and the past participle both add *-ed* to the base form. Whenever a new verb is added to English, it follows this pattern:

> base form: *eyeball*
> past tense: *eyeballed* (*I eyeballed the new contract*)
> past participle: *eyeballed* (*I have often eyeballed new contracts*)

But this pattern was not always the dominant one for English. Old English had a much more complicated way of forming the past tense and the past participle which was unpredictable even then, and many of our current forms are holdovers from long ago. As a consequence, we can never be sure whether the past tense or the past participle will use the suffix *-ed,* nor can we be sure that the past tense and the past participle will be the same form. Here are some patterns that occur frequently:

past tense and past participle are the same, but do not add *-ed*

Base form	Past tense	Past participle
catch	*caught*	*caught*
hit	*hit*	*hit*
buy	*bought*	*bought*
bring	*brought*	*brought*
have	*had*	*had*
keep	*kept*	*kept*
sleep	*slept*	*slept*
swing	*swung*	*swung*

past tense and past participle both change the vowel of the base form, but differ from each other

sing	*sang*	*sung*
drink	*drank*	*drunk*
swim	*swam*	*swum*

past tense changes the vowel, and the past participle adds the suffix *-en* or *-n* to the base form

take	*took*	*taken*
see	*saw*	*seen*
fall	*fell*	*fallen*
know	*knew*	*known*

past tense changes the vowel, and the past participle shortens the vowel of the base form and adds the suffix -en

write	*wrote*	*written*
drive	*drove*	*driven*
ride	*rode*	*ridden*

past tense changes the vowel, and the past participle adds -en to the past tense form

speak	*spoke*	*spoken*
break	*broke*	*broken*

Still other combinations don't lend themselves to easy description:

do	*did*	*done*
go	*went*	*gone*
be	*was, were*	*been*

It is easy to see why speakers of English have trouble remembering the past tense and the past participles of irregular verbs. One common nonstandard usage results from assuming that the past tense and the past participle are the same, just as they are in the regular pattern. So you might hear people say such nonstandard sentences as

(14) I seen it before.
We done it already.

These assume that the past participle also serves as the past tense. In other cases, people assume that the past tense also serves as the past participle and say sentences like

(15) He has ran a mile.
She has went for milk.

DISCUSSION EXERCISES 4.4

1. Although people may be judged uneducated for using sentences like those in (14) and (15), their meaning is understood. Why do you think people get the intended meaning despite the confusion of past tense and past participle?

2. Because confusion of past tense and past participle carries with it some social stigma, educated people are sensitive about their usage. Given the range of unpredictability of these forms, we all fall prey to anxiety about some verbs. Can you think of any that you are unsure of? Did any of the ones listed above surprise you?

3. If you can't think of any, you might consider the verb *sneak,* or *lie* and *lay.* Does everyone agree on the past tense and past participle forms of these verbs?

Given the variability of irregular past tense and past participle forms, you can see that they would be unstable in the language. Language users, as you know, prefer simple, regular patterns to follow. We certainly do not lose any ability to communicate if we make an irregular verb fit the regular pattern, and this is precisely what speakers of English have been doing for centuries. There used to be many more irregular verbs in the language than there are now. Gradually, the irregular verbs get replaced by regular ones. The most common ones are heard so frequently that people tend to retain them in standard English, but less common irregular verbs are highly vulnerable to regularization. We take for granted now that *climb, walk, drag, help, ache, laugh,* and *yield* are regular verbs, but they are among many that became regular over time. This process continues into modern English.

When a regular form is replacing an irregular form, both are used for a period of time. Here again is fertile ground for linguistic anxiety. Not only are we uncomfortable with two ways of saying the same thing, but we also know that regularizations are considered uneducated when they first appear. (If you doubt this, think again of your reaction to someone who says *I knowed it.*) So if we hear two different past tense forms or two different past participles for the same verb, we want to know which is "correct." But in the absence of an absolute authority, we have to make judgments about whether a new form is considered standard or whether an older form is considered old-fashioned. At a certain point in the transition from old to new, the two forms coexist and no such judgments can be made. Judgments are clearer before and after this point. No one wonders anymore whether the past tense of *laugh* is *low* or *laughed.* But no such clear judgment can be made about *dream,* for example. Is it more correct to say *I dreamt* than *I dreamed?* There is nothing about people's usage or people's reactions to their usage that would lead us to choose one over the other.

DISCUSSION EXERCISES 4.5

1. Are the following verbs regular or irregular in their past tense and past participle forms? *plead, stride, strive, sweep, dive, creep, shine, leap, kneel, slay, light, strike.* (See Reflection 12 at the end of the chapter.)

2. If you find that there are competing forms, what would help you decide if only one or both were considered standard?

3. Consider the verbs *lie* (as in *lie down*) and *lay* (as in *lay an egg*). They are undoubtedly in a period of transition. These are the forms that have been considered standard until now:

   lie: past tense *lay*   past participle *lain*
   lay: past tense *laid*   past participle *laid*

   What evidence is there that people don't always use these verbs as described above? What is your own assessment of the status of this alternate usage?

WHAT ARE SOME COMMON SUBCATEGORIES OF VERBS?

The characteristics of verbs that we have described apply generally to verbs, but just as is the case for nouns, there are different types of verbs. Some exhibit more of the typical verb properties than others. In our discussion so far, the kind of verb we had in mind was a **main verb.** Main verbs are what we usually think of as verbs: they express actions or states of being; they have all of the five inflectional forms we described; and they can occur alone, independent of any other verb. The underlined word in each of the following sentences is a main verb:

(16) Mike <u>studies</u> statistics.
      My aunt <u>collapsed</u> in the hallway.
      Cary <u>looks</u> healthy.

There is another subcategory of verb called **helping verbs.** These, as their name suggests, are used to support a main verb and do not occur by themselves in sentences. Helping verbs come in two types, **auxiliary verbs** and **modal verbs** (also called **modal auxiliaries**).

There are three auxiliary verbs in English: *be, do,* and *have.* They occur together with a main verb in sentences, and when an auxiliary verb is present, the main verb occurs in one of its nonfinite forms: the present participle, the past participle, or the bare infinitive. The sentences below will give you an idea of how auxiliary verbs function in sentences.

(17) I <u>am</u> waiting for an answer.
      <u>Do</u> you think it will rain?
      <u>Have</u> you seen the report?
      The car <u>was</u> washed by the students.

Call them Non-modals

You will notice that the auxiliary verbs carry no meaning of their own; it is the main verb that carries the meaning of the action or the state. The job of the auxiliary verb in these sentences is to indicate the time of the action, since the nonfinite verb forms cannot do this by themselves.

DISCUSSION EXERCISES 4.6

1. Show how you can change the time of the action in the sentences in (17) by changing the time of the auxiliary verb.
2. Sometimes in conversations auxiliary verbs will occur in sentences without a main verb, as in *Yes I am* or *He did.* Does this contradict our claim that auxiliary verbs must occur with a main verb?

(continued)

3. Although *be, do,* and *have* are the three auxiliary verbs of English, they may also function as main verbs. What makes the following underlined verbs main verbs, and not auxiliaries?

Barbara <u>did</u> her homework every night.
The cats <u>are</u> playful.
I <u>have</u> enough money to take a trip.

As speakers of English, you are also aware that the auxiliary verbs all have certain irregularities. Because we use them so much, we have not weeded out their irregularities. *Do* is irregular in the past tense (*did*), the past participle (*done*), and the third-person-singular present tense (*does*). *Have* is irregular in the past tense (*had*), the past participle (*had*), and the third-person-singular present tense (*has*). (*Have* used to be more regular, but the pronunciation of the sound *v* sometimes got lost in the middle of words.) The verb *be* is the most irregular of all verbs and requires a closer look.

The first thing we notice about the verb *to be* is that it has more different finite forms than the other verbs. Following are all its forms:

infinitive: *to be*
present participle: *being*
past participle: *been*
present tense: *am, is, are*
past tense: *was, were*

You'll notice that in the present tense there is a choice of three different forms, while all other verbs have only two. In the past tense there is a choice of two forms, while all other verbs in the language have only one.

DISCUSSION EXERCISES 4.7

1. Because *to be* is so irregular, people may try to make it more regular in its usage. One common nonstandard usage occurs in sentences like *We was so happy, They was laughing, You was lying to me.* How can these be explained as an attempt to make *be* more like other verbs?

2. Do you ever hear attempts to simplify the present tense of the verb *be?* What would be some examples of this?

3. There is one other way in which the verb *be* is irregular. There are sentences that look like this: *If I were you, I wouldn't do that.* You'll notice that *were* in this sentence seems out of place because we would not say *I were happy,* for example. Many people attempt to regularize this usage and say *If I was you. . . .* Where does this usage fall on your scale of acceptability? (For more on this, see Reflection 3.)

The other kind of helping verb is a **modal.** There are nine modal verbs in English: *will, would, shall, should, can, could, may, might, must.* (*ought to* is sometimes added to this list) They each have only one form: there is no **to shall* or **musting* or **woulded,* for example. Like the auxiliaries, they always occur with a main verb:

(18) Jan must leave now.
     Tom might be absent.
     Fran should tell him.

But unlike the auxiliaries, they do carry some meaning of their own. In fact they carry a wide range of different meanings and nuances of meaning that we learn as we learn English, but the meanings are very hard to spell out in exact and predictable terms. Consider the meanings conveyed by the modal in each of the following:

(19) Chuck will sell his house. (future certainty)
     As a child, Irene would hide in the garden. (repeated past activity)
     The toddler might hurt himself. (possibility)
     The child may eat now. (possibility or permission)
     I should call her. (obligation)
     He can swim a mile. (ability)
     They should arrive by seven. (probability)

You will notice that some may carry more than one meaning, so, spoken in isolation, the sentence might mean more than one thing, such as *The child may eat now.* We usually know from the context which meaning was intended.

DISCUSSION EXERCISES 4.8

1. What is the meaning of the modal in each of the sentences in (18)?

2. Which modal carries the meaning of necessity? past ability? advisability? Give some examples of sentences that demonstrate these meanings.

3. What meanings are conveyed by *could* in the sentence *She could swim ten miles?* (Hint: expand the sentence to put it in a larger context.)

4. One of the few grammar rules explicitly handed down from one generation to the next is the rule about *can* and *may: can* is for ability, *may* is for permission. To what extent do you think this rule is in effect in modern English usage?

5. There is an obsolete grammar rule about *will* vs *shall* that is not in effect in modern American English. Do you know what it is? The answer appears in Reflection 2 at the end of the chapter.

There are two other important uses for modal verbs. They occur in the second part of what are called *hypothetical if-then* statements (although *then* is optional). This is the type of sentence we discussed in Discussion Exercise 4.7, question 3. As you can see from the examples in (20), this construction does not necessarily involve the verb *be*.

(20) If you had the money, (then) you <u>could</u> go to Europe.
If Dan applied himself, (then) he <u>might</u> get good grades.
If Carla smiled more, (then) she <u>would</u> seem kinder.

The *if* part of the statement says something that is contrary to fact (you don't have the money, Dan is not applying himself, and Carla doesn't smile more); the *then* part expresses a condition that would result if it were a fact. We say that the modals in the *then* part function as **conditionals.**

Another use for some modals is to soften commands and make them seem less blunt or rude. Here they tend to lose their individual meanings and are more or less interchangeable:

(21) Could you help me?
Can you help me?
Might you help me?
Would you help me?

You will notice that each of these has a literal meaning and can be answered literally:

(22) Could you help me? I could yesterday, but I can't today, or I could if I had the time.
Can you help me? Yes, I am physically capable of helping you.
Might you help me? I might if I saw something in it for me.
Would you help me? I would if I were a more generous person.

But there is another use for these questions that requires no verbal response at all. Opening a door or relieving someone of a heavy package might be a sufficient response if you interpret them as commands for assistance (albeit softened and polite) rather than requests for information.

DISCUSSION EXERCISES 4.9

1. Soften the following commands by using a modal:

   Get me a beer!
   Stop talking!
   Lend me five dollars!

2. Explain how these statements could mean different things in different contexts:

   You might change your attitude.
   You may want to check your spelling.

(continued)

3. Sometimes modals are used as conditionals with no accompanying *if*-statement, but there is still an implied *if*-statement. Supply an appropriate *if*-statement for the following conditionals:

You could get better grades.
I would not do that.
He would do anything for her.

WHAT IS VERB TENSE?

*[handwritten margin note: * only 2 tenses because the forms have enflection reinflection. — pres. — past (future not a tense but a time)]*

Verbs, as we already know, are those words that tell us the time of the action. We are used to thinking of the **time** of the verb as the **tense** of the verb, but they are not exactly the same thing. Let's talk about *time* first. English has three different times that we associate with verbs: present, past, and future. The present, despite its name, does not refer to activities going on at the moment. Rather, it refers to general facts and activities that include right now but cover a much wider range of time. The following examples will give you some idea of the present time:

(23) Lauren loves the Red Wings.
Jane reads historical novels.
The workers punch time cards.
This car needs a brake job.
The Bronx is part of New York.

The past refers to an action or fact prior to the time of utterance:

(24) I studied French in Paris.
The enemy invaded at dawn.
It snowed yesterday.
They bought a new house.
Betty left in a huff.

The future, of course, refers to an action or fact subsequent to the time it is said or written:

(25) You will regret this.
The police officer will file a report.
The world will end next Friday.
My aunt will visit us in June.

These three times make up the **simple tenses.** So, if you thought time and tense were the same thing, you were right up until this point. We can talk about the times we described above as the **simple present tense,** the **simple past tense** and the **simple future tense.**

DISCUSSION EXERCISES 4.10

1. Given what we already know about verbs, it is easy for us to describe how each of these tenses is formed. We know that if the subject of the present tense verb is a singular noun phrase or *he, she, it,* we must add the suffix *-s.* What form does the verb take otherwise?

2. The past, in its regular formation, adds the suffix *-ed* to the base form. Does it matter what the subject is? Give some examples of regular past tense verbs. What are some exceptions?

3. The future tense is expressed with the modal *will.* What form of the verb follows *will?* Does it matter what the subject is? Are there any exceptions?

The simple tenses allow us to talk about actions occurring at a variety of times relative to when we utter or write them, but they are limited in what they can express about the time of an action. For example, as we saw above, the simple tenses do not let us talk about something happening right now. If I say *Jane reads historical novels,* it doesn't tell me what she is doing right now. Similarly, if I wanted to describe an event as background to another event, I couldn't do it with the simple tenses, nor could I indicate the relative order of two events if they both occurred in the past. To give us a richer and more complete way of referring to the time of actions, English provides us with what is called **aspect.** *Aspect* never occurs on its own; rather, it combines with time to form the **complex tenses.** Thus, English has three times that may occur on their own to express the simple tenses, or they may combine with aspect to form the complex tenses:

key

> **Time (Present, Past, Future) = Simple Tense**
> **Time + Aspect = Complex Tense**

To understand what this means, we need to understand what aspect is, and that is best accomplished by illustration.

two aspects —

There are two different aspects in English, the **progressive aspect** and the **perfect aspect.** The *progressive* aspect allows us to describe actions as backgrounds to other actions, or actions in progress. The following examples will show you how the progressive aspect works.

(26) As I speak, Mary is writing her letter of resignation.
    When Pat arrived home, the children were playing quietly.

Although the progressive may occur without another action overtly expressed, another "anchor" action is always implied:

(27) My roommate was snoring (when I passed his room).
    The kitten is hiding (as I say this).

You will notice that the progressive aspect involves the use of the present participle of the verb, but the present participle cannot occur as a verb all by itself. We wouldn't say *My roommate snoring* or *The kitten hiding*. The present participle is a nonfinite verb form, meaning it cannot carry time. So what we do is use it together with the auxiliary verb *be* to express the progressive aspect. When a time is attached to the verb *be*, the progressive tenses are formed, as indicated below:

 Progressive Tenses = (Be + Time) + Present Participle

Since there are three different times, there are three different progressive tenses. The tense will change as you change the time of the verb *be*, as you can see in the following set of sentences.

(28) She <u>is</u> waiting: present progressive tense
She <u>was</u> waiting: past progressive tense
She <u>will be</u> waiting: future progressive tense

DISCUSSION EXERCISES 4.11

1. Use the frame *the boy study Spanish* and give the sentence in the simple present, the simple past, the simple future, the present progressive, the past progressive, and the future progressive.

2. Change the subject to *the boys* and do the same thing. What changes do you have to make?

3. Tell the tense of the verb in each of the following sentences:

   The house lacks character.
   Polly was asking for a cracker.
   The storm will pass in an hour.
   We were expecting trouble.
   My uncle will be staying with us.
   The chef is preparing a banquet.
   Lightning destroyed the barn.

4. Sometimes one tense can express a time ordinarily reserved for another tense. For example, *I leave tomorrow* uses the present tense but actually expresses a future time. What tense is used in each of the following? Can it express a time outside its normal function?

   Paul is studying French at school.
   Sarah feels ill right now.
   The Germanic tribes invade England in AD 449 and drive out the Celts.
   So then he says, "Leave me alone."

   The last two examples illustrate what is sometimes referred to as the *historical present*.

The second aspect of English is the *perfect* aspect, which serves to associate an action with a later action. Consider the following sentences, all of which contain the perfect aspect:

> (29) I <u>have seen</u> that movie already.
> The woman <u>had left</u> by the time her sister arrived.
> By our next class, you <u>will have read</u> the chapter.

Let's look at the first of these sentences, *I have seen that movie.* If we think of events occurring along a timeline, we can see where this action falls relative to the present:

PAST	PRESENT
I see that movie (perfect aspect)	

At first glance, it does not seem different from the simple past, *I saw that movie,* but there are subtle differences. I might say *I saw that movie* even if it happened twenty years ago. It simply means that the event happened sometime before now. But *I have seen that movie* implies that it is recent, a past event with connections to the present. Now let's look at a timeline for the second sentence in (29), *The woman had left by the time her sister arrived.*

PAST		PRESENT
The woman leaves (perfect aspect)	Her sister arrives	

In this case, the woman's leaving is an event in the past associated with another event in the past, but a later one. The earlier event is expressed using the perfect aspect. The perfect, of course, does not have to express a past event at all, just one that happens before another event. Consider the third sentence in (29), *By our next class, you will have read the chapter.* Now the timeline looks like this, with both events in the future.

PRESENT	FUTURE	
	You read the chapter (perfect aspect)	The class meets

If you compare the three timelines, you will see that in each instance the event expressed using the perfect is associated with some *later* event.

To express the perfect tenses, we use the auxiliary verb *have* and the past participle of the main verb. We form the perfect tenses as illustrated below:

 Perfect Tenses = (Have + Time) + Past Participle

The auxiliary verb *have* carries the time of the action, giving rise to three more complex tenses:

(30) She <u>has waited</u>: present perfect tense
She <u>had waited</u>: past perfect tense
She <u>will have waited</u>: future perfect tense

Notice that the time we attach to *have* is the same as the time of the later event: the present perfect is associated with the present, the past perfect with the past and the future perfect with the future.

DISCUSSION EXERCISES 4.12

1. The use of the perfect tenses in isolation seems odd because they imply some connection to a later time or event. Use each of the sentences in (30) in a larger sentence that makes the connection clearer.

2. Use the frame *his friend rents the cabin* and give the sentence in the present perfect tense, the past perfect tense, and the future perfect tense.

3. Change the subject to *his friends* and do the same thing. What changes do you have to make?

4. The name of the present perfect tense may seem confusing to you, since it expresses a past event. Just keep in mind that it is called *present perfect* because it establishes a connection between a past event and the present. In what sense is there a connection to the present in each of the following?

   The wind has knocked over that tree.
   The secretary has left.
   A bird has built a nest in the rafters.

5. Name the tense in each of the following:

   He had prepared for this exam.
   The novelist has lost her motivation.
   By Monday, the ship will have reached the island.
   They have surrendered.

According to the formulas we have given for expressing verb tense in English, there should be nine different tenses: each of the three times standing alone as a tense (simple tenses), and each of the three times combined with one of the aspects (complex tenses). You may think that these provide more than enough opportunity to describe the time of an action, but English gives us still three more complex tenses, because a verb may have both aspects in its tense at the same time. The sentences in (31) are examples of how we use both aspects at once.

(31) I <u>have been working</u> for a long time.
     She <u>had been living</u> in New Mexico.

You will notice that in the first, the auxiliary verb *have* is followed by the past participle *been,* expressing the perfect aspect. But *been* also serves as the auxiliary verb for the present participle *waiting,* expressing the progressive aspect. Time only appears on the first auxiliary verb, and *been* does double duty as part of the perfect and part of the progressive. Since there are three times, we have three more complex tenses:

(32) She <u>has been waiting</u>: present perfect progressive
     She <u>had been waiting</u>: past perfect progressive
     She <u>will have been waiting</u>: future perfect progressive

All in all, English verbs may occur in twelve different tenses:

simple tenses	complex tenses
simple present	present progressive
simple past	past progressive
simple future	future progressive
	present perfect
	past perfect
	future perfect
	present perfect progressive
	past perfect progressive
	future perfect progressive

Now you know why they call it tense!

DISCUSSION EXERCISES 4.13

1. Use the frame *the girl worry for nothing* and give the sentence in the present perfect progressive, the past perfect progressive, and the future perfect progressive.

2. Change the subject to *the girls* and do the same thing. What changes do you have to make?   *(continued)*

3. Put each of the sentences you have just created in a larger sentence where the use of the tense makes sense.

4. Identify the tense of the verb in each of the following sentences:

By morning, Sam will have been waiting for thirty-six hours.

My in-laws have been organizing a party for us.

Until the war, London had been a wealthy metropolis.

He has not been anticipating any trouble.

Before yesterday, I had not thought about the trip.

WHAT MAKES UP A VERB PHRASE?

When you look at a verb in a sentence, regardless of its tense, you will see that it may occur with modifiers. The verb and its modifiers make up a constituent known as a **verb phrase.** The verb is the head of the verb phrase and the permissible modifiers depend on the subcategory of main verb. The most important subcategories of main verb are **intransitive, transitive,** and **linking.** We have encountered all of these in earlier discussions, but not by name. *[subcateg ones of main verb]*

Intransitive verbs are those that can stand all by themselves in their *[main verb]* phrases. They may have modifiers, but they don't require them, just as some nouns may stand as the sole element in the noun phrase. The sentences in (33) all have intransitive verbs.

(33) The children laughed.
   My heart stopped.
   The tree swayed.
   The roof collapsed.

We *could* add modifiers to these verbs, additional words that tell something more about the action, such as in the sentences in (34).

(34) The children laughed at the clown.
   My heart stopped when I saw them.
   The tree swayed in the wind.
   The roof collapsed under the weight of the snow.

But intransitive verbs do not *need* additional modifiers. They may stand all by themselves and constitute their own verb phrase. So we can say that *laughed* in the first sentence in (33) is an intransitive verb, it is the head of its verb phrase, and it makes up the entire verb phrase.

Transitive verbs, on the other hand, require a following noun phrase, as in the sentences in (35). *[or direct object]*

(35) The pitcher threw the ball.
   His father bought a new suit.
   Sally sold vegetables.

We talked about these required noun phrases in Chapter 3: they are the direct objects. So, transitive verbs are those verbs that require direct objects, and it is sometimes said that transitive verbs transfer their action onto the direct object. If we removed the direct object noun phrases from the sentences in (35), the sentences would be incomplete. The transitive verb and its direct object make up the verb phrases in these sentences. Again, we could include other modifiers in the verb phrase, but the only two that are required are the verb and the following noun phrase.

*trans.
verb
phrases
verb +
direct
obj.*

DISCUSSION EXERCISES 4.14

1. What is the verb phrase in each of the following sentences? Is the verb transitive or intransitive? How do you know?

   The bell rings at 5:00 P.M. every day.

   Those children play all afternoon.

   Cats catch mice by instinct.

   The cynic snickered.

   His answer surprised us.

   Keith caught a cold last week.

2. There are many verbs in English that can be intransitive or transitive, depending on the sentence. So, we often cannot say whether a verb is transitive or intransitive unless we see how it is used in a sentence. For example, compare the pairs of sentences below.

   The window broke.   The paper tore.
   He broke the window.   He tore the paper.

   Are *broke* and *tore* transitive or intransitive? How can it be argued that they may be both?

3. There is some difference of opinion about whether to call verbs like *eat* and *read* in the sentences below transitive or intransitive.

   My family eats at 6:00 P.M.

   She reads at bedtime.

   The argument for calling them intransitive is that they can stand all alone in their verb phrases. What is the argument for calling them transitive?

The third important subcategory of main verb is a *linking* verb. Linking verbs do what their name suggests: they link a subject with a description of that subject. The one linking verb that we have encountered so far is *to be*. When this verb is the main verb, it is linking, as in the following sentences:

(36) The cow was contented.
      The beans are in the pot.

I am unhappy.
She has been the president.

There are a variety of constituents that can follow a linking verb, including adjectives, prepositional phrases, and noun phrases. <u>Linking verbs never stand alone in their verb phrase since, after all, their function is to "link" the subject to something else.</u> There are other linking verbs in English as well, most of them used to describe senses or perceptions. The sentences in (37) illustrate some additional linking verbs.

(37) Mary <u>feels</u> tired.
My goldfish <u>seems</u> lethargic.
The soup <u>tastes</u> funny.
This beer <u>smells</u> sour.
He <u>became</u> angry.
This paper <u>looks</u> messy.
Their music <u>sounds</u> terrible.
The situation <u>appeared</u> hopeless.

linking verbs

DISCUSSION EXERCISES 4.15

1. If you are thinking that the verbs in the above examples are not always linking verbs, you are right. Some of them may be transitive, and some may be intransitive. Consider each of the underlined verbs and see if you can create another sentence in which the verb is either transitive or intransitive, not linking.

2. Tell whether the underlined verb in each of the sentences below is intransitive, transitive, or linking.
   That man <u>appeared</u> in my dream.
   I <u>felt</u> so happy today.
   Linda <u>lost</u> her contact lens.
   He <u>feels</u> your pain.
   Do you <u>taste</u> the pepper in this stew?
   The lawyer <u>seemed</u> nervous.
   I <u>question</u> your motives.
   We <u>smelled</u> smoke.
   The room <u>smelled</u> smoky.

WHAT ARE NONFINITE VERB PHRASES?

finite verb phrase carries tense

So far in our description of the verb phrase, we have been assuming that the verb of the phrase carries tense, so we can call it a **finite verb phrase**. But it is also possible to have a verb phrase in which the verb is in one of its nonfinite forms and there is no tense expressed. These are called **nonfinite verb phrases** and often occur at the beginning of a sentence. As you will see in the sentences below, nonfinite verb phrases are like other verb phrases in terms of their modifiers. They may have direct objects, prepositional phrases, or any other modifier that appears in finite (tensed) verb phrases.

(38) Having abdicated his throne, the king felt relieved.
Smelling the poison, the princess refused to eat her soup.
Dismissed from class, the children ran in all directions.
Having eaten dinner, we were able to relax.
To have friends, a person must be a friend.
To feel fulfilled, most people need meaningful work.

What is interesting about these nonfinite verb phrases is that they do not have subjects of their own; they have to "borrow" the subject from the rest of the sentence. We know from the rest of the sentence that the king abdicated his throne, the princess smelled the poison, the children were dismissed from class, we ate dinner, a person has friends, and most people are the ones feeling fulfilled.

One common nonstandard usage involves a nonfinite verb phrase that cannot borrow the subject from the rest of the sentence. These are the famous **dangling participles.** Following are some examples:

(39) Running for the bus, my book fell in the mud.
Having eaten dinner, the turkey carcass was put in the refrigerator.
Dismissed from class, the parents picked up their children.
Worried about opposition, the editorial was censored.

The meanings of these sentences are not hard to figure out, but technically the nonfinite verb phrases "dangle" because the book didn't run for the bus, the turkey carcass didn't eat dinner, the parents were presumably not the ones dismissed from class, and the editorial was not worried.

COMPOUNDS

Verbs and verb phrases, like nouns and noun phrases, can be conjoined to form compounds. Again, like nouns and noun phrases, they are linked together by means of coordinating conjunctions, either simple or correlative, to form another constituent of the same type. Some examples of compound verbs are given in (40); compound verb phrases can be seen in (41):

(40) The florist cut and dried the flowers.
This machine neither collates nor staples documents.
Everyone either slipped or fell on the ice.

(41) The secretary arranged the meeting and invited the guests.
He works hard all day but plays at night.
The doctor either lost the x-rays or forgot to read them.

DISCUSSION EXERCISES 4.16

1. What is the finite verb phrase in each of the following sentences? What is the nonfinite verb phrase?

   Having received another rejection letter, I gave up writing poetry.
   Discovering the hidden treasure, Kelly jumped for joy.
   Lowered onto the floor, the bench looked smaller.
   Insulted by his cousin's remarks, Peter left the room.

2. Which of these nonfinite verb phrases are dangling participles? Can you rephrase the sentences so they don't dangle?

   Having written the best poem, the prize was given to Elaine.
   Being a sloppy writer, Ian's notes were hard to read.
   Realizing that he had insulted her, Jeff apologized to Carol.
   Expecting the worst, my grades surprised my parents.

3. The examples of the compounds in (40) and (41) are all of finite verbs and verb phrases. But nonfinite verb forms can also form compounds. Give examples of sentences with a compound present participle, a compound infinitive, and a compound past participle. Expand each of these into a compound nonfinite verb phrase.

WHAT IS SUBJECT-VERB AGREEMENT?

Now that we have a better understanding of noun phrases and verb phrases, we can talk about an important cross-referencing rule of English called **subject-verb agreement.** You might remember that in Chapter 2 we introduced the idea of the clause. A clause is a combination of a noun phrase and a verb phrase. The noun phrase of the clause is called the subject, and the verb phrase is called the predicate. All sentences, then, are made up of subjects and predicates. (To refresh your memory, turn back to Chapter 3, Discussion Exercise 3.8, question 2.) The rule of *subject-verb agreement* says that the verb of the predicate must agree with the subject noun phrase in person and number. We already know what **number** means: if the subject is a singular noun phrase, the verb must be marked as singular; if the subject noun phrase is plural, the verb must be plural as well. All of the following sentences are nonstandard because they violate number agreement.

(42) The boy save his money.
     My plants is dying.
     It are on the table.
     His answers sounds ridiculous.

Person is also relevant to the agreement rule. Person refers to the role of the noun phrase or pronoun in the conversation: **first person** is the speaker (or writer); **second person** is the person spoken to; and **third person** refers to anything spoken about. In more concrete terms, the pronouns *I* and *we* are first person, *you* is second person, and any noun phrase or pronoun that is being spoken about is third person. All subjects have both person and number. For example, *I* is first person singular, *we* is first person plural.

DISCUSSION EXERCISES 4.17

1. What is the person and number of the subject in each of the following sentences?

   All people need compassion.
   You should take a break.
   This dog is a stray.
   We agreed to disagree.
   I won't report it this time.
   The answers are in the book.
   My sister arrived last night.

2. Which of these would you judge to be in violation of the subject-verb agreement rule?

   She bring her lunch every day.
   They expects to leave tomorrow.
   She dislikes dishonest people.
   The soldiers is returning from war.
   I does not agree with you.
   We have a problem.

The rule of subject-verb agreement is not something we need to pay attention to all the time, because in many cases the verb stays the same for all subjects, regardless of person and number. In the simple past tense, for example, we don't have to think about which verb goes with which subject, because the verb doesn't change its form. So when do we need to pay attention to the rule? One case that does need special attention is the verb *to be*, because it changes more than other verbs do. In the simple present tense, for example, there are three different forms:

	singular	plural
first person	*am*	*are*
second person	*are*	*are*
third person	*is*	*are*

In the simple past tense, *to be* also requires special notice. Unlike any other verb in the language, it has two different forms from which we must choose.

	singular	plural
first person	*was*	*were*
second person	*were*	*were*
third person	*was*	*were*

DISCUSSION EXERCISES 4.18

1. What makes these violations of the standard English rule of subject-verb agreement?

   They was laughing at me.
   You is supposed to be my friend.
   His parents is coming for dinner.
   We wasn't invited to the party.

2. Give the standard English versions of the above sentences. Are there any differences in meaning between the standard and the nonstandard versions?

Other than the verb *to be*, the only other place where the rule of subject-verb agreement shows some effect is in the simple present tense. As we have already said, most of the time the verb in the present tense is merely the same as the base form. But if the subject is third person singular, we must add the suffix -*s* to the base form of the verb. *The girl sees the boy* versus *The girls see the boy.* (Note that -*s* marks nouns as plural, but verbs as singular!) Not every dialect of English adds the -*s* to the verb in the present tense. It carries no meaning and upsets what is otherwise a neat pattern. But standard English still requires us to use it. We usually have no trouble recognizing when a subject is third person, but we sometimes have trouble recognizing whether the subject is singular or plural.

One situation in which the number of the subject might be difficult to determine is where the subject contains more than one noun phrase. If it is a compound noun phrase with *and*, we treat the subject as plural: *The man and the woman are working.* But the agreement requirement is different if there are two noun phrases joined by *(either) or,* or *(neither) nor,* as in (43), often called a **disjunction.**

(43) Either my sister or my brother is picking me up.
Neither the man nor the woman works here.
You or your friends are expected to show up.

Here we might be inclined to think of these subject noun phrases as plural also, but standard English requires us to view them separately and imposes the following rule: *the noun phrase closest to the verb determines the agreement.* If you look again at the sentences in (43), you will see how that works. Sometimes following this rule gives rise to sentences that are awkward to the ear, like *Either he or I am to blame,* and we might avoid the problem by rephrasing the sentence: *Either he is to blame or I am,* for example.

The next set of sentences illustrates another situation in which it may not be clear to us what the number of the subject is.

(44) One of the professors requires a term paper.
      Each of the children receives a gift at Christmas.

Although the subjects are *one of the professors* and *each of the children,* it is only the head of the noun phrase that determines the agreement. That means the verb must agree with *one* and *each,* both of which are singular. This is an especially difficult rule to follow for two reasons. First, the meaning of the subject may be plural, as in *each of the children;* second, we are used to thinking of the noun phrase right before the verb as the subject. This rule of agreement goes counter to our intuitions about how English works and so it is often violated, especially in speaking. The same problem arises if the head of the noun phrase is a singular noun, as in (45), and nonstandard sentences like the following are commonplace.

(45) The range of answers were interesting.
      The intelligence of the children amaze me.
      The use of cameras are prohibited.

A third situation that goes counter to our intuitions about subject-verb agreement occurs in sentences that begin with *there.* Consider the pairs of sentences in (46).

(46) A book is on the table.   Three books are on the table.
      There is a book on the table.   There are three books on the table.

The meaning of each pair is the same; the only difference is that in the second sentence of each pair, the subject has been moved behind the verb and the expletive *there* has been put in its place. No matter whether it has been moved or not, the subject noun phrase determines the person and number of the verb. But, given its location in the sentence, there is a strong temptation to treat *there* as if it were the subject. The result is nonstandard but very common sentences like *There's three books on the table,* where *there's* is a contraction of *there is.*

Subject-verb agreement is not a difficult rule to follow as long as it doesn't collide with other things we know and expect about English: we expect the subject to appear before the verb; we expect the grammatical number and the meaning number to be the same; we expect that if there is more than one noun phrase in the subject it will be plural. These are all reasonable expectations, and they work most of the time for English. But there are instances in which the standard rule of subject-verb agreement requires that we set aside those expectations and figure it out instead. We are more successful at this in writing, since we have time to reflect, and less successful in speaking, where we speak and formulate our thoughts simultaneously.

DISCUSSION EXERCISES 4.19

1. Each of these sentences violate the standard English rule of subject-verb agreement. Tell what the violation is and what leads people to make the error. What is the standard version of each sentence?

   Neither my mother nor my father are going.
   Either Sue or I are supposed to respond.
   There's too many people in this room.
   Each of you have to take the exam.
   One of the dogs keep barking all night.
   Everyone in my family attend the reunions.
   There's three reasons for rejecting this offer.
   Neither you nor I are to blame.

2. The above instructions are written in nonstandard English. Did you notice? Let's hope so.

3. Similar to sentences like *Each of the children receives a gift* are sentences like

   All of the children receive gifts.
   Both of the children receive gifts.
   Why don't these sentences cause subject-verb agreement problems for us?

4. There are many nouns, called *collective nouns,* that are grammatically singular but have plural meaning, like *group, committee,* and *team.* In American English, they usually require a singular verb: *the group is meeting, the team is playing.* In British English they may have plural verb agreement: *the team are playing.* Even in American English there are some collective nouns that can be thought of as singular or plural, such as *faculty: the faculty is responsible, the faculty are responsible.* Can you think of others that allow this fluctuation in number?

5. In his *New York Times Magazine* column called "On Language" (February 19, 1995), William Safire objects to President Clinton's statement "There's the talkers and there's the doers." What do you think Safire's complaint is?

6. This headline appeared in a local newspaper:

   The enlightening power of the arts are overblown.

   What rule of grammar does it violate?

You have now crossed an important threshold in the study of English grammar. Noun phrases and verb phrases are the basic building blocks of sentences. Once you understand what they are made of and how they behave, you have a grounding in how the language works generally. Much of what we will say in the remaining chapters of the book will build on and deepen this understanding. In the next chapter we will consider pronouns, which in most respects can be considered a special kind of noun phrase.

REFLECTIONS

1. It may seem strange to you that only third-person-singular subjects require a suffix on the verb. In fact, there was a time when all forms of the verb required suffixes, but most of them were lost over time. You can still see remnants of these earlier suffixes in most versions of the Bible and in earlier literary writing: *thou hast* (you have), for example. You will also notice that the -(*e*)*s* suffix used to compete with -(*e*)*th* as the third-person-singular verb ending. Look up Portia's famous speech in Shakespeare's *The Merchant of Venice* that begins "The quality of mercy is not strained. . . ." How does this speech illustrate that these two suffixes competed during Shakespeare's time?

2. In her column titled "Word Court" in the *Atlantic Monthly* (March 1996), Barbara Wallraff tells us about the rule of *will* vs *shall:* "The traditional distinction made in England is that in the first person *will* has to do with willpower— that is, it denotes intentionality— and *shall* with simple futurity, whereas the second and third persons reverse the pattern." She goes on to explain the difference in meaning between *I shall drown; no one will save me,* and *I will drown; no one shall save me.* Can you figure it out?

3. You will remember from the discussion in the chapter that there is fluctuation in *hypothetical if-then* statements between the standard *if I were you* and the nonstandard *if I was you.* The explanation behind this unexpected form of *be* is that it is in a verb form called the *subjunctive,* a term you might be familiar with if you have studied Spanish or French. English doesn't use the subjunctive very much anymore, but it still appears in the *if* part of *hypothetical if-then* statements. You'll notice that the stigma of *was* diminishes greatly if the *if* statement is something other than *if I were you.* Consider, for example, *If the weather was better, we could have a picnic.* Does this sound nonstandard to you?

4. The distinction in meaning between the present perfect tense and the simple past tense can be very subtle, and in some cases they are used interchangeably. There is probably no difference at all between *I ate the pie* and *I have eaten the pie.* But notice that if you want to pinpoint the action at a specific time in the past, a difference emerges. Suppose you wanted to add *yesterday.* Could you add it to both? Which sounds odd? Why do you think the two tenses are not equally compatible with expressions like *yesterday, last week,* etc.?

5. The three main subcategories of verbs are transitive (requires a direct object), intransitive (can stand alone), and linking (requires a subject complement). But there are some verbs that don't fit neatly into any of these categories. For example, what requirement is there for the use of *be* with the meaning "be located," as in *He is in his seat?* What about the verb *put,* or the verb *lie* meaning "stretch out one's body"?

6. The verb *to act* can be either intransitive or linking. Consider the sentences

> He acts odd.
>
> He acts oddly.

Describe some behavior of his that would fit each of these descriptions.

7. It is possible for nonfinite verb phrases to have their own subjects. These are known as *absolutes* and occur only in very formal English. Which are the absolutes in the following?

> The king having abdicated his throne, the peasants rejoiced.
>
> The students having passed their exams, the partying began.

You will notice that in these there is no requirement that the nonfinite verb phrase be linked to the subject of the finite verb phrase. In the novel *Alias Grace* (Nan A. Talese, A Division of Random House, New York: Doubleday, 1996), the author, Margaret Atwood, uses this construction with unusual frequency. These are just two examples out of many:

> "The captain having been notified, two sailors came to carry my mother up onto the deck." (p. 120)
>
> ". . . and when I looked the next day, she being out of the room, I found that it was a gold ring." (p. 172)

8. Dangling participles are actually part of a larger category of **dangling modifiers.** Modifiers at the beginning of a sentence are supposed to connect to the following subject; if they can't, they "dangle." What makes each of these a dangling modifier?

> Unhappy with the election results, another vote was taken.
>
> Located a block from home, it was easy for me to get to work.

There was a time when a sentence like the following was considered to have a dangling modifier:

> Due to the storm, the school was closed.

In what sense can this modifier be consider dangling? What is your own judgment about this sentence? Listen for this construction in everyday usage. Do you know anyone who considers it to be nonstandard?

9. There is always more to say about dangling modifiers. When they are at the beginning of the sentence, modifiers must "borrow" the subject. But when they are at the end, they may borrow the subject *or* the noun phrase closest to them. So, some sentences may have two meanings:

> I saw the boy looking through my window.

Who was looking through the window? There is nothing grammatically wrong with this sentence, but you need to be aware in your own usage that it can have two different interpretations.

10. You will find people struggling with agreement problems in sentences like the following:

> The number of students <u>is</u> growing.
>
> A number of students <u>are</u> coming.

Although they look very much alike, they have different structures. In the first, *number* is the head noun and is singular, so the verb is singular. In the second, *a number of* acts like a determiner, comparable to *several,* and the head of the noun phrase is *students.* Since *students* is plural, the verb is plural. Try to explain this to someone without using grammatical jargon.

11. Some nouns are singular in meaning but plural in form and require the verb to be plural. Some examples are *scissors, pants, trousers.* Why do you think these nouns have plural form?

12. The following is from a modern novel: "He shone his own flashlight upward then, so that two beams shone against the mast now." (David Guterson, *Snow Falling On Cedars,* Vintage Books: New York, 1995, p. 452)

This is from another modern novel: "It lasted fine. It throve . . ."
(Wallace Stegner, *Crossing to Safety,* Penguin Books: New York,
1987, p. 103)
Does the past tense usage in these passages match your own?

13. A character in still another modern novel asks the following:

> "Is that because you understand I have to ask if you or your sister know where Hawkins is?" (Alice Hoffman, *Practical Magic,* Berkley Books: New York, 1995, p. 275)

What grammar rule does this question violate?

14. The following were collected from newspapers, textbooks, websites, and university student writing. What do they all have in common? Why is this particular usage in English so common?

> "Recent analysis of the structure of discourse in western courts have stressed the careful sequencing of speech turns."
>
> "The rule of r-lessness states that the 'R' in words are pronounced only if they come before a vowel."
>
> "One of the morphemes are the result of the natural change in language and the other is borrowed from another language."
>
> "The choice between the pronouns 'who' and 'whom' often present a problem for the English speaker."
>
> "I think teaching them these things are an important part in promoting skills they will need for the 21st century."
>
> ". . . the report concludes that a range of effective treatments exist for nearly all mental disorders."
>
> "I thought that the comparison of the words *pail* and *bucket* were quite interesting."

". . . the dialects that are spoken in various parts of the United States is heavily influenced by the geographic location of people more than commonly thought."

"The distinction between particles and prepositions are that particles can be moved to the end of the sentence. . . ."

"The meaning of the words are changed."

"Each of the words above explain how this German word is formed in the mouth."

"In order to be sure that in the future the meaning of documents are clear . . . ."

"Investors are already beginning to see signs that the impact of pre-announcements are diminishing."

15. As we saw in Discussion Exercise 4.3, question 5, it is very common for nouns to be made into verbs, although they are often frowned upon when they are first introduced. For example, in the recent past, grammatical purists have objected to sentences like the following:

Contact his relatives.

How will this impact your business?

Loan me ten dollars.

In each case, what do you think is the basis for the objection?

16. Does your dictionary list *transition, wordsmith, interface,* and *e-mail* as verbs? Can you use all of them as verbs in the same sentence? Does it make you sound like a corporate executive?

17. An author in a gardening magazine says that she "could wheelbarrow only 20 bricks at a time." A University of Michigan publication says, "Many other University organizations are partnering with U-M Online . . . ." An Olympics TV announcer said, "No American has medaled in this event." An author of a scholarly article writes ". . . most other participants will membership themselves as 'middle-men' . . . ." In what way is their use of English innovative?

18. Trace the history of the verbs *to xerox* and *to fax.*

PRACTICE EXERCISES FOR CHAPTER 4 (Answers on p. 225)

1. Identify the nonfinite verb forms in the following sentences. Tell whether each is a present participle, a past participle, or an infinitive.

   1. I need to ask you a few questions.
   2. She was looking for her sister.
   3. Eric hasn't considered all his options.
   4. They will be expecting you at seven o'clock.

(continued)

    5. Having been informed of the results. Mary regretted her actions.

    6. John is driving his father to the airport.

    7. To be truthful, I don't like your new haircut.

    8. Judy can't leave yet.

    9. Sitting in my living room, I can see his parked car.

    10. By next week, we will have been living here one year.

2. Which of the following *-ing* words are present participles and which are gerunds?

    1. My children enjoy visiting their grandparents.

    2. They are painting the bedrooms today.

    3. Ted was taking a walk.

    4. You are being a nuisance.

    5. Seeing is believing.

    6. She has been listening to the radio.

    7. You can learn this by memorizing the tables.

    8. Canvassing the neighborhood is a good way to get votes.

    9. Canvassing the neighborhood, I discovered a lot of Republicans.

    10. He wrote a book about breeding horses.

3. Which of the following are generally accepted as standard and which are generally considered to be nonstandard?

    1. Vickie has wrote a letter to her congresswoman.

    2. He has ran the marathon two years in a row.

    3. Lay down and close your eyes.

    4. The baby has drunk all her milk.

    5. I have never swum in this lake.

    6. They pleaded with her to stop.

    7. Jerry has went home.

    8. We have seen that exhibit.

    9. She has lain in her bed all day.

    10. He swang the bat.

4. Identify all the verbs in the following sentences. Which are main and which are helping? Of the helping verbs, which are auxiliaries and which are modals?

    1. You can leave your shoes at the door.

    2. We are all happy for you.

    3. His watch is running fast.

    4. This man has no enemies.

    5. I have been expecting you.

    6. She would wait by the telephone for hours.

    7. Cathy has had a cold all week.

(continued)

8. Ruth has been having second thoughts.
9. We must stop all this bickering.
10. Must you leave the door open?

5. Take the frame *Mary go home* and create a sentence in each of the following tenses:

simple present: _____

simple past: _____

simple future: _____

present progressive: _____

past progressive: _____

future progressive: _____

present perfect: _____

past perfect: _____

future perfect: _____

present perfect progressive: _____

past perfect progressive: _____

future perfect progressive: _____

6. Name the tense of the verb in each of the following sentences:
   1. She bought her ticket.
   2. I will have been waiting for an hour.
   3. We meet up north every year.
   4. He has agreed to go.
   5. She had already left.
   6. They will accept the invitation.
   7. You were grinning.
   8. I have been expecting you.
   9. They will have eaten by then.
   10. We had been studying.

7. Tell whether the main verb in each sentence is transitive, intransitive, or linking.
   1. The plane flew over the mountain.
   2. The pilot flew the plane.
   3. The passengers seemed calm.
   4. A flight attendant appeared with beverages and peanuts.
   5. One child felt sick.
   6. Everyone was frightened.
   7. I saw the approaching storm.
   8. A little girl sobbed quietly.

(continued)

9. The plane landed safely.

10. We all cheered.

8. Which of these sentences have dangling participles?

   1. Realizing that he would be late, Mike began to run.
   2. Having left her keys at home, Barbara couldn't get into her office.
   3. Neglecting to floss daily, Ben's teeth began to rot.
   4. Fortified with vitamins, I drink plenty of whole milk.
   5. Expecting the worst, we were pleasantly surprised.

9. Which of the following violate the rule of subject-verb agreement?

   1. Neither Roberta nor her children are coming.
   2. Either Sue or I are supposed to respond.
   3. There's too many people in this room.
   4. Each of you have to take the exam.
   5. Both of the men are here.
   6. Neither my husband nor I am to blame.
   7. One of the neighbors keep yelling.
   8. Allen and Joe lives on this street.
   9. Everyone in my family attend these reunions.
   10. Neither my aunt nor my uncle are coming to my graduation.

10. Make up a sentence that meets each description. It doesn't matter what tense of the verb you choose.

   1. *may* expresses permission
   2. *be* is a linking verb
   3. *feel* is a transitive verb
   4. *could* is a conditional
   5. *must* expresses probability
   6. a modal softens a command
   7. *look* is a linking verb
   8. *look* is an intransitive verb
   9. *taste* is a transitive verb
   10. *bend* is an intransitive verb

11. Find an example of each of the following in the *Believers* selection below:

   an infinitive

   be used as a linking verb

   a verb in the past perfect tense

   a compound verb phrase

   a direct object noun phrase

   a compound noun phrase

(continued)

a verb in the simple past tense

an object of a preposition

a modal verb

a past participle

a subject noun phrase

a present participle

Somehow, my Mickle Street story had created the wrong tone or put some element into the air that the other guests were forced to ponder. A silence without depth or extension drifted down over us like an invisible black fabric. You would have thought that I had committed a terrible social blunder, courageous in its rudeness. The night sky was dimly visible overhead, and I had had too much to drink, so that when I looked up, the stars appeared to be swirling, or blindly racing some sickening stellar soapbox derby, right to left, right to left." (Baxter: "Reincarnation" p. 17)

12. Identify the violations of formal standard English in the following letter:

Dear Chris,

I am getting more and more excited as the day of our trip gets closer. Having been to Paris before, the image of the city is very vivid in my mind. Last night I looked through my photo's and seen all the places I visited before. I have went there twice now, so this time I will take less photos. Neither you nor my sister have been there, so I know that the variety of museums and restaurants are going to fascinate you.

Fondly,
Pat

FIVE

PRONOUNS

WHAT ARE PRONOUNS?

Pronouns are words that, for the most part, take the place of or stand for noun phrases. Sentence (1) contains a noun phrase and a *pronoun* that takes its place.

(1) The elderly man sat on the bench until he was asked to leave.

The elderly man is a noun phrase and *he* is the pronoun that takes its place, in the sense that it enables us to avoid repeating the noun phrase. You can see that pronouns make communication efficient. It would be awkward and burdensome to have to repeat whole noun phrases in conversation: *The elderly man sat on the bench until the elderly man was asked to leave.* In fact, since we expect people to use pronouns to avoid repetition, when the noun phrase is repeated we tend to assume that it refers to two different things.

The noun phrase that the pronoun stands for is known as the **antecedent** of the pronoun. In sentence (1), *the elderly man* is the antecedent of the pronoun *he*. Normally, of course, the pronoun follows its antecedent. We use a noun phrase and then a pronoun to avoid repetition of the noun phrase. But there are some situations in which the pronoun can come first. In the examples below, the antecedent follows the pronoun (in at least one interpretation of the sentence).

(2) After he was asked to leave, the elderly man began to sob.
    When she saw the mess, my mother called the police.

In some cases the antecedent of a pronoun is not a noun phrase, but rather a whole sentence, as in (3).

(3) I hate to say it, but you didn't pass the exam.

And there are some pronouns that do not have grammatical antecedents at all. Instead, they refer directly to the participants in a conversation. In the sentences of (4), *I, we,* and *you* are pronouns, but they do not have grammatical antecedents. That is, they refer to the speakers and listeners and are not being used to avoid repetition of a noun phrase.

(4) <u>I</u> question your sincerity.
<u>We</u> enjoyed our vacation.
<u>You</u> must knock before entering.

You will remember from Chapter 4 that these are called first- and second-person pronouns; only the third-person pronouns can have true antecedents.

DISCUSSION EXERCISES 5.1

1. Tell what the antecedent is for each of the underlined pronouns. Remember that some pronouns do not have antecedents.

   Ken bought a coat, but <u>it</u> doesn't fit.
   Although <u>he</u> doesn't know <u>it</u> yet, Jon is taking Kate to the prom.
   Ted and Lora said that <u>they</u> would come to the party.
   I am embarrassed to say <u>it,</u> but *you* have spinach in your teeth.
   We found two pennies and put <u>them</u> in the bank.

2. Some people say that pronouns take the place of *nouns.* Can you demonstrate that this is not correct?

3. Other lexical categories also have pro-forms, that is, words that are used to avoid repetition. They are not as varied and complex as the pronouns, so they don't lend themselves to similar in-depth study. Can you pick out the pro-forms in the following sentences? What repetition do they avoid?

   The fish is in the bowl and the snail is there also.
   When Kathy left the room, her brother did so too.
   The puppy is nervous, but being so doesn't affect his appetite.

4. You will remember from Chapter 3 that the word *it* also has a placeholder function when no other grammatical subject is available. In which of the sentences below is *it* a true pronoun and in which is *it* a placeholder? Could any be both?

   It has been snowing all winter.
   Put it in the closet.
   It is too hot to walk.
   It is easy to see that you're happy.
   It isn't the one I asked for.

PERSONAL PRONOUNS

You will see as we go along that there are many different kinds of pronouns, each with a different function. The ones that generally come to mind first are the **personal pronouns.** As we have already mentioned, these are distinguished by *person;* that is, they can be first person, referring to the speaker; second person, referring to the listener; or third person, referring to whatever is being talked about. They also have *number:* they may be singular or plural. For example, *I* is a first-person-singular pronoun, *they* is a third-person-plural pronoun. Some personal pronouns are also distinguished by *gender.* If I asked you to tell me what the third-person- singular personal pronoun is, you would have to say *he, she,* or *it.* If I wanted you to be more specific, I would have to specify gender as well: pronouns that refer to females are *feminine;* those that refer to males are *masculine;* those that refer to things are *neuter.* The gender of English pronouns is called *natural gender* because the use of the pronoun corresponds to the sex of the antecedent. If you know a language other than English, you might be familiar with *grammatical gender.* In Spanish and French, for example, nouns are arbitrarily assigned gender; in English *table* and *feather* are both neuter because they are inanimate things, but in Spanish and French they happen to have feminine gender (which affects the choice of adjective and article). English used to have grammatical gender as well, but it has been lost over time. When we use pronouns, we choose the ones that match their antecedents (or the conversational participants they stand for) in person, number, and gender.

The one other feature that distinguishes personal pronouns is **case.** Case refers to the function of the pronoun in a sentence, which is independent of the function of its antecedent. There are three cases: **subject** (or **subjective**), **object** (or **objective**), and **possessive.** Consider the underlined pronouns in the sentences in (5).

(5) <u>He</u> found the missing key.
The idea intrigued <u>him</u>.
<u>His</u> father was kind.

These pronouns are all third-person-singular, but the first is a subject, the second an object, and the third a possessive pronoun.

DISCUSSION EXERCISES 5.2

1. Personal pronouns are distinguished by person, number, gender, and case. Fill in the grid below to show all the personal pronouns of English. Use the following frames to guide your choices:

_____ saw the boy.   (subject)

The boy saw _____.   (object)

_____ cat is in the tree.   (possessive)

(continued)

	subject	object	possessive
singular			
first person			
second person			
third person			
masculine			
feminine			
neuter			
plural			
first person			
second person			
third person			

2. You might remember that we encountered the possessive pronouns when we were talking about the determiners. *My, your, his, her, our,* and *their* are possessive pronouns that fall into the determiner system and modify the head noun of the noun phrase, in exactly the same way that possessive noun phrases do. For example, *his* in *his house* might stand for *that man's.* But possessive noun phrases can also stand alone and do not have to be determiners.

This manuscript is the essayist's.
The fault is John's and Ted's.
This piece of property is that woman's.

If you want to replace these noun phrases with possessive pronouns, you must use the **free-standing form** of the pronoun. Fill in the sentences below with the free-standing form of the possessive pronoun that corresponds to the possessive pronoun determiner.

Example:	This is my book.	The book is mine.
	This is your book.	The book is _____.
	This is his book.	The book is _____.
	This is her book.	The book is _____.
	This is its book.	The book is _____.
	This is our book.	The book is _____.
	This is their book.	The book is _____.

3. Which possessive pronoun does not have a free-standing form? Which determiner and free-standing possessive pronouns are the same?

4. You will notice that the possessive pronoun *its* is spelled without an apostrophe, but it is often seen spelled incorrectly with an apostrophe. Why do you think this is such a common spelling error? Does it surprise you to learn that at one time it was an acceptable spelling?

If you look at the grid you have prepared, you will notice some interesting features of the pronoun system. One is that there is no difference between the second-person-singular and the second-person-plural pronouns. This is a relatively recent development in English, which used to have a separate set of second-person-singular pronouns—*thou* (subject), *thee* (object), and *thy, thine* (possessive)—that are no longer used in modern English. If you listen to people in conversation, you will notice that they often still need this distinction even though modern standard English does not supply it. For many speakers of English, *you all* (or *y'all*) serves as the plural in casual speech (although for some it can also be singular). Some of us make do with *you guys* or *you people,* or even the sorely stigmatized *youse,* formed on the basis of analogy with noun plurals. Standard English is clearly deficient from the standpoint of second-person pronouns, so people devise strategies for bypassing the deficiency and communicating what they need to communicate. It is a principle of human language behavior that people do not like to sacrifice meaning to follow the rules of standard grammar and, when standard grammar fails us, we find other ways to get our meaning across.

Another characteristic of our pronoun system that often leads to awkwardness in usage is the absence of a gender-neutral third-person-singular human pronoun. The problem arises in sentences like those in (6).

(6) If anyone wants to go, _____ should sign up now.
You should see a doctor and ask _____ to X-ray your arm.
Some person left _____ umbrella in the closet.

The pronoun in the blank has to refer to humans, so it cannot be the neuter pronoun *it.* That leaves us only the masculine and feminine pronouns, but in these sentences we don't know the sex of the antecedent. So what are our choices for filling in the blanks? People resolve this dilemma in different ways. The eighteenth-century grammarians suggested using the masculine pronouns, arguing that they covered both sexes, in much the same way that words like *mankind* are said to refer to all people. This was never a popular choice because to most speakers the masculine pronouns are simply masculine, but you will still see some grammatical purists adhering to this rule. In more recent years the use of masculine pronouns to include both sexes has been labeled sexist language and is frowned upon by the editors of many scholarly books and journals. Unfortunately, there is no fully acceptable substitute. Some people will use *he or she* (or *him or her* or *his or her* for object and possessive pronouns, respectively). There are also some written variations of these like *he/she* or *s/he.* Anyone who tries to use these combinations discovers how awkward they can be, especially if the pronoun needs to be repeated several times. In scholarly writing, authors may alternate the use of masculine and feminine pronouns, sometimes with a prefatory explanation of their choice. Another option that is sometimes available to us, but not always, is to change the antecedent to a plural noun phrase. That solves the problem, because the plural third-person pronouns are gender-neutral, as we see in (7).

(7) If people want to go, <u>they</u> should sign up.
    When students work hard we should reward <u>them.</u>
    Children must bring notes from <u>their</u> parents.

Probably the most popular choice among speakers of English for resolving this dilemma is to use the plural gender-neutral pronouns *they, them,* and *their,* even when the antecedent is singular. As you would guess, this usage is more common in speaking than in writing, but it seems to be gaining ground on all fronts in recent years and may soon be considered standard.

DISCUSSION EXERCISES 5.3

1. Why is the standard English absence of a distinction between a singular and a plural second-person pronoun a particular handicap to people who wait on tables in restaurants? How would you resolve the problem if you were a server?

2. How would you fill in the blanks in the following sentences? Explain your choices.

   No competent lawyer would advise ___ client to lie on the stand.
   When a child learns to speak ___ can make ___ wishes known.
   Someone knocked, but I told ___ you weren't in.
   Any person who travels abroad needs to have ___ passports validated.
   If you see anyone, ask ___ what ___ are doing here.

3. To solve the gender-neutral pronoun problem, some people have suggested that we introduce a new pronoun into English. One such suggestion is *em,* as in *if anyone calls tell em I'm asleep.* What do you think of this as a solution? Why do you think it hasn't caught on?

4. If someone told you that an anonymous donor gave all his money to the university, would you think that the donor might be female? Should you be able to get this meaning according to the eighteenth-century rules for pronoun usage? Explain.

Probably the most serious usage problem in our pronoun system is the distinction between subject and object pronouns. You remember from Chapter 3 that we signal whether a noun phrase is a subject or an object by where we put it in the sentence. We do not have to change the form of the noun phrase. So *the girl* in (8) is a subject if we put it before the verb and an object if we put it after the verb.

(8) The girl caught the ball.
    Jeff saw the girl.

But our pronoun system says that not only do we need to locate the pronouns appropriately to mark their grammatical function, we also must choose a different form of the pronoun for each function. If we change *the girl* in (8) to a pronoun, it will be *she* for the first sentence but *her* for the second: *she caught the ball, Jeff saw her.*

The standard English rule for subject and object pronouns is simple in principle: use subject pronouns for subjects and object pronouns for objects (direct, indirect, and objects of prepositions). Adult speakers of English apply this rule easily in simple frames such as the ones that were given in Discussion Exercise 5.2 to help you fill in the grid of pronouns. But let's look at some situations in which the choice seems to be harder. Suppose the pronoun is part of a compound, as in (9).

(9) He and I are building a fort.

He and *I* are both part of the subject, so standard English requires subject pronouns. But if you observe people's usage, you will hear other variations of this compound: *him and me, me and him, him and I.* That is, for compound subjects there is a tendency for some people to use at least one object pronoun. This usage is considered uneducated and is often corrected by adults: "It's not *him and me*, it's *he and I*." In an attempt to correct this, many people overcorrect, or hypercorrect, and use sentences like (10).

(10) She is proud of he and I.

Sentence (10) is nonstandard, of course, because *of* is a preposition, and the pronoun(s) following it is the object of the preposition, therefore requiring the objective form.

DISCUSSION EXERCISES 5.4

1. To refresh your memory, make a list of all the subject and object personal pronouns, labeling them according to person, number, and gender. Which subjects and objects have the same form?

2. Fill in the blanks with subject or object pronouns, according to the standard English rules of pronoun selection.

   You and _____ (I, me) are sitting together.
   ___ (He, Him) and ___ (she, her) will arrive soon.
   Deliver this letter to ___ (him, he) and his sister.
   This is a story about ___ (her, she) and ___ (we, us).
   They spotted you and ___ (I, me).

(continued)

3. Would you say *this is a secret between you and I* or *this is a secret between you and me?* Explain your choice.

4. Even if someone says *Him and me are friends,* using object instead of subject pronouns, we still understand the pronouns to be subjects. Why do you think that is so?

5. Rather than signaling function, it may be that subject and object pronouns in compounds have come to signal levels of formality: object pronouns are casual, informal, intimate, while subject pronouns are formal and maybe even stuffy. Does this fit your own perceptions of their usage? What is your image of the person who says *her and me took a trip* as compared to the one who says *she and I took a trip?* How do you judge the person who says *I saw he and she at the concert?*

6. If a compound pronoun contains a first-person pronoun, it is preferred that this pronoun be placed last: *He and I* rather than *I and he,* for example. Have you ever been given an explanation for this ordering?

Besides compounds, there are two other situations in which the standard English rules for pronoun usage are not universally followed, even by the most educated. One deals with the use of pronouns after the verb *to be.* Which of the two answers in (11) is standard, for example?

(11) Which one is the thief? This is him.
       This is he.

You will probably hear both, as did the eighteenth-century grammarians. Needing to find a rule that decided which was correct, the grammarians used Latin as a model; constructions such as these in Latin require the nominative case or, in terms of English grammar, subject pronouns. So, *this is he* is the strictly formal standard English answer to the question. Many of us follow this rule in formal situations, such as when answering the telephone (*this is she, this is he*), but we tend not to extend it to our everyday usage. How many of us in answer to the question *Where are the books I lent you?* say *Those are they on the table?* We are apparently comfortable with placing subject pronouns at the beginning of sentences, where we expect to find subjects, but our comfort level drops precipitously when we are asked to put subject pronouns somewhere else in the sentence.

The other situation in which the formal standard rule collides with our intuitive sense about how English works is in comparisons. Which of the two sentences in (12) is "correct"?

(12) I am taller than him.
       I am taller than he.

The eighteenth-century grammarians were faced with the same question. They reasoned that there was an implied continuation of the sentence: *I am taller than he is tall.* Therefore, they concluded, we should use whatever pronoun fits into the implied continuation. According to this rule, the second of the two choices in (12) is "correct." It is easy to see why speakers of English tend to favor the first choice. Unless you happen to have been told the rule for continuing the sentence in your mind, you would not be likely to figure it out for yourself, and putting subject pronouns at the end of the sentence seems highly unnatural to us.

DISCUSSION EXERCISES 5.5

1. Choose one of the two pronouns given to complete each sentence. Explain your choice. Would the setting in which you said it make a difference in your choice?

   Who is it? It is ___ (I, me).
   Which are my keys? Those are ___ (they, them).
   Are you happier than ___ (she, her)?
   Which one is David? This is ___ (he, him).
   You know more than ___ (we, us) about this.

2. Suppose you were one of the eighteenth-century grammarians involved in discussions about comparisons and pronouns. Could you make a plausible argument that *I am taller than him* should be correct? You were asked to do the same thing in Chapter 1. Your new knowledge of pronouns and pronoun usage should enable you to make a more convincing argument now.

3. Imagine yourself knocking on someone's door. They say *Who is it?* Do you say *It is I* or *It's me?* What is the effect of each? Do you think you would choose to violate the standard English rule? You might be interested to know that standard French uses the equivalent of "it's me," *c'est moi.*

4. How did the author resolve the gender-neutral pronoun problem in the previous question? Do you think the author of a grammar book should resolve the problem in this way? What would you have done?

REFLEXIVE PRONOUNS

Reflexive pronouns end in *-self* or *-selves.* In many ways they are like the personal pronouns, but they are used only under certain conditions. One of those conditions is illustrated in the sentences in (13).

(13) Keith likes him.
     Keith likes himself.

You notice that when we use the personal pronoun *him,* we know that *Keith* and *him* are two different people. But when we use the reflexive pronoun, we know

Know several examples in which the pronouns have a different function !

that *Keith* and *himself* refer to the same person. So, one occasion on which we use a reflexive pronoun is when the subject and an object in a sentence refer to the same entity.

Another purpose of reflexive pronouns is to provide contrast, as in (14).

(14) My whole family is Republican, but I myself am a Democrat.

Here the reflexives do not function as pronouns in a technical sense, since they are not replacing a noun phrase, but rather are repeating it for the sake of emphasis or contrast.

A third use of reflexive pronouns is illustrated in (15).

(15) The women built the garage (by) themselves.

As you can see, here the reflexive pronoun carries the meaning of "alone, without accompaniment," again not technically a pronoun function since it is not replacing a noun phrase.

DISCUSSION EXERCISES 5.6

1. What is the function of the reflexive pronoun in each of the following sentences?

   Todd cooked dinner himself.
   Irene saw herself as an activist.
   The nurse gave himself an injection.
   The island itself is calm, but the surrounding seas are dangerous.
   I myself prefer cats.

2. There is some apparent overlap in the use of personal and reflexive pronouns, as illustrated here.

   As for me, I will vote my conscience.
   As for myself, I will vote my conscience.

   Do you detect any difference in meaning between the two sentences?

3. Many people use reflexive rather than personal pronouns in compounds, such as

   I accept this award on behalf of my wife and myself.
   My family and myself like to vacation at the lake.

   These are sometimes called *unmotivated reflexives* and are considered nonstandard by many. What do you think prompts people to use reflexive pronouns in these situations?

4. What two meanings does the following sentence have? *When he gets drunk he can hardly stand himself.*

You have undoubtedly noticed that reflexive pronouns come in a variety of forms and that they agree in person, number, and gender with their antecedents. Every native speaker knows this and would never use ungrammatical sentences like those in (16).

(16) *The boys blamed itself.
      *The fire extinguished themselves.

The full set of reflexive pronouns is as follows:

	singular	plural
first person	myself	ourselves
second person	yourself	yourselves
third person		
masculine	himself	
feminine	herself	{themselves
neuter	itself	

These pronouns are a good example of how people in their everyday use of English strive to make sense of its grammatical system. The formation of the reflexive pronouns generally follows a pattern:

Reflexive Pronoun = Possessive Pronoun (Determiner Form) + *self* (singular)
+ *selves* (plural)

But two of the reflexive pronouns are glaring exceptions to this pattern: *himself* and *themselves*. These use the object pronouns, not the possessives. Some people will discard these in favor of the forms that fit the regular pattern.

(17) He did it hisself.
      They considered theirselves lucky.

These are stigmatized forms, but you certainly can't fault their logic!

There are other deviations from the standard set of reflexive pronouns in people's linguistic behavior. *-Self* and *-selves* distinguish singular from plural, but this is redundant information, since the number is already expressed in the first part of the pronoun. It is not uncommon to hear sentences like those in (18)

(18) We saw it ourself.
      Let them do it themself.

in which *-self* is used as the generalized reflexive suffix. Again, this usage leads to a simpler system with no loss of meaning. Although they are judged ungrammatical at this time in the history of English, all of the reflexive pronouns in (17) and (18) are good candidates for becoming acceptable in the future.

DISCUSSION EXERCISES 5.7

1. Keeping the previous chart out of sight, choose the standard English reflexive pronoun for each sentence.

   The horse injured ___.
   Jim has confidence in ___.
   I caught ___ in a lie.
   Those people should consider ___ lucky.
   We don't blame ___.

2. Explain the grammatical reasoning behind the creation of the nonstandard pronoun *theirself* as in *They built it theirself.*

3. Consider the following sentence:

   If a person wants to succeed in life they should take care of themself first.

   Although *themself* does not exist as a pronoun in standard English, it makes particular sense to use it in sentences like this. Why?

RECIPROCAL PRONOUNS

Reciprocal pronouns are similar to reflexive pronouns in that they are used when the subject and object refer to the same entity. The only difference is in the way the action is distributed. The sentences in (19) show the difference.

(19) The lawyers respect themselves.   (reflexive)
      The lawyers respect each other.   (reciprocal)

As you can see, with reciprocal pronouns the subjects are always plural and the action (feeling, etc.) is distributed from one entity to another. There are only two reciprocal pronouns: *each other* and *one another.* In modern English they are used interchangeably, but historically there was a difference between them. *Each other* was used for two entities, and *one another* was used for more than two. Thus at one time the sentences of (20) had different meanings.

(20) The houses are close to each other.   (only two)
      The houses are close to one another. (more than two)

This distinction reflects an older grammatical sensitivity to the difference between two and more than two that is now fading from English. (See Reflection 1 at the end of this chapter.)

DEMONSTRATIVE PRONOUNS

Demonstrative pronouns are easy to talk about because we have already encountered demonstratives as determiners. We know there are four of them

Demonstrative Pron.

and they indicate location relative to the speaker as well as number: *this, these, that, those.* As determiners they modify a head noun in a noun phrase: *this book, that car.* As pronouns, they take the place of a noun phrase, as in the examples in (21).

> (21) This is an interesting fact.
>   Who told you that?
>   Shall I order these?
>   I need those for my presentation.

this
these
that
those

Like first- and second-person pronouns, they may occur without grammatical antecedents and can refer directly to something in the context of the conversation.

RELATIVE PRONOUNS

who
whom
whose
which
that

Relative pronouns are used in constructions called **relative clauses,** which we will explore in detail in Chapter 12. Basically, a *relative clause* is a sentence that has been incorporated into another sentence. When a noun phrase in the first sentence is repeated in the relative clause, the one in the relative clause is replaced by a relative pronoun. For example, I might want to tell you *I know the woman,* but you will not know which woman I mean unless I tell you more. I might try to fix that by adding another sentence, as follows:

> (22) I know the woman. The woman won the prize.

As described above, English provides us with a way to incorporate the second sentence into the first and to eliminate the repetition of the noun phrase. So, instead of two choppy sentences with an ill-defined connection between them, like those in (22), we can change the second to a relative clause and incorporate it into the first. When we do this, we replace the repeated noun phrase with a relative pronoun. The resulting sentence is (23).

> (23) I know the woman who won the prize.

The object noun phrase in (23) can be described visually like this:

ex.
When did you see?
because
You saw someone (whom)
obj.

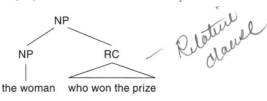

Relative clause

The noun phrase (NP) that the relative clause (RC) describes is called the **head of the relative clause.** In (23) *the woman* is the *head of the relative clause* and *who,* of course, is the relative pronoun. There are five different relative pronouns in English, as illustrated by the sentences in (24).

ex.
the man whom you saw
because you said the man
object (whom)

(24) We admired the boy <u>who</u> (or <u>that</u>) caught the fish.
      She approves of the man <u>whom</u> (or <u>that</u>) you intend to marry.
      The child <u>whose</u> puppy ran away is sad.
      The house <u>which</u> (or <u>that</u>) is for sale needs a new roof.

How do we know which relative pronoun to choose? One thing you will notice from the examples is that you need to pay attention to whether the head of the relative clause is human or nonhuman. Setting aside the pronoun *that* for the moment, we see that if the head of the relative clause is human, the relative pronoun is *who, whom,* or *whose.* If it is nonhuman, it is generally *which.* That still leaves the question of how we choose among the human ones. In (25), we "unravel" the relative clauses of (24) to help you see what determines the choice of human relative pronouns.

(25) We admired the boy. <u>The boy</u> caught the fish (*who*).
      She approves of the man. You intend to marry <u>the man</u> (*whom*).
      The child is sad. The <u>child's</u> puppy ran away (*whose*).

You can see now that human relative pronouns are marked for case, just like the personal pronouns, and you choose the pronoun according to its function in the relative clause. In the first it is a subject, so we use *who;* in the second it is an object, so we use *whom;* and in the third it is a possessive, so we use *whose.* We see also from the examples of (24) that the pronoun *that* can generally be used in place of all the relative pronouns except *whose.* (But see Reflection 12 and Chapter 12, pp. 206-207.) It is important to stress that the case of the head noun phrase is not relevant to this choice. If you look again at the first example in (25), you will see that *who* is chosen because *the boy* is a subject in the sentence that becomes the relative clause. Its case in the first sentence (which happens to be objective) simply doesn't matter.

DISCUSSION EXERCISES 5.8

1. Identify the relative clause in each of the following sentences. Then identify the relative pronoun and tell which noun phrase is the head of the relative clause.

    I met the clerk who sold you that car.
    The dog that you trained has gone berserk.
    Any person that agrees with you is a fool.
    The dentist whom you recommended accepted my insurance.
    She is the teacher whose class you visited.

(continued)

2. The choice between *who* and *whom* is a difficult one for speakers of English because all relative pronouns are placed at the beginning of the relative clause regardless of their function. Normally, we identify subjects and objects by word order, but we can't do that for relative clauses. Instead, we have to mentally "unravel" the clause to see where the repeated noun phrase was before the clause became incorporated. Figure out whether standard English requires *who* or *whom* in the following sentences.

> Example: The child __ you scolded is crying.
> Unraveled: The child is crying. You scolded <u>the child.</u>
> Answer: *whom*

> The dancer ___ fell will be out of the show.
> We respect the people ___ you have chosen.
> The woman ___ sold me this blouse works in another department now.
> I pity the person ___ they convicted.
> Let me be the one ___ congratulates you first.

3. For many speakers of English (but not all) a test for whether the relative pronoun should be *who* or *whom* is to see if you can leave it out. *Whom* can be omitted with no change of meaning, but *who* cannot. Try this test with the sentences in Exercise 2. Do you need to change any of your answers?

4. As you have probably observed, *whom* is dropping out of English, at least in informal, conversational English. *Whom* now carries with it an air of formality that seems inappropriate to most for more casual contexts. Rephrase the following sentences to illustrate the various strategies people use for avoiding *whom*. Do any of these strategies mark speakers as uneducated?

> This is the actor whom the talent agent discovered.
> I recognize the woman whom you insulted.
> Tell me the people whom you would like to invite.

INTERROGATIVE PRONOUNS

Interrogative pronouns are those question words that ask about the identity of a noun phrase. You will be happy to learn that they are very similar to the relative pronouns in both form and principles of usage. Like the relatives, they are sensitive to the distinction between human and nonhuman. The three human ones are *who? whom?* and *whose?* The nonhuman one is *what? Which?* is used when a choice is implied and is either human or nonhuman. The sentences in (26) illustrate their use.

> (26) Who is making that noise?   (human subject)
>   Whom did you invite?   (human object)
>   Whose is this?   (human possessive)
>   What is making that noise?   (nonhuman subject)

What do you want?   (nonhuman object)
Which do you prefer?   (choice implied)

Like the relative pronouns, interrogative pronouns always occur at the beginning of the sentence, so you need to unravel the question to see whether a subject or an object is being questioned. As you might well expect, the choice between *who* and *whom* is equally problematic for questions, and many speakers use *who* for both without serious consequences.

DISCUSSION EXERCISES 5.9

1. Fill in the appropriate interrogative pronoun as specified.

   ___ did you see?   (human object)
   ___ did he steal?   (human possessive)
   ___ is going on?   (nonhuman subject)
   ___ told you that?   (human subject)
   ___ do you want?   (implied choice-object)
   ___ can I trust?   (human object)
   ___ is better?   (implied choice-subject)
   ___ is his problem?   (nonhuman subject complement—figure it out!)
   ___ shall I say is here?   (human subject)
   ___ costs more?   (implied choice-subject)

2. Notice that some of these pronouns can also be determiners. Which ones? Give some examples.

3. Interrogative *pronouns* are used to seek the identity of a noun phrase. Other interrogative words are used to elicit other kinds of information. What information is being sought in each of the following?

   Where is she?
   Why can't you do it?
   When does the movie begin?
   How does this work?

UNIVERSAL AND INDEFINITE PRONOUNS

Universal pronouns are words that represent all-inclusive noun phrases: *each,* *all,* and combinations of *every* with *one, body,* and *thing.* Grammatically all of them except *all* are singular, even though their meaning is plural. Notice the singular verbs in the sentences in (27):

(27)   Each has its own place.
       Everyone in my family is rich.
       Everybody likes music.
       Everything looks good.

They may themselves act as the antecedents of other pronouns, but because they are plural in meaning they are often referred to by plural pronouns.

(28) Everyone in my family is rich. They own several homes apiece.

Indefinite pronouns, as their name suggests, generally refer to indefinite entities or quantities. Included in this group are *some* and *any,* and the various combinations of *some* and *any* plus *one, body,* and *thing. None* is also an indefinite pronoun, but shortens to *no* if it combines with something else. Quantities such as *many, several, enough, few,* and *less* also fall under this category, as does the indefinite *one* as in *one ought to listen to one's elders.*

DISCUSSION EXERCISES 5.10

1. Identify the universal and the indefinite pronouns in the following sentences.

   Everyone needs love.
   I don't need anything.
   Nothing pleases you.
   Some may appreciate this.
   Few arrived on time.
   Do you have enough?
   One ought to respect the law.
   Nobody heard the news.
   She dropped something into the river.
   All can sing but none can dance.

2. Which pronoun would you use when *someone* and *anyone* serve as antecedents? Give sentences that illustrate your choice.

3. Many of the universal and indefinite pronouns can also serve as determiners. Pick three and for each demonstrate that it can be a pronoun or a determiner.

4. The word *all* can be a universal pronoun, a determiner, or a predeterminer. Illustrate this with example sentences.

At this point, with the understanding you have gained of pronouns and how they work, you can probably identify all the major players and actions in the sentence "mini-drama." In the next two chapters, we explore in depth those lexical categories that give added richness and variety to the basic components of sentences: adjectives and adverbs, particles and prepositions.

REFLECTIONS

1. English pronouns used to have three numbers: singular, *dual*, and plural. There was a separate set of pronouns that referred specifically to two things. We have lost dual number in pronouns, but there are still some ways in which English grammar remains sensitive to the distinction between two and more than two. For example, there may be a secret *between* two people, but if more than two people share it the secret is *among* them. Can you think of any other differences based on the dual-plural distinction? You may have trouble thinking of them because this number distinction has already been lost in many people's usage.

2. In some people's speech, certain inanimate objects are assigned female gender, such as ships and cars. Why do you think these objects are assumed to be female?

3. The following appeared in a letter to a newspaper advice columnist: "We love to eat out and enjoy trying new restaurants. Nine times out of 10 our server . . . refers to us throughout the meal as 'You guys.' We find this annoying. Even if we get excellent service, we will tip less if the server calls us 'You guys.' There must be others out there who feel as we do, or do you think we are too stuffy?"

Several years later another letter appeared with the same complaint. The server's use of "would you guys like another drink?" and "Are you guys going to have some dessert?" was found to be "unprofessional" and "offensive," as was a flight attendant's request, "If you guys would sit down, we could get this plane away from the gate." The advice columnist advises people who use "you guys" in this way to "shape up." How would you respond to this complaint, given your understanding of the English pronoun system?

Additional note: If you listen to people who use *you guys* as a second-person plural pronoun, you will also hear a new possessive form that goes along with it: *you guys'* as in "Here's you guys' bill."

4. The following appeared on a letter of recommendation form from a large midwestern university: "*May we have your candid judgment of this applicant's qualifications and promise for the successful completion of their chosen graduate program.*" An e-mail list from another major university states: "*Your query matched a student that cannot be listed because they have not registered an e-mail address.*" How might a grammatical purist react to these statements? What do they tell us about the acceptability of plural pronouns with singular gender-neutral antecedents?

5. How do the following suggest that the choice of a gender-neutral pronoun is in a state of flux in standard English?

"For example, if you go into a convenience store to buy some cat food and you can't find it on the shelves, and you ask the salesperson if they have any cat food, he or she will reply. . . ." (Ian Frazier, "The Positive Negative," *The Atlantic Monthly,* June 1997, p. 24.)

"A slave could claim that he or she was the child of a free person, had once lived in a free state, or that they had once been granted their freedom." (From an exhibit about the Dred Scott case on the walls of the Old Courthouse in St. Louis, Missouri.)

If you wonder about the acceptability of competing grammatical choices, the best way to find out is to put them to the test. Try out various options for gender-neutral pronoun replacement in papers you write for other courses and see how your instructors react to them. It's risky, but it's all in the name of science!

6. What do you think would prompt a prominent television talk-show host to say "*I couldn't be happier for you and he,*" a prominent politician to say "*I have great respect for he and his family,*" or a public television classical music announcer to say a composer "*composed music for performance by she and her sister*"? (We are interested in the grammar, not the meaning.)

7. Listen for the usage of subject and object pronouns in popular music. Do you find any deviations from the rules of standard English? What is the effect of this usage?

8. Another pronoun usage problem occurs in double constructions of a pronoun and a noun phrase, as in *We Americans love our automobiles.* Which of these do you think are standard?

Us tall guys can't find pants to fit.

We girls should give a party for her.

Take us loyal followers with you.

You are so kind to we weary travelers.

9. The eighteenth-century solution to the comparison question is not entirely without merit even if it doesn't fit the way people actually use English. There are circumstances in which the choice of pronoun, subject or object, could make a difference in the meaning of the sentence. What is the implied continuation of the sentence in each of the following?

Mary likes Tom more than me.

Mary likes Tom more than I.

10. There are some verbs that are inherently reflexive; that is, they can or must be followed by a reflexive pronoun that has no particular meaning or function. *Behave* is such verb: *The children behaved themselves.* Can you think of others?

11. One oddity of English relative pronouns is that we do not have a nonhuman possessive pronoun parallel to *whose*. *Which* can be a nonhuman subject or object, but not a possessive. So what do we do if we want to say the following as a relative clause construction?

I found the book. The book's cover is torn.

Survey students in your class to see how they would say this. The most common response is to rephrase it so that it is no longer a relative clause: *I found the book with the torn cover,* for example. But is there a way to preserve the relative clause?

12. There are various editorial preferences concerning the use of *that* as opposed to the other relative pronouns. Consult some grammar handbooks or style manuals to see if you can detect a pattern of preference. If they phrase their concerns in terms of restrictive and nonrestrictive relative clauses, you will probably need to wait until the end of the course to understand these explanations.

13. Many people think that the question *"Whom shall I say is calling?"* sounds highly educated and formal. Does it meet the requirements of standard English? Try to unravel it to see whether the interrogative pronoun should be *who* or *whom.* An ad in a local newspaper urged people to vote "for the political party whom you believe will deliver results." Does this relative pronoun usage conform to standard English?

14. There is some disagreement about the number of *none.* Is it singular or plural? Would you say *None of them are invited* or *None of them is invited?* Consult several traditional grammar handbooks and ask a few people what they think. Does a consensus emerge from your findings?

15. An airline company sent out a mailer to its customers defending the reliability of its planes. The same type of plane is used by other airlines and, says the mailer, "they, like we, have total confidence in this workhorse of the industry. . . ." In what way is this sentence a violation of the rules of standard English?

16. A character in Toni Morrison's novel *Song of Solomon* says, "Don't you city boys know how to handle yourself?" (New York: A Signet Book, New American Library, 1977, p. 284.) What makes this nonstandard? Why is its meaning clear nevertheless?

17. In our discussion of personal pronouns, we said that first- and second-person pronouns do not necessarily have grammatical antecedents. Later we said that demonstrative pronouns also do not necessarily have them. What other kinds of pronouns do not have to have grammatical antecedents?

PRACTICE EXERCISES FOR CHAPTER 5 (Answers on p. 226)

1. What is the antecedent of each personal pronoun in the following sentences? If the pronoun has no grammatical antecedent, tell what it refers to.
   1. Max lost his book but found it in the garden.
   2. Leslie said that we should be friends.
   3. The agency called Alice and offered her a job.
   4. Don't do the exercise if you find it too difficult.

(continued)

    5. My dentist charges too much.

    6. The classes met for two weeks, so I signed up for them.

    7. Joe lied to Sally, so she divorced him.

    8. If you find the missing letter, send it to me.

    9. When he heard the news, my uncle hugged me.

    10. When you get to England, give us a call.

2. Give the personal pronoun that corresponds to the description.

    1. first-person-singular subject

    2. third-person-plural object

    3. second-person-singular possessive

    4. third-person-singular feminine subject

    5. third-person-singular masculine object

    6. first-person-plural object

    7. second-person-plural object

    8. third-person-singular neuter possessive

    9. first-person-plural possessive

    10. third-person-plural subject

3. Replace the underlined possessive noun phrases with their corresponding free-standing possessive pronouns.

    1. <u>My watch</u> is running slow.

    2. She found <u>your slippers</u> under the bed.

    3. The students turned in <u>their assignments</u>.

    4. <u>His villa</u> is situated on a cliff.

    5. No one wanted to answer <u>her question</u>.

4. Tell whether the following sentences are standard or nonstandard according to the strictest standard English rules for pronoun usage.

    1. Bob and I will meet you in an hour.

    2. It is an honor for my husband and I to be here.

    3. You are much smarter than him.

    4. Seth and me went fishing last week.

    5. This is her in the photograph.

    6. We met him and her at a party.

    7. They were more frightened than we.

    8. Him and I tied for first place.

    9. Let this remain between you and I.

    10. My son likes to visit her and her sisters.

5. Give the reflexive pronoun that corresponds to each description.

    1. first-person-plural

    2. third-person-singular feminine

(continued)

   3. third-person-plural

   4. second-person-plural

   5. first-person-singular

6. What function is served by the reflexive pronoun in each sentence?

   1. I found myself all alone.

   2. She herself is very tolerant.

   3. They went to the movies by themselves.

   4. He himself prefers to memorize his speeches.

   5. Those doctors consider themselves experts in bone repair.

7. Replace the relative pronoun *that* in each of the following sentences with *who* or *whom,* following the traditional rules of standard English.

   1. This is the person that lost his notebook.

   2. We contacted the builder that you recommended.

   3. Here comes the woman that I have been expecting.

   4. I pity the child that has been crying all morning.

   5. I pity the child that the others teased all morning.

   6. Are these the students that will be taking the course?

   7. He is the person that helped me.

   8. Is Jan the person that you saw behind the curtain?

   9. Philip is the student that scored highest on the exam.

   10. I learned it from the teacher that retired last year.

8. Fill in the appropriate interrogative pronouns:

   1. ___ did you have for breakfast? (nonhuman object)

   2. ___ went to the museum? (human subject)

   3. ___ is better? (subject, implied choice)

   4. ___ can you trust these days? (human object)

   5. ___ did the storm destroy? (human possessive)

9. Identify the pronoun (ignore the personal pronouns) in each sentence and tell whether it is *reciprocal, demonstrative, relative, indefinite,* or *universal.*

   1. Everyone can learn this sport.

   2. The children know each other.

   3. I admire the drawing that you did.

   4. This isn't easy for the losers.

   5. Phyllis didn't see anyone in the office.

   6. The soldiers protected one another.

   7. One shouldn't expect too much.

   8. Each shall have a chance.

   9. The citizens will obey the rules that are approved by the majority.

   10. Nobody is blameless.

(continued)

10. Identify every pronoun in the following sentences and give as much information as you can about their form and function.
    1. Can somebody help me?
    2. What can I do for you?
    3. Whose is this?
    4. Everyone came to my party.
    5. She bought the computer that they suggested.

11. Find an example of each of the following in the *Believers* selection that follows.

    a subject pronoun

    a possessive pronoun

    a relative pronoun

    a place where a relative pronoun has been omitted

    a pronoun that precedes its antecedent

    an intransitive verb

    a transitive verb

    a compound noun phrase

    a past perfect tense

    a simple past

    an object of a preposition

       As he finally broke his way out of the wood, Father Pielke stepped over a hip-high sandbar willow he hadn't seen that caught his ankle. He didn't fall. His balance had always been good. But his temporary disorientation and his limp caused him to drop his asparagus spears as he emerged into the sunshine. (Baxter: "Believers" p. 183.)

12. Identify the violations of formal standard English in the following letter:

    Dear Chris,

    Our big adventure starts tomorrow! My uncle, he knows more than us about the route to the airport, so he will drive you, my family, and I to the airport. He is the same person whom, I believe, will pick us up when we return. Wait for my family and myself in front of your house at 8:00 a.m. sharp. Me and my father will sit in the front seat, and the rest of you guys can sit in the back. Neither my mother nor my sister mind riding in the back, and it causes less complications if we agree in advance. Have you already began to pack? Don't forget your guidebook's. Having waited so long, its hard to believe that the time has actually came!

                                                    Affectionately,
                                                    Pat

SIX

ADJECTIVES AND ADVERBS

WHAT ARE ADJECTIVES? ✓

Adjectives are more easily identified by their function than by their form. Their main job is to *modify* nouns. This means they may be used to provide added description to a noun for purposes of embellishment or to help distinguish it from other nouns. All of the underlined words in the sentences in (1) are considered adjectives.

(1) The <u>tall</u> man left but the <u>short</u> one stayed.
A <u>certain</u> woman is needed for this <u>complicated</u> job.
A <u>mere</u> child could not solve this <u>amazing</u> mystery.

As you can see, there is no particular marking that makes a word look like an adjective, so adjectives are not easy to identify merely by how they look. <u>There are, however, certain derivational suffixes that turn roots into adjectives</u>, and when one of these appears, the lexical category is transparent. Some of these are *-ive (pensive, native)*, *-able (portable, communicable)*, *-ible (responsible, edible)*, *-al (rational, political)*, *-ful (thoughtful, careful)*, and *-ish (boyish, childish)*. There are also some derivational prefixes that can turn a positive adjective into a negative one: *un-(happy)*, *dis-(satisfied)*, *in-(competent)*, *ir-(regular)*, *il-(legible)*, *im-(mature)*.

Many (but not all) adjectives also have inflectional markings for **comparative** and **superlative.** The comparative form is used to compare two different nouns, the superlative to compare more than two (note again the dual-plural distinction). The sentences in (2) illustrate the comparative and the superlative of the adjective *smart*.

(2) Katy is smart, but Jill is smarter.
Of the three women, Beth is (the) smartest.

You see that the comparative inflectional suffix is *-er* and the superlative suffix is *-est*. It has probably occurred to you that not all adjectives are permitted to add these suffixes. In some cases we must use the words *more* and *most* to indicate the comparative and superlative, respectively, as in (3).

(3) Dan is more responsible than Jack.
    This is the most beautiful landscape painting in the museum.

How do we decide whether to use the suffixes or the words *more* and *most?* There are some general guidelines, although they are subject to change over time and there is a lot of fluctuation in people's usage. In present day English, the guidelines are as follows:

> One-syllable adjectives add the suffixes: *taller, slimmer, coldest.*
>
> Adjectives of three or more syllables use *more* and *most: more responsible, most enviable.*
>
> Adjectives of two syllables add the suffixes if they end in *-y (happier, loveliest);* otherwise they use *more* and *most (more honest, most handsome).*

DISCUSSION EXERCISES 6.1

[handwritten margin notes: assimilation, prosody & set II some; un-happy, in-competent, immature, dis-satisfied]

1. List some additional derivational suffixes for adjectives with examples of words that use them. Think, for example, about the suffixes that indicate nationalities. *expensive , bloody* *[handwritten]*

2. Can you think of any other prefixes that turn a positive adjective into a negative one? How do we know which prefix goes with which adjective? Which is the one that people are likely to use if they're not sure?

3. There are some exceptions to the rule of adding *-er* and *-est* to one-syllable adjective roots, most notably the adjectives *good* and *bad.* What are their comparative and superlative forms? *better/best   worse/worst* *[handwritten]*

4. You will find the most fluctuation in the comparison of two-syllable adjectives. What are your judgments about each of the following pairs? Does everyone agree?

    He is handsomer than my brother.
    He is more handsome than my brother.
    This is my happiest experience yet.
    This is my most happy experience yet.

5. The comparative and superlative markers *more* and *most* have negative counterparts. What are they?

   We have been assuming in our discussion so far that adjectives generally lend themselves to comparison, but this is true only of one subset of adjectives, called **gradable adjectives.** *Gradable adjectives have the capacity for degrees in their meaning, so not only can they be compared, but they can also be modified by other words,* such as *very, quite, somewhat,* and *exceedingly,* called **intensifiers.** There are other adjectives, called **nongradable adjectives** that do not lend themselves to comparison or modification. They are absolute in their meaning and have no degrees. *Perfect* is an example of a nongradable adjective. Something is either perfect or it isn't and there are no steps in between. Other examples of nongradable adjectives are *married, pregnant, square, silent,* and *indestructible.* In theory, the distinction between gradable and nongradable adjectives is clear, but in practice it is often blurred. People have a tendency in their use of English to move adjectives from the nongradable to the gradable category, which entails some shift in their meaning. A good example of this is the word *unique.* Historically, it meant "one-of-a-kind," which would make it nongradable. But people frequently use it with comparisons and modifiers, with a shift in meaning to "unusual," as in the sentences in (4).

(4)   This is the most unique shop in the city.
      Her idea is more unique than yours.

There are grammatical purists who object to this shifting of category and see it as one more example of the decay of the English language, but for the most part it is a common element of language change and part of the normal development of the language.

DISCUSSION EXERCISES 6.2

1. Which of the following adjectives are gradable and which are nongradable? Are there any that are debatable? *reversible, speculative, quiet, special, intentional, supreme*

2. The adjectives *married* and *pregnant* are often used in conversational English as gradable adjectives. Give examples of this usage and tell what shift of meaning occurs when each is used as a gradable adjective.

3. Are comparative adjectives gradable? Are superlatives? How do you test this?

4. A store in Michigan advertises itself as "Michigan's most historic jeweller." What do you think the intended meaning is?

5. There are some intensifiers that can occur with nongradable adjectives, such as *almost, not quite,* and *not really.* Why are these compatible with nongradable adjectives?

HOW DO ADJECTIVES MODIFY NOUNS?

As we have said, the function of adjectives is to modify nouns. This function is carried out in a number of different ways. When the adjective is part of the same noun phrase as the noun, as in *the happy children,* or *the wild west,* we say that the adjective is an **attributive adjective.** When the adjective occurs in its *attributive function,* within the noun phrase, it usually directly precedes the noun. If you look again at the formula for noun phrases that we gave in Chapter 3, you can now fill in another detail: an optional adjective before the noun.

But adjectives may also modify a noun from outside the noun phrase, as in the examples in (5).

(5) The cost is <u>excessive.</u>
    The children are <u>happy.</u>
    We considered the issue <u>unimportant.</u>

In these sentences the adjective does not share a noun phrase with the noun it modifies; rather, it is part of the predicate (see Chapter 4) and is called a **predicate adjective.** *Predicate adjectives* are commonly linked to a subject noun phrase via a linking verb: these adjectives are called **subject complements,** as illustrated in (6).

(6) Our house seems empty.
    The horses appear nervous.
    His father sounds worried.
    This soup tastes funny.
    You were impressive.

Predicate adjectives can also modify object noun phrases, as in the third sentence in (5) or the sentences in (7).

(7) I found the news <u>unsettling.</u>
    She judged the report <u>inadequate.</u>
    The doctor pronounced the patient <u>cured.</u>

The adjectives in these sentences are called **object complements.** Notice that although they are next to the nouns they modify, they are not part of the noun phrase and do not form a constituent with the noun phrase. To summarize, there are two adjective functions: attributive and predicate. Predicate adjectives are of two types, subject complements and object complements, depending on what they modify. (Note that subject and object complements can also be noun phrases, as was discussed in Chapter 3.)

There is one other very interesting fact about the way adjectives modify nouns in English. If there are several nouns present in a noun phrase, an adjective may either modify the noun closest to it or all of them. Consider the sentence in (8).

(8) Sensitive men and women are the best pet-sitters.

The sentence can refer to women and sensitive men, or to sensitive men and sensitive women. In other words, the sentence is ambiguous. Linguistically speaking, this is not a negative judgment about the sentence. **Linguistic ambiguity** is a common feature of language and simply refers to the fact that a sentence may be interpreted in more than one way. We often don't notice when a sentence is ambiguous because the context makes it clear which meaning was intended. But sometimes the listener must seek clarification. If I tell my host that I can't eat fried fish or chicken, the host might want to check with me before serving grilled chicken, for example.

DISCUSSION EXERCISES 6.3

1. Tell whether the underlined adjectives in the following sentences are attributive or predicate adjectives.

The <u>angry</u> mother scolded the child. *at. adj.*
The music sounds <u>funny.</u> *adj pred.*
I consider him <u>intelligent.</u> *adj pred*
He taught this <u>lazy</u> boy algebra. *attributive*
You are <u>intimidating.</u> *pred.*
We encountered an <u>enthusiastic</u> crowd. *attributive*
The jury judged her <u>innocent.</u> *predicate*
This stew tastes <u>terrible.</u> *pred.*
My <u>elderly</u> aunt just died. *attributive*
They have <u>talented</u> relatives. *attributive*

2. For all those you labeled predicate adjectives, tell which are subject complements and which are object complements.

3. Most adjectives can be either attributive or predicate, but a few are restricted in their usage. What is the restriction on *sole, afraid, mere?* What is odd about the adjective *certain?* *→ only attributive* *only attributive*

4. The sentence *They are amusing children* is ambiguous. That is, it has more than one possible meaning. Under one interpretation, *amusing* is an attributive adjective. What is it under the second interpretation?

5. What makes the following sentences ambiguous?

She is a rare butterfly collector. *modifies either*
Look at the messy child's handwriting.
Send me more beautiful pictures.
I stopped at the pleasant vicar's cottage.
She attended a little girls' school.

6. An interesting fact about English is that a noun may take on the role of an adjective and modify another noun. In what sense is *brick* functioning as an adjective in the noun phrase *the brick house?* Can you think of another example? *the highschool teacher ~ the brick wall*

Test
ambiguous sentence

WHAT ARE ADJECTIVE PHRASES?

Adjectives serve as the heads of **adjective phrases** and can be accompanied by modifiers of their own. The most typical modifier of the adjective is the intensifier, as in the sentences in (9).

(9) I am extremely upset.
  This is somewhat unusual.

Adj Phrases = Adj + modifiers (intensifiers)

The news is quite shocking.
We are very excited.

In each of these sentences, the adjective phrase is a subject complement. It can also be an object complement, as in (10).

(10) He considered the questions very annoying.

In addition, the adjective phrase can be attributive, as in (11).

(11) That is a somewhat unusual request.

Adjective phrases can also be formed by completing an adjective. Some examples of these are illustrated in the sentences in (12).

(12) She was afraid to respond. *Adj phrase*
      I am sorry to upset you.
      They are adept at lying.   *adj. complement: finish meaning of prev. adj.*
      We are full of hope.
      He is ready for anything.

The underlined portions of the sentences in (12) finish off the meaning of the preceding adjective and are called **adjective complements.**

Adjectives can also form phrases by "stacking up." Unlike other lexical categories, adjectives may appear in a string, as illustrated in (13).

(13) The big red house.
      A thin blue line.
      A tall dark handsome stranger.

Both adjectives and adjective phrases freely form compounds, as can be seen in (14).

(14) The day was bright and breezy.
      He was both somewhat lazy and mildly indifferent.
      The idea was offbeat but brilliant.
      The device was not only extremely practical but very cheap.
      The lecture was neither enlightening nor entertaining.
      A number can be either cardinal or ordinal.
      They are poor yet happy.

DISCUSSION EXERCISES 6.4

1. What makes up the adjective phrase in each of the following sentences?

I found a small glass bottle.
These results are interestingly deceptive.
She considered your remark quite amusing.
Anne seems unusually cheerful today.

(continued)

A rather odd character appeared at my door.

He is suspicious of doctors.

You should be kind to others.

The gardener planted a short round prickly bush in my courtyard.

2. What is the function of the adjective phrase in each of the previous sentences: attributive, subject complement, or object complement?

3. You will notice that compounds with *but* and *yet* indicate something contrary to one's expectations. If you say they are *poor yet happy,* you are implying that those two characteristics don't normally go together. Sometimes these implications can be insulting, such as when a woman is described as *beautiful but smart.* Can you think of other common combinations that might offend in the same way?

WHAT ARE ADVERBS?

It is difficult to talk about **adverbs** as a category because several different things are given the name *adverb* in grammatical description. Most people think of adverbs as those words that modify verbs. This type of adverb tells where, when, or how an action is carried out. The underlined words in the sentences in (15) are adverbs.

(15) We saw the film yesterday.
Sharon flew home to see her folks.
She graciously accepted my invitation.

These are broadly categorized as adverbs of time, adverbs of place, and adverbs of manner, respectively.

Another type of adverb, one we have already encountered, is the *intensifier.* Intensifiers modify adjectives and are part of adjective phrases: *very quiet, quite sincere.* But intensifiers can also modify adverbs of manner, as in the following:

Intensifiers = Adv.
+ are part of adj.
phrases

(16) The dog ate quite greedily.
They responded very enthusiastically.
He typed amazingly quickly.

In each of these sentences the verb is modified by an adverb that tells the way in which the action was performed. But each of these adverbs is itself modified by another kind of adverb, an intensifier.

A third common type of adverb modifies an entire sentence and is referred to as a **sentence adverb.** These normally occur at the beginning of a sentence and inject some commentary on the part of the speaker. A few examples appear in the following sentences:

(17) Fortunately, it didn't rain the day of our picnic.
Consequently, Mary had to find another babysitter.
Moreover, I couldn't afford to spend the money.

Other common sentence adverbs are *therefore, however, furthermore,* and *nevertheless.*
Adverbs, then, perform four distinct functions:

1. modify verbs: time, place, manner
2. modify adjectives: intensifiers
3. modify other adverbs: intensifiers
4. modify sentences: sentence adverbs

DISCUSSION EXERCISES 6.5

1. Identify the adverbs in the following sentences and tell what kind they are. Are there any sentences that have more than one adverb?

   Amazingly, we got all the answers right.
   Betty searched laboriously through the manuscripts.
   You are being very silly.
   I'll see you tomorrow.
   However, the value of your stocks are down.
   The politician spoke quite sincerely.
   Stay here for the night.
   The child sobbed uncontrollably.
   Truthfully, I don't want to help you.
   Slowly, Maxine approached the bobcat.

   manner or sentence adverb

2. Did you notice the subject-verb agreement error in the above exercise? Let's hope so.

3. Adverbs have somewhat more order flexibility than other lexical categories. What other positions could the underlined adverbs occupy without changing the meaning of the sentence or making it sound odd?

   <u>Therefore</u>, Al can't attend the lecture.
   Cary inched <u>carefully</u> around the debris.
   Mildred listened <u>attentively</u> to his arguments.

4. What kind of adverb is *easily* in *Easily, she lifted the child from his crib?* Explain your choice.

   both manner & sentence adv.

5. In formal standard English, the words *real* and *right* are not normally used as intensifiers with adjectives and most adverbs. What would be examples of this nonstandard usage? But it is also true that *right* is standard with certain adverbs of time and place. Can you think of any?

Although the similarities are not overwhelming, many adverbs share certain common properties. For one, adverbs of all categories may have the derivational suffix *-ly,* which is added to an adjective root to form the adverb. This *-ly* is a remnant of the Old English suffix *-lic* ("like," pronounced "*leech*"). So *happily,* for example, is historically *happy-like,* as in "*She laughed happy-like.*" Another common property is that, like adjectives, many of them can be made comparative or superlative.

(18) She runs quickly, but he runs more quickly.
        My aunt worked most diligently of all to keep the family together.

You will notice that adverb comparatives and superlatives are typically formed with the words *more* and *most* rather than the suffixes *-er* and *-est*. But this is just a consequence of the fact that most adverbs have more than one syllable. There are a few one syllable adverbs, and these do add the suffixes. Consider the sentences in (19).

(19) Joe works hard, but Gloria works harder.
        Clint sings loud, but Charlie sings louder.
        Jay runs fast, Pat runs faster, and Chuck runs (the) fastest of all.

These one syllable adverbs (*hard, fast, loud, slow*) are known as **flat adverbs** and have exactly the same form as their corresponding adjectives.

DISCUSSION EXERCISES 6.6

1. Give sentences that contain the specified forms: the comparative of *fast, merrily, readily;* the superlative of *loud, charmingly, noisily.*

2. Give an example of a sentence with an adverb that ends in *-ly* and

   modifies a verb
   modifies an adjective
   modifies another adverb   *She runs extreanly slowly*
   modifies a sentence   *hopefully, shill come .*

3. Is the underlined word in each sentence an adjective or an adverb? How do you know?

   The choir sings too <u>loud.</u>   *adv.*
   The band sounds too <u>loud.</u>   *Adj Linking verb*
   The men work <u>hard.</u>   *Adv*

(continued)

The rock feels <u>hard.</u> *Adj. —linking*
The race car is <u>fast.</u> *Adj.*
The athlete runs <u>fast.</u> *Adv.*
The turtle seems <u>slow.</u> *Adj – linking*
The turtle walks <u>slow.</u> *Adv*

4. The flat adverbs are irregular in that they don't behave like other adverbs. Do you have any evidence that people are trying to make any of them regular? Has standard English accepted any of the regularizations?

5. *Right* and *wrong* can be adjectives: *the right answer, the wrong address.* Can they also be adverbs?

IS ALL WELL AND GOOD?

One of the problem areas in the use of adverbs involves the adjectives *good* and *bad* and their corresponding adverb forms. As we all know, they do not follow the regular pattern. The standard English pattern is as follows:

		Comparative	Superlative
Adjective:	*good*	*better*	*best*
Adverb:	*well*	*better*	*best*
Adjective:	*bad*	*worse*	*worst*
Adverb:	*badly*	*worse*	*worst*

The sentences in (20) illustrate the pattern.

(20) This cake is <u>good</u>, this one is <u>better</u>, and this one is <u>best</u> of all.
This car runs <u>well</u>, this one runs <u>better</u>, and this one runs <u>best</u> of all.
This cake is <u>bad</u>, this one is <u>worse</u>, and this one is <u>worst</u> of all.
This car runs <u>badly</u>, this one runs <u>worse</u>, and this one runs <u>worst</u> of all.

Perhaps because the forms and meanings are so similar, there is some tendency to confuse the adjective and adverb forms. The most stigmatized version of this is the use of the adjectives *good* and *bad* for their corresponding adverbs, as in (21).

(21) That child reads good.
That child spells bad.

This confusion is aggravated by the fact that the word *well* can also be an adjective, meaning "in good health," and has the same comparative and superlative forms as *good*.

(22) I was <u>ill</u> yesterday, but I am <u>well</u> today.
I was <u>ill</u> yesterday, but I am <u>better</u> today.
I was <u>ill</u> Saturday, <u>better</u> Sunday, and <u>best</u> of all on Monday.

DISCUSSION EXERCISES 6.7

1. Tell whether the underlined word is an adjective or an adverb.

The music sounds <u>good</u>. *Adj.*
The weather is <u>better</u> today. *Adj*
Jack feels <u>better</u> today. *Adj*
Johnny reads <u>better</u> this year. *Adv.*
The cheese tastes <u>bad</u>. *Adj. Adv.*
He reacted <u>badly</u> to the news. *Adv.*
You sing very <u>well</u>. *Adv.*
My mother is <u>well</u> today. *Adj.*

2. Which of the following are standard English? Which aren't? Explain your answers.

I feel so badly about the accident. *S/B bad*
The soup tasted well. *STB good*
The machine runs well. ✓
Mary never danced bad. *badly*
He did good on his exam. *well*
As a volunteer, he does good for the community. *depending on meaning*
Jan felt good about her party. ✓
Does the music sound good? ✓

Many speakers of English are sensitive to the stigma associated with the use of *good* and *bad* for *well* and *badly,* but we have difficulty sorting out standard usage, probably because of the similarity of the structures in which they appear. As you probably figured out from Exercise 6.7, there are two typical verb phrase patterns in English, illustrated as follows:

Action Verb + Adverb: *run quickly, dance well, work hard*
Linking Verb + Adjective: *feel happy, be ready, seem good*

You will recognize the second formula as the subject complement construction. We often rely on word order to help us decide the choice of word in English, but word order won't help us in this situation. Instead, we must pay attention to the type of verb that occurs in the verb phrase and choose the following word accordingly. Aside from not being able to rely on word order, we are met with a host of other obstacles in making this choice: <u>well can be an adjective or an adverb; the flat adverbs and the adjectives look the same; and</u> some verbs can be action or linking, such as *feel.* As a linking verb, it is followed by an adjective: *feel good.* As an action verb, it is used with an adverb: *feel the cloth gently.* It is not at all surprising that we find a great deal of variation in the use of adjectives and adverbs, especially with *good, bad, well,* and *badly.* As a result of all this variation, we will probably see some changes in standard English as time goes by. For example, many educated people say *I feel badly.* Technically speaking, this is nonstandard if *feel* is intended as a linking verb. But many people know that *bad* is nonstandard in *the child spells bad,* for example, and aren't willing to risk the negative judgment. This hypercorrection is so widespread that for many it is the only acceptable way of expressing this idea.

DISCUSSION EXERCISES 6.8

1. Explain how the following could be standard or nonstandard, depending on the intended meaning.

   He feels badly today.
   She looked excitedly.
   Tom sounds well.

2. What is your opinion of the statement: *I feel strongly about that?* Is it standard? Is there another way to say it? How do you think it is viewed generally?

3. Some speakers of English use *poorly* as the adverb corresponding to *bad.* Give an example of this usage. Do you ever hear it used as an adjective?

4. Is the word *lovely* an adjective or an adverb? How do you know? What about *kindly* and *friendly?* If they are adjectives, what are their corresponding adverbs?

WHAT ARE ADVERB PHRASES?

An adverb acts as the head of an **adverb phrase** and has modifiers similar to modifiers of adjectives. One type of adverb phrase that we have mentioned before contains an intensifier, essentially an adverb modifying an adverb, as in (23).

(23) Lou speaks rather fast.
       Proceed very cautiously.

Adverb phrases may also be formed with **adverb complements,** words that complete the meaning of the adverb, as in (24).

(24) Fortunately <u>for us</u>, the package arrived early.
       Mike works harder <u>than a beaver.</u>
       She walked (<u>as</u>) haughtily <u>as a queen.</u>

There are other constructions that perform adverbial functions that are neither adverbs nor adverb phrases. We will see some examples of these in the next chapter on prepositions and prepositional phrases.

DISCUSSION EXERCISES 6.9

1. Identify the adverb phrase in each of the following:

   Her cat rather quickly learned to catch mice.
   The deer runs faster than the antelope.
   This tailor very meticulously removed the stitches.
   The patient stared as blankly as a zombie.
   Fortunately for him, the meter reader never returned.

2. For each phrase you identified above, tell which is the head adverb and which are the modifiers.

3. Both adverbs and adverb phrases may form compounds. What would be an example of a compound adverb? a compound adverb phrase?

REFLECTIONS

1. Why do you think the tendency is so strong to use both *more* and *most* along with the comparative and superlative suffixes (in children's speech especially): **this is more better; *he's the most handsomest man in the world*? These constructions were not always considered nonstandard. Why do you think the eighteenth-century grammarians judged them to be ungrammatical?

2. Before English settled on *-est* as the superlative suffix, it had a number of other competing superlative suffixes, including *-ost, -ist,* and *-m.* Some people combined *-ost* and *-m* to form another suffix, *-most* (which looked just like the free-standing superlative word). Can you think of any modern-day words that use *-most* as the superlative suffix?

3. A politician was recently quoted as saying, "They have selected the least qualified of the two." A recent newspaper article refers to "the youngest of two sons." In what way do these statements violate the rules of formal standard English? Do you think these are isolated errors or part of a larger change in the English language?

4. Consider these two statements, the first from a television sitcom, the second quoting a program coordinator in a local newspaper:

> "She lives on a very fixed income."
> "It seems very seamless to the community."

On what grounds might a grammatical purist object to them?

5. A 1987 Supreme Court decision rested on the interpretation of the following instructions to a jury: "You must not be swayed by mere sentiment, conjecture, sympathy, passion, prejudice, public opinion or public feeling." The justices were divided on the question of whether *mere* modifies only *sentiment* or the whole list that follows. What do you think? If you want to know more about this case and its outcome, read Lawrence M. Solan, *The Language of Judges* (Chicago: The University of Chicago Press, 1993).

6. Words that end in *-ing* can have multiple functions. What is the lexical category of *talking* in each of the following?

> This is a talking mailbox.
>
> Talking relieves tension.
>
> I am talking about you.

7. There are interesting questions about the order in which adjectives are allowed to stack up. For example, it is more natural to say *the little red brick house* than it is to say *the brick red little house.* Can you detect any pattern in the preferred ordering?

8. In Old English, adverbs were formed by adding the suffix *-e* to adjectives. Eventually the *-e* dropped off and people replaced it with *-lic* ("like"), which later reduced to *-ly.* The flat adverbs are the ones that did not pick up *-lic* after *-e* dropped off. But users of English continue to bring these flat adverbs into the fold by creating new forms with *-ly.* So now *slow* and *slowly* are both adverbs, and *slow* will undoubtedly fall into disuse as an adverb over time. *Soft* used to be a flat adverb. Can you find any dictionary that still acknowledges its status as an adverb? What about *quick?* Are these flat adverbs more or less acceptable in their comparative forms: *softer, quicker, louder, slower?*

9. Do you think the stigma attached to using adjectives for adverbs has contributed to the creation of the new adverbs *slowly* and *loudly?* Explain. Ask a few educated people to judge the acceptability of *he runs slow* vs *he runs slowly.* Do you see any pattern in their responses?

10. Explain what this means: "We do well by doing good." What are the grammatical categories of *well* and *good* in these sentences?

11. Some grammatical purists object to the use of *hopefully* as a sentence adverb, as in *Hopefully, more communication will lead to greater understanding.* Why do you think they disapprove of this usage? (Hint: compare it to *fortunately.*)

12. What is your opinion of *a good paying job* as opposed to *a well paying job?* Are they equally acceptable alternatives? Which should be the only acceptable one according to strictly formal English?

13. Here's another chance to play advice columnist. How would you respond to the person who wrote: "So many well-educated people say, 'I feel badly,' when we know that 'feel' is like the verb 'to be,' which *never* takes an adverb. Either you feel good or you feel bad. I cringe every time I hear 'badly.' "

14. What do you think of the Apple computer company's slogan: "Act Quick, Think Different"?

15. Using nouns as adjectives is a highly productive process in English usage. Consider this: A holder for pencils may be called a *pencil holder*. Here, *pencil* takes on the function of an adjective. Labels for pencil holders might be called *pencil holder labels*. Here, *pencil holder* takes on the function of an adjective. What would you call a tray for storing pencil holder labels? Can you keep the process going? A real-life example of this process is the following: *Academic Plan Implementation Monitoring Committee.* Can you unravel its meaning? What about *workplace violence prevention training?*

16. Can you explain why *I've heard more vicious rumors* is ambiguous in standard English but *I've heard less vicious rumors* is not?

PRACTICE EXERCISES FOR CHAPTER 6 (Answers on p. 228)

1. Which of the following words are adjectives? For each gradable adjective, give the comparative and superlative forms: *salivate, spectacular, rigid, mossy, partially, incandescence, verifiable, bland.*

2. Make the following adjectives negative by adding negative prefixes: *literate, acceptable, fortunate, reversible, mobile, functional, connected, polite, distinct.*

3. Identify every adjective in the following sentences. Tell whether each is *gradable* or *nongradable, attributive* or *predicate.*
   1. My only son became depressed after his favorite dog died.
   2. The strong boxer toppled his weaker opponent.
   3. The foundation of this incredible structure is not stable.
   4. The angry cook tasted the ruined pudding.
   5. The pudding tasted sour.
   6. Her dear friend rented a little cabin in the woods.
   7. We sell frames that are circular, square, and rectangular.
   8. They considered the elderly man incompetent, but they were wrong.
   9. Your thoughtful gift made Jane happy.
   10. She seems incapable of change.

4. Identify the adjective phrases in the following sentences. What function does the whole phrase perform: attributive, subject complement, or object complement?
   1. They seem very nervous.
   2. The engine is about to explode.
   3. My sister considers my boyfriend extremely lazy.

(continued)

4. We are pleased to inform you of the results.
5. The big colorful leafy tree was blown over by the ferocious wind.
6. She is inclined to tell the truth.
7. I consider your question highly impertinent.
8. He noticed a tiny little spot on the brand new rug.
9. Very generous people allow their overly needy friends to take advantage of them.
10. This old battered building needs renovation.

5. Identify the adverbs in the following sentences and tell what lexical category they modify. Sentences may have more than one adverb.
   1. The president ruled quite responsibly.
   2. Nevertheless, I can't float you a loan.
   3. The scientists are extremely excited about the findings.
   4. You arrived too late.
   5. Yesterday I danced quite well.
   6. It's not possible, therefore, to plan the trip.
   7. You waited so patiently.
   8. This day has been quite lovely.
   9. The dog happily bit the bully.
   10. The sofa will remain, however.

6. Choose the standard English word for the blank in each sentence. For which are both acceptable?
   1. The engine sounds ___ (good, well).
   2. The pony runs ___ (slow, slowly).
   3. I feel ___ (bad, badly).
   4. You talk too ___ (loud, loudly).
   5. The class performed ___ (well, good) today.
   6. She looked ___ (good, well).
   7. He did ___ (good, well).
   8. They worked so ___ (hard, hardly).
   9. The bread feels ___ (soft, softly).
   10. He doesn't feel ___ (well, good).

7. Pick out the adverb phrases in the following sentences.
   1. She quite impudently asked my weight.
   2. Did they play loud enough?
   3. I can guess your age very easily.
   4. The cat approached rather tentatively.
   5. Nan writes better than her brother.
   6. The baby talked well for her age.
   7. I answered as civilly as I could.

(continued)

8. He sang surprisingly well.
9. They responded as quickly as possible.
10. She works extraordinarily fast.

8. What are the two meanings of *Visiting relatives can be fun*? Name the lexical category of *visiting* under each of these interpretations.

9. Find an example of each of the following in the *Believers* selection that follows.

an adverb of manner

an intensifier

an attributive adjective

a noun used as an adjective

an adjective phrase

a subject complement

a sentence adverb

a personal pronoun

a possessive pronoun

a linking verb

an object of a preposition

an intransitive verb

a demonstrative determiner

Jodie sat where she was for a moment, painfully resisting the impulse to go rummaging through Walton's medicine cabinet and desk and dresser drawers. Instead, she brought a chair over next to him, sat down in it, and studied his face. Although it wasn't an unusual face, at this distance certain features about it were certainly noteworthy. The line where the beard began on his cheek—he was cleanshaven—was so straight that it seemed to have been implanted there with a ruler. He had two tiny, almost microscopic, pieces of dandruff in his eyebrows. His lashes were rather long, for a man. His lower lip was also rather full, but his upper lip was so small and flat at the bottom that you might not notice it unless you looked carefully. (Baxter: "Kiss Away," p. 12.)

10. Identify the violations of formal standard English in the following letter:

Dear Chris,

Wasn't the trip to Paris real nice? I wish we could of stayed their longer. I feel badly about not getting to see the Eiffel Tower, but at least me and you saw it from a distance. What was your most favorite sight? Mine was the Cluny Museum, with all those very unique tapestries. I thought it was the best of the two museums I visited. I'm sorry we got lost the last day. Usually I can read maps pretty good. If I was you, I would have those photo's developed soon. Hopefully, we can get together one of these days and share our memory's.

Love,
Pat

SEVEN

PREPOSITIONS AND PARTICLES

WHAT ARE PREPOSITIONS?

Prepositions are words, usually small words, that indicate the relationship of a noun phrase to the rest of the sentence. This may seem like a strange definition to you, given that we devoted a whole chapter to describing noun phrases and their functions without talking about prepositions at all. You will remember that noun phrases can be subjects, direct objects, indirect objects, and complements, and that their position in the sentence tells us the particular roles they play in the sentence. Prepositions allow noun phrases to relate to the rest of the sentence in a variety of other ways. For example, the noun phrase *my place* in the first sentence of (1) is a location, but it needs the preposition *at* to fit it into the sentence as a location. Similarly, *the night* in the second sentence expresses a time, with the help of the preposition *during*. *Love* in the third sentence is a purpose, expressed as such by the use of the preposition *for*.

> (1) Let's have dinner <u>at</u> my place.
> The club met <u>during</u> the night.
> She did it all <u>for</u> love.

Some other noun phrase functions that can be expressed with the help of prepositions are illustrated in (2).

> (2) He left <u>with</u> Bob.   (accompaniment)
> She cut the rope <u>with</u> a knife.   (means)
> I walked <u>into</u> the room.   (direction)
> They hid the heirlooms <u>of</u> the family.   (possession)
> The mistake was made <u>by</u> you.   (agent)

There is no pattern to how prepositions indicate noun phrase function, but native speakers of English have learned them by adulthood, so you do not have to memorize them. If you want to teach preposition use to speakers of other languages, then you have a problem. Consider how all the different prepositions in the sentences in (3) indicate location.

(3) We live <u>in</u> the United States.
     We live <u>on</u> Beacon Street.
     We live <u>at</u> the corner of Hollywood and Vine.

Consider also how the preposition *by,* as illustrated in the sentences in (4), can have several different functions.

(4) I'll be there by noon.   (time)
     Meet me by the fountain.   (place)
     He passed the exam by cheating.   (means)
     The house was built by my father.   (agent)

DISCUSSION EXERCISES 7.1

1. Describe as accurately as you can the noun phrase functions signalled by the prepositions in the following sentences:

    We met them on the slopes.
    He felled the tree with an axe.
    The car disappeared over the hill.
    I'll see you at noon.
    She said to meet her near the fountain.
    It flies like an arrow.
    He went to the party with his brother.
    They prepared for their exams.
    The dog ran into the yard.
    Don't open a can of worms.

2. Preposition use is highly unpredictable and may even vary from region to region within the United States. Do you wait *on line* or *in line?* Do you become *sick to your stomach* or *sick at your stomach?* Are you aware of other fluctuations in preposition use?

WHAT ARE PREPOSITIONAL PHRASES?

Prepositions always occur with a following noun phrase (or pronoun), called the object of the preposition (see Chapter 3). Together they make up a constituent called a **prepositional phrase,** which fits into a sentence in one of two ways. It can modify a noun or it can modify a verb. When it modifies a noun, we say it has an adjectival function. In its adjectival function, it can be part of a noun phrase, modifying the head noun, as illustrated in (5).

(5) The boy <u>with the kite</u> is having fun.

✱ A prepositional phrase can also be a subject complement, as in (6).

> (6) The king is <u>without mercy</u>.

On the other hand, when the prepositional phrase modifies a verb, we say that it performs an adverbial function. In its adverbial function it often tells the time or place or means of the action, as in (7).

> (7) We met them <u>at noon</u>.
> We met them <u>on the corner</u>.
> We got there <u>by bus</u>.

✱ It is <u>important to keep in mind that the job of a preposition is to signal</u> a role for a noun phrase. Once the two join together to form a prepositional phrase, the whole phrase acts either like an adjective, modifying nouns, or like an adverb, modifying verbs.

DISCUSSION EXERCISES 7.2

1. Identify the prepositional phrase in each of the following sentences. Tell whether its function is adjectival or adverbial.

   The ashes blew into her eyes. *Adv.*
   Let's go to the movies. *Adv.*
   The people in this neighborhood are friendly. *adj*
   I don't believe the price of that sweater. *Adj.*
   Take me to your leader. *Adv.*
   Please arrive on time. *Adv.*
   A woman with a mysterious smile left this package. *Adj.*
   The purpose of this exercise is evident. *Adj.*

2. Sentences like the following present a problem for grammatical analysis.

   The ship is at sea.   *adj or Adv*   *depending on interp*   *Adv—location*   *Adj. Sub. comp*
   The accident was at the intersection.

   Are the prepositional phrases performing an adjectival or an adverbial function? Why is the answer not as clear-cut as it is for the previous sentences?

3. Explain why the following sentence can have two different meanings.

   The astronomer saw her colleague with the telescope.   *could modify either*

Prepositional phrases, like other constituents, hold together in sentences. The noun phrase and the preposition together form answers to questions.

(8) Where do you live?

> On the corner of Hollywood and Vine.
> In Texas.
> At the intersection of Main and Elm.

Prepositional phrases also move around as a unit.

(9) I saw him <u>near the fountain</u>.
It was <u>near the fountain</u> that I saw him.

And they can often be replaced by single pro-forms such as *here, there,* and *then.*

But there are also grammatical forces that work to separate a preposition from its following noun phrase. Sometimes we need to move a noun phrase (or more likely a pronoun) to the beginning of its clause, specifically in questions and in relative clauses. Let's look again at those two cases. If I know, for example, that you could see someone, but I don't know the identity of that person, the question might form in my mind as in (10).

(10) You could see whom?

For ordinary questions, standard English requires that we move *whom* to the beginning of the sentence.

(11) Whom could you see?

Now suppose the question in my mind is (12).

(12) You were speaking to whom?

If I move only *whom,* I am left with (13).

(13) Whom were you speaking to?

The preposition that is left behind is called a **deferred preposition.** Formal standard English frowns upon deferred prepositions; many of us are aware that somewhere out there is a rule that tells us not to end a sentence with a preposition. The standard English solution is to bring the preposition forward along with the noun phrase, giving us (14).

[handwritten marginal note: Test prep. phrases by: ① Entire constituent can be moved ② Question can be answered with prep phrase.]

(14) To whom were you speaking?

We see a parallel situation with relative clauses, which also require the pronoun to be moved to the front of the clause. Suppose we wanted to combine the two sentences in (15) into one sentence with a relative clause.

(15) I know the man. You were speaking to the man.

If we moved the relative pronoun alone, the result would be (16).

(16) I know the man whom you were speaking to.

This leaves *to* behind as a deferred preposition. Again, formal standard English requires that the preposition be brought forward as well, giving (17).

(17) I know the man to whom you were speaking.

Prepositional phrases often nest inside other constituents. Consider, for example, the following sentence:

(18) I sat near the boy in the overalls.

This sentence contains the prepositional phrase *near the boy in the overalls,* which performs the adverbial function of place. Inside this prepositional phrase is the noun phrase *the boy in the overalls* (the object of the preposition *near*), and inside this noun phrase is the prepositional phrase *with the overalls* (which in turn contains the noun phrase *the overalls*). Graphically, the structure of *near the boy in the overalls* looks like this:

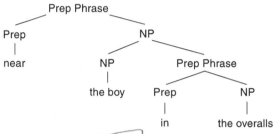

We might also describe this nesting structure using brackets, as illustrated:

near [the boy [in [the overalls]]]

DISCUSSION EXERCISES 7.3

1. Identify the prepositional phrases in the sentences in Discussion Exercises 7.1 question 1. Show that they are constituents by applying some of the constituent tests we described.

2. We have described the formal standard English rule for deferred prepositions, but we also know that deferred prepositions are not highly stigmatized and sound more natural in more casual uses of English. *Whom* is also highly formal and using *who* in its place is acceptable in less formal English. That gives us a variety of ways to express the mental question expressed in (12). What are they?

3. For relative clauses we often have the additional options of replacing *whom* with *that* or leaving it out altogether. What are the various less formal options for expressing (15) with a relative clause?

4. Illustrate the nesting of constituents in *She laughed at the man in the red hat.*

WHAT ARE PARTICLES?

A **particle** is the second element of a two-part transitive verb. *Particles* are often confused with prepositions because the two word classes look very much alike. Many words can be either prepositions or particles, and they seem to occupy the same position in sentences. The sentences in (19) help to illustrate the differences between them.

(19) Dorothy turned down the brick road.
Dorothy turned down the invitation.

Down in the first sentence is a preposition. It forms a constituent with the noun phrase *the brick road,* and so can stand as the answer to a question: *Where did Dorothy turn?* The whole prepositional phrase moves as a unit, giving us sentences like *It was down the brick road that Dorothy turned,* and it can be replaced with a pro-form as in *Dorothy turned there. Down* in the second sentence is not a preposition; it is a particle. You'll notice that *down the invitation* does not hold together as a constituent: it cannot be a freestanding answer to a question, nor can it move around together or be replaced by a pro-form. *Down,* rather, forms a grouping with *turned:* together they make up a two-part transitive verb. There are other single-word verbs that could take their place: *refused,* for example. If we were to capture the constituent structure of the two sentences in (19) visually, they would look like this:

Preposition: Dorothy turned [down the brick road].
Particle: Dorothy [turned down] the invitation.

Another interesting fact about particles is that they are permitted to move away from their verbs by a special rule called **particle movement.** Particle movement allows us to move the particle behind the object noun phrase, giving us another way to say the same thing. Thus, *Dorothy turned down the invitation* can also be said as (20).

(20) Dorothy turned the invitation down.

You notice that we do not have to worry here about the rule against deferred prepositions, because *down* is not a preposition in this sentence.

DISCUSSION EXERCISES 7.4

1. Tell whether the underlined word in each sentence is a particle or a preposition. How do you know?

She looked <u>over</u> the contract.
I found it <u>over</u> the rainbow.
They ran <u>down</u> the street.

(continued)

He burned down the house *particle*
Turn in your assignment. *particle*
Sit in your seat. *Prep. phr.*
She turned off the ignition. *Part.*
She turned off the beaten path. *prep*
It flew out the window. *prep*
I put out the garbage.

2. Demonstrate that the word *up* can be a preposition or a particle.

3. Explain in grammatical terms why the following sentence has more than one meaning.

   He slipped in the alcohol.

4. How does the rule of particle-movement work if the object noun phrase is a pronoun? That is, suppose instead of saying *She turned down the invitation,* we replaced *the invitation* with the pronoun *it.* Does it make a difference in the application of the particle movement rule?

5. Both prepositions and prepositional phrases can form compounds. What would be an example of each? Can particles form compounds?

It may be disconcerting to find time after time that words can play more than one role in grammar. We are sometimes led to believe that grammar is a naming exercise, that all we need to do is learn what things are called and label them correctly. By now it should be apparent to you that that isn't how language works and that understanding the grammatical structure of a sentence involves analyzing how words relate to other words in the sentence. What something is called depends on the context in which it appears. As users of the language we have the ability to sort out the various possible interpretations of words and sentences and choose the ones appropriate for the occasion on which they are uttered. As students of grammar we need to be able to call up all the possible grammatical interpretations of words and sentences. We must also understand that the forces of language change can alter those analyses over time.

Now that we have learned how to sort out all the individual word classes and the constituents they form, we are prepared to move on to an examination of clauses. Clauses are combinations of noun phrases and verb phrases that play a vital role in English grammar as the primary building blocks of sentences.

REFLECTIONS

1. In Chapter 3 we said that indirect object noun phrases are preceded by the prepositions *to* or *for: I gave the book to Bill, I bought the book for*

Bill. You will remember that some linguists have argued that these are merely examples of prepositional phrases and should not have a special designation as indirect object. Is there any reason to single them out as different from other prepositional phrases?

2. As we have mentioned, prepositional phrases can be embedded inside other constituents. How would you analyze the structure of the following sentence? Can it have more than one analysis?

Put it in the drawer of the desk near the window.

3. The best way to learn how people judge deferred prepositions is to ask them. Ask several speakers of standard English to comment on the following sentences:

For which doctor are you waiting?
Which doctor are you waiting for?

You might ask: Are they both grammatical? Would you use them in different settings? Does one seem more natural than the other?

4. Speculate about why the eighteenth-century grammarians ruled against deferred prepositions. What reasons can you come up with? Do these reasons collide with the fact that moved particles are perfectly acceptable?

5. The previous question contains a deferred preposition. What is it? How else could the question be formulated?

6. Children may say things like "Take out it." What have they not yet mastered about English?

7. There are some two-part verbs that do not use particles. The following sentence has two interpretations:

We decided on the boat.

Under one interpretation, *on the boat* is a prepositional phrase telling the location of the decision. Under the other, *decided on* is a two-part verb with the meaning "chose." But there is no interpretation in which *on* is a particle. Can you demonstrate that it isn't a particle?

Note also that there are some intransitive verbs that have two parts, such as *catch up, sit up, give in, lie down.* Some grammarians will call the second part of these verbs "particles" but designate them as "inseparable particles" as distinct from the kind that can move behind direct objects.

8. In addition to being particles and prepositions, some words, like *up, in,* and *out,* can also be adverbs. When they are adverbs, they can be replaced by the adverb pro-forms *here* and *there.* Can you give examples of these words used as adverbs?

9. Can you demonstrate that the word *down* can be a preposition, a particle, an adjective, a verb, a noun, or an adverb?

10. What would be the most formal version of this sentence?

Address your level of speech according to who you are speaking to.

PRACTICE EXERCISES FOR CHAPTER 7 (Answers on p. 229)

1. Which noun phrases (or pronouns) are objects of prepositions in the following sentences? (Note that the *to* that is part of the infinitive is not considered a preposition.)
   1. I like to take vacations in the springtime.
   2. My favorite times are at the seashore.
   3. This secret is between you and me.
   4. You are under no obligation to testify.
   5. I'll get there by hook or by crook.
   6. Like us, they eat dinner early.
   7. I can't wait until my birthday.
   8. He's waiting for the right moment.
   9. Let's meet after class.
   10. You can succeed by working hard.

2. Is the function of the prepositional phrase in each of the following sentences adjectival or adverbial? Are there any that could be argued both ways?
   1. The dog with the flea collar is scratching.
   2. My father takes a nap in the afternoon.
   3. Let's ask the guard in the red helmet.
   4. The pot is on the counter.
   5. The box under the tree is a present.
   6. You've opened a can of worms.
   7. She hammered the nails into the board.
   8. By tomorrow, the job will be finished.
   9. He stood before the judge.
   10. My best suit is at the dry cleaners.

3. What are the two meanings of the following sentence? Which function of the prepositional phrase corresponds to which meaning?

   He found the speeding motorist with the electronic sensor.

4. What are the prepositional phrases in the following sentence? Which are embedded within another prepositional phrase?

   The puppy crawled into a pipe under the house around the corner.

5. Give the most formal version of each of the following sentences by moving the deferred preposition and making other necessary adjustments.
   1. Who are you looking for?
   2. That's the book she was talking about.
   3. Is this the pot I'm supposed to cook it in?

(continued)

4. I need to call the friends I'm going with.
5. Which actor are you standing in for?
6. I fear the world we live in.
7. Is this the channel that the news is broadcast on?
8. Which bench did they sit on?
9. This is the hill we rolled down as children.
10. Which cliff did she jump off?

6. Perform particle movement on each of the following sentences.
    1. She turned off the ignition.
    2. Linda took out the trash.
    3. The teacher brought in the books.
    4. The librarian looked up the address for me.
    5. Lois put on her new dress.
    6. Arsonists burned down the building.
    7. The children turned in their parents to the police.
    8. Please hand in your homework.
    9. They turned down our offer.
    10. Hand over your money!

7. Which of the underlined words are particles and which are prepositions? Could any be either?
    1. Sally brought <u>in</u> the mail.
    2. Ed looked <u>over</u> the newspaper.
    3. Put the flowers <u>in</u> the vase.
    4. The cashier rang <u>up</u> the wrong amount.
    5. Please turn <u>off</u> the light.
    6. Ethel put <u>on</u> her new hat.
    7. He looked <u>up</u> the street.
    8. They found <u>out</u> the truth.
    9. Let's jump <u>off</u> the bed.
    10. There's a pot of gold <u>over</u> the rainbow.

8. For which of the following has particle movement applied obligatorily? Why?
    1. She put the cat out.
    2. The lawyer turned them in.
    3. Turn the engine off.
    4. Don't write him off.
    5. Please turn the volume down.
    6. He let himself in.
    7. I tuned her out.

(continued)

8. He put the shoes on.
9. They found it out too late.
10. Take them off.

9. Which of the underlined words are prepositions, which are particles, and which are adverbs?
   1. Let's go <u>out</u> tonight.
   2. Please take <u>out</u> the garbage.
   3. He ran <u>out</u> the door.
   4. Clyde hobbled <u>up</u> the street.
   5. Look <u>up</u> and you'll see a helicopter.
   6. Turn <u>up</u> the volume.
   7. They called <u>in</u> a consultant.
   8. We met <u>in</u> a bar.
   9. Come <u>in</u> from the rain.

10. Find an example of each of the following in the *Believers* selection that follows.
   a particle
   a preposition
   a prepositional phrase
   an object of a preposition
   a sentence adverb
   a noun used as an adjective
   an intensifier
   an adjective complement
   a subject complement

   A few days later, when she picked up the developed film, she was delighted to see that the photograph of the sugar maple was good enough to frame. The super night shot, however, was terribly blurred in it: streaks of light crossed the sky, like meteors, and the west gate of the park had the appearance of fiery brown gelatin. (Baxter: "The Exposure," p. 88.)

11. Identify the violations of formal standard English in the following letter:

   Dear Chris,

   I seen you yesterday from across the street. I thought you were buying a present. Who were you buying it for? My birthday isn't until next month. Ha, ha. Seriously, the thank-you note that you sent to my family and I was very gracious. Each of us have a special feeling for you. Either my sister or my mother are planning to invite you on our trip next year. But no one enjoyed the trip this year more than me. By the way, I took my drivers test yesterday. I did real horrible, but they passed me anyway, so now you and me can drive places together. Just let me know where you want to drive to!

   Love and hugs,
   Pat

EIGHT

CLAUSE TYPE: VOICE

WHAT IS GRAMMATICAL VOICE?

There are two voices in English: the **active voice** and the **passive voice.** Voice has to do with the arrangement of the players or actors in the sentence or, more accurately, the clause. The difference between active and passive voice is relevant when there are two players surrounding the action, that is, when there is a transitive verb with a subject and a direct object. Normally the linear order of elements is subject + verb + direct object, or very loosely construed, doer + action + receiver. All of the sentences in (1) show this order.

(1) An agent delivered the goods.
     My friend witnessed the accident.
     That pitcher threw the ball.
     The waiter poured the water.

You are already familiar with clauses of this type. All the sentences in (1) are in the *active voice.* We have not had occasion until now to name this as the active voice, since this is the normal, expected line-up of grammatical relations. Most of our examples so far have been in the active voice, and we have not had any reason to contrast them with other arrangements.

But there is another possible arrangement in English in which the order of elements is receiver + action + doer: this arrangement is known as the *passive voice.* We need to stop for a moment to consider what this means. Clearly, we don't mean that we are completely free to rearrange the noun phrases in a sentence. As speakers of English, we know that we cannot do that. Consider the sentences in (2), for example.

(2) The dog bit the child.
     The child bit the dog.

If we merely have the doer and the receiver change places, we have a new sentence with a different meaning and the doer of the action is still the subject. Both of these are in the active voice. If we want a clause to be in the passive voice, we have to signal that we intend for the first noun phrase to be understood as the receiver, not the doer, of the action. That is, we have to alert our listener (or reader) to intercept the normal interpretation and replace it with one in which the noun phrases don't have their normal or expected functions. We have several different ways in which we signal the passive voice, all evident in the sentences in (3), which are the passive versions of the sentences in (2),

(3) The child was bitten by the dog.
    The dog was bitten by the child.

You will notice that there are certain systematic changes in structure as we go from the active voice to the passive voice.

DISCUSSION EXERCISES 8.1

1. Which of the following clauses are in the active voice and which are in the passive voice?

   The announcer reported the results of the election.
   A small child started the fire.
   He was frightened by the loud noise.
   The deer was killed by the hunter.
   My sister won the contest.
   The secretary shredded the documents.
   Basketball is enjoyed by everyone.
   My sister ordered this package.
   The game was stopped by the referee.
   The detective discovered the evidence.

2. Although we have not yet discussed the details of how we turn active into passive clauses, your native ability in English will enable you to do it instinctively. See how quickly you can turn each of the following active clauses into their passive equivalents. Make sure you preserve the meaning of the original active clause.

   The little dog buried the dirty old bone.
   My nasty uncle Pete fired the servant.
   The archaeologist on the dig uncovered the ruins of the ancient city.
   Sailors consume large quantities of fish.
   Good music soothes our souls.
   That teacher taught chemistry and physics.
   The local newspaper published my letter complaining about trash collection.
   The cat cornered the terrified mouse.
   An honest stranger returned my lost wallet.
   Your attitude surprises me.

HOW IS THE PASSIVE VOICE FORMED?

What is it that we are doing when we turn the active into the passive voice? One thing we do is switch the positions of the active voice subject (doer) and the active voice direct object (receiver). In fact, you will remember that one of the tests for direct objects described in Chapter 3 was the passive test, which involved placing the direct object in the position of the subject. But we have already seen that this exchange is not enough to signal the passive voice. So what else do we do? We see that we also insert the preposition *by* in front of the doer of the action. This is how the elements line up in the passive as compared to the active voice:

Active Voice: **Doer + Action + Receiver**

Passive Voice: **Receiver + Action + by Doer**

＊ good way to explain

In addition, we express the action in a different way. For the passive voice, we insert the verb *to be,* an auxiliary verb, and we put the main verb into its past participle form.

Active Voice: **Doer + Action + Receiver**
                      tensed main verb

Passive Voice: **Receiver + Action + by Doer**
                      to be + past participle of main verb

DISCUSSION EXERCISES 8.2

1. Write out the passive versions of Discussion Exercise 8.1, question 2. What does it mean to say that *to be* functions as an auxiliary? What is its function?

2. To retain the same meaning from active to passive, the verb *to be* must carry the same tense as the main verb of the active sentence. Most of the examples we have given are in the simple past, but almost all tenses have corresponding passives. What are the corresponding passive sentences of the following?

   The proctor has administered the test.
   The whole town will remember you.
   The post office will have delivered the package by then.
   The researchers had expected those results.
   My cousin is building this house.
   The assistant was grading the exams.

3. What is the tense of *to be* in each of the passive sentences you have created above? (Refer to Chapter 4 if you need help on this.)

(continued)

4. For most speakers of English, the following active sentences do not have corresponding passive forms. (Try to make them passive!) What do they all have in common?

   They have been forging many checks.
   The class will have been studying the complex tenses.
   The employer had been reviewing the files.

[handwritten note in margin: "They are perfect prog. already "b"]

5. The verb *to get* may serve as the auxiliary instead of *to be* in the passive voice, usually in less formal contexts. Turn each of the sentences in Discussion Exercise 8.1, question 2 into its corresponding *get-* passive. Is there a meaning difference between the *be-* passive and the *get-* passive?

HOW ARE GRAMMATICAL RELATIONS DETERMINED IN THE PASSIVE VOICE?

Although it is useful to talk about "doers" and "receivers" when we compare the passive to the active voice, we need to rethink our use of these terms as definitions for subjects and direct objects. They raise some questions in the active voice, but they are most problematic in the passive voice. If we think of the subject of the sentence as the noun phrase before the verb, the noun phrase that the verb agrees with, *and* the doer of the action, there will rarely be one noun phrase in a passive clause that meets all three criteria. Whereas the active voice tends to assign all these characteristics to the same noun phrase, the passive voice tends to distribute them between two different noun phrases. In (4), for example, the noun phrase *that company* meets all three criteria because the clause is in the active voice.

(4) That company built very fancy houses.

But consider (5), its passive version.

(5) Very fancy houses were built by that company.

Here *very fancy houses* precedes the verb and the verb agrees with it, but *that company* is still the doer of the action. To simplify the definition of subject, we will say that the subject is the noun phrase that precedes the verb and the noun phrase that the verb agrees with, recognizing that the doer of the action may be another noun phrase.

Similarly, we must reexamine our criteria for identifying the direct object. By the same reasoning, receiver of the action may shift from one noun phrase to another. The more fixed and reliable definition of direct object is the noun phrase that immediately follows a transitive verb in the active voice. In (4), for example, *very fancy houses* is the direct object. But in (5), its passive version, there is no direct object. The direct object of (4) has become a subject and the subject of (4) has become the object of a preposition.

DISCUSSION EXERCISES 8.3

1. We said that the verbs in (4) and (5) agree with their subjects. Demonstrate this by changing the subject in each so that the verb must also change.

2. What is the grammatical function of each noun phrase in the following active clauses?

   The reporter discovered two new pieces of evidence.
   A large number of people tolerate dishonest behavior.
   Many potential employers reject sloppy resumes. Do
   His students planted a memorial garden.
   Thousands of tourists visited the museum exhibit.

3. Describe the functions of the noun phrases in the following passive clauses.

   Two new pieces of evidence were discovered by the reporter.
   Dishonest behavior is tolerated by a large number of people.
   Sloppy resumes are rejected by many potential employers.
   A memorial garden was planted by his students.
   The museum exhibit was visited by thousands of tourists.

4. Normally, the two noun phrases that get reversed in the passive voice are the active subject and direct object. One exception to this is illustrated by the following sentence:

   The clerk was given a second chance by the sympathetic customer.

   What makes this sentence an exception to the reversal rule?

5. How does *the clerk* come to occupy subject position in the sentence above? If you are having trouble answering this question, think of indirect object inversion. It will also help to review the section on grammatical relations in Chapter 3.

6. Name the function of each noun phrase in the following sentences:

   My father gave a dozen roses to my mother.
   My father gave my mother a dozen roses.
   A dozen roses were given to my mother by my father.
   My mother was given a dozen roses by my father.

7. Sometimes even in active clauses doers and receivers aren't the same as subjects and objects, respectively. Consider the following sentence:

   The doctors received the supplies.

   Which noun phrase is the subject? the direct object? the doer? the receiver? What is the passive form of this sentence?

WHY DO WE NEED THE PASSIVE VOICE?

The passive voice adds nothing to the ability of English to express meaning. When we turn an active sentence into its passive counterpart, we rearrange the noun phrases, but the meaning is left intact. This raises an interesting question: why would a language have two ways of expressing the same meaning? Is the passive voice merely a redundant structure in the language, a frivolous and unnecessary addition that serves only to complicate the lives of students of grammar and contributes nothing to the expressive power of its users? Or is there a legitimate function of the passive voice independent of the literal meaning it conveys? You are undoubtedly expecting a "yes" answer to this last question, so let's explore what a "yes" answer means.

Although there is no literal meaning difference between a clause in the active voice and its corresponding passive, there are still some differences, primarily of focus or emphasis. The passive voice allows us to put an object in a more prominent position in the clause and play down the importance of the subject. The subject position, the first noun phrase in the clause, is the most prominent. If we put the active voice object there, it takes on more importance. Similarly, the active voice subject, by being made the object of a preposition at the end of the clause, isn't even one of the "major players" anymore. Being able to realign the importance of subject and object noun phrases is a handy tool for us in communication. Suppose, for example, that we are having a lengthy conversation about your Aunt Tillie. If I ask you "what finally happened to your Aunt Tillie?" you might answer as in (6).

(6) She was arrested by the police and sent to jail for mail fraud.

It wouldn't be wrong to say this in the active voice, as in (7).

(7) The police arrested her and sent her to jail for mail fraud.

But saying it this way would take the focus off Aunt Tillie and interrupt the continuity of the conversation. So stylistically the passive voice is a useful alternative to the active voice even though it doesn't change the meaning.

DISCUSSION EXERCISES 8.4

1. Construct a conversational context in which the following passive sentences would be an appropriate alternative to the active voice.

   The reports were found by the cleaning staff.
   My printer is being repaired by a computer expert.

(continued)

The bad news had been anticipated by most of us.

Foreign automobiles are sold by that dealer.

The textbook was chosen by the principal.

2. Students are sometimes discouraged by teachers from using the passive voice in their writing. Why do you think this is so?

3. Change the above statement to the active voice. Does this change how you would answer the question that follows it?

WHAT IS A TRUNCATED PASSIVE?

There is another very important difference between the active and the passive voice. Not only does the passive voice allow us to diminish the importance of the active voice subject, it allows us to leave it out entirely. Consider the sentences in (8), for example.

(8) The suspects were brought in for questioning.
    Her car was wrecked in the accident.
    His name has been eliminated from the list.
    You are expected to arrive on time.

These are called **truncated passives** because the subject of the corresponding active clause is left unexpressed, in contrast to the **full passive,** in which the subject is expressed as the object of the preposition *by*. In each of the clauses in (8) there is an implied doer, but we are not forced to express it in grammatical terms. The option of talking about an action without expressing a doer is normally not available to us in the active voice, and that is what makes the passive voice truly useful to us.

Under what circumstances would we prefer to use a truncated passive? In some cases it allows us to avoid laying blame or taking responsibility.

(9) Mistakes were made.
    The cake was left out in the rain.

In other cases we may know the result of an action, but the doer is unknown to us.

(10) The window was broken during the night.
     A monument was erected in her honor.

And in some cases the doer is obvious, so expressing it would be redundant.

(11) The governor's address was delivered at 9:00 P.M.
     All my money was lost on a bad gambling bet.

For good or for evil, the truncated passive is a popular construction, used widely even by those who themselves frown upon the use of the passive voice.

DISCUSSION EXERCISES 8.5

1. Turn the following active clauses into truncated passives.

   Someone left that dog out all night.
   A thief stole all my jewels.
   I ruined your valuable painting.
   Everyone respects my family.
   The treasurer gave the treasurer's report at the end of the meeting.

2. Do any of the truncated passives you created seem preferable to the full passive? Why?

3. Turn the following truncated passives into full passives by supplying a doer.

   He was arrested and searched.
   The books were read to the children.
   Your car got wrecked.
   The show was canceled.
   The land got developed.

4. Some of the examples in Question 3 remind us that the verb *get* can be used as the auxiliary verb in the passive voice instead of *be.* But it also can be an active, transitive verb meaning "acquire" or a linking verb meaning "become." What is *get* in each of the following: auxiliary, transitive, or linking?

   She got a new puppy last night.
   Ellen gets red in the face when you compliment her.
   The problem got resolved by the lawyers.
   They got admitted for free.
   Harry got accepted by the army.
   Steve got a letter from his uncle.
   Everyone got angry.

5. Truncated passives may look very much like sentences with subject complements. Compare these two sentences:

   The door was opened.   (truncated passive)
   The door was open.   (linking verb + subject complement)

What makes the following sentence ambiguous?

   The door was closed.

What are the two meanings of *The contestant was withdrawn? The meat was frozen*?

We have seen in this chapter that the way we form clauses depends in part on the purposes they serve in communication. In the next chapter, we explore in more detail the connection between the form of a clause and its communicative function.

REFLECTIONS

1. In addition to the active and passive voice, there is an uncommon voice, sometimes referred to as the *middle voice*. Some examples of the middle voice are the following:

> These pants iron easily.

> This book reads well.

Why do you think grammarians call this the *middle voice?*

2. In modern English we cannot freely rearrange the noun phrases of a clause unless we also add the signals of the passive voice to the clause. But in Old English it was possible to rearrange the noun phrases of a clause without changing the meaning and without marking it as passive. Consult a history of the English language to find out why it was possible to do this then but not now.

3. The progressive tenses were not used regularly in English until the late eighteenth century, which might explain why they still do not combine readily with the passive voice. Some are more acceptable than others in modern English, as illustrated in Discussion Exercises 8.2. Present and past progressive have acceptable passives: *The house is (was) being built by the contractor.* What about the future progressive? Does it have a corresponding passive? Can you give an example of it?

4. As we saw in this chapter, there are some verbs in English that are inherently passive in their meaning, like *receive*. It follows the usual pattern for active and passive voice, but there is no doer associated with *receive*, whether active or passive.

> His friend received the package.

> The package was received by his friend.

Can you think of other verbs that are like *receive* in this respect?

5. Here is a quote from a modern British novel. Would you combine the progressive and the passive in this way?

> "Paternal concern seems to be being overridden now by other considerations, she retorted." Penelope Lively, *Passing On* (New York: Harper Perennial, 1991), p. 195.

6. Select about five pages from a textbook or an article in a journal. How many examples of the passive voice do you find, both full and truncated?

PRACTICE EXERCISES FOR CHAPTER 8 (Answers on p. 231)

1. Turn each of the following active sentences into its corresponding full passive, using the verb *to be* as the auxiliary verb.
    1. The realty company sold our house.
    2. The storm caused widespread destruction.
    3. This job requires great sensitivity.
    4. Mixing the two chemicals created an explosion.
    5. A consulting firm is hiring a new chancellor.
    6. Our president will deliver the speech tomorrow.
    7. The librarian left a book at the circulation desk.
    8. Many people have witnessed their cruelty.
    9. The family purchased a week's worth of groceries with your gift.
    10. A retired outfielder threw the first ball.
2. Which of the above have equally acceptable *get*-passives?
3. Name the grammatical functions of the noun phrases in each of the following.
    1. The teller handed the customer a roll of bills.
    2. Your proposal has been accepted by management.
    3. The stagecoach was robbed by the bandits.
    4. That unhappy child demands constant attention.
    5. The customer was handed a roll of bills by the teller.
    6. The book was returned to the library by the sheepish patron.
    7. Your party will meet you by the fountain.
    8. Many intelligent people admire good writing.
    9. The suspect was informed of his rights by the police.
    10. Free cheese is distributed by the government.
4. Restructure the following sentence so that the indirect object becomes the grammatical subject.
    The doctor gave a clean bill of health to the nervous patient.
5. Make a truncated passive out of each of the following.
    1. One should avoid the passive voice.
    2. Someone chopped down that old tree.
    3. People expect you to dress appropriately.
    4. The legislators passed the bill by a vote of 50–37.
    5. The trash collectors pick up the trash on Tuesdays.
    6. This TV station broadcasts the news at 6:00 every evening.
    7. The opposing team defeated the Yankees.
    8. The storekeeper will open the store early tomorrow.

(continued)

9. The police obtained a warrant to search the house.

10. Everyone prefers laser printers.

6. Why are the full and truncated passives corresponding to the above sentences so close in meaning?

7. Make the following truncated passives full passives by providing a doer.

1. Lunch should be eaten in the cafeteria.
2. The animals were released from their cages.
3. Her cries for help were ignored.
4. The law was repealed.
5. The bell was rung one last time.
6. My car will be repaired.
7. The rules of the competition were rarely understood.
8. Our mail is being sorted right now.
9. Her gardens were planted in May.
10. The students were told to begin the exam.

8. Label the function of each noun phrase in the following sentence.

   The child was given a handful of coins by the magician.

9. Give the active sentence that corresponds to the sentence in 8, and name the functions of the noun phrases.

10. Which of the following are ambiguous? Describe the two possible structures for the ambiguous ones.

1. The animals were frightened.
2. His clothes were torn.
3. The traffic was heavy.
4. The doors were open.
5. The doors were closed.
6. We were amused.
7. Class was dismissed.
8. The children were ready.
9. The movie was exciting.
10. The dog was tied to a tree.

11. Find an example of each of the following in the *Believers* selection that follows.

   three truncated passive clauses

   an infinitival phrase used as a direct object

   a compound determiner

   an object of a preposition

   a verb in the present perfect tense

   an interrogative pronoun

   an indefinite pronoun

   an adverb

(continued)

It was arranged, the trip, intermediaries were empowered to transfer cash to the archdiocese, bishops and archbishops and cardinals were no doubt enlisted, and somehow they were persuaded to release my father from his pastoral duties to accompany the Jordans. I haven't gone prowling through the records of the archdiocese to find out what was promised in whispers to whom, and I won't, because even if they decided to let me look in those records, if they had a lick of shrewdness, and I hope they did, the Church functionaries would have had the sense to destroy each and every document related to Father Pielke's trip to Germany in June and July of 1938, a subject of no great pride to anyone now:. . . (Baxter: "Believers," p. 222)

12. Identify the violations of formal standard English in the following letter:

Dear Chris:

Yesterday I run into our tour guide from Paris. What a surprise! He was having trouble ordering a meal in a restaurant. He speaks fluent, but his pronounciation is awful. Just between you and I, I don't think he learned his verbs real good either. Neither the server nor the chef were able to understand him. I felt badly for him, because the choice of menu items were extensive, but he couldn't order nothing! I helped him, and I think that next time he will make less mistakes. What are friends for?

Hope to see you soon,
Pat

NINE

CLAUSE TYPE: DISCOURSE FUNCTION

WHAT IS DISCOURSE FUNCTION?

There are many reasons for communicating, and English helps us to signal those reasons by providing us with a range of clause types. As we saw in the last chapter, we can alter the voice of a clause to signal the relative prominence among the noun phrases. Beyond that, we have different clause types that tell our listeners the purpose we have in addressing them. Those different purposes are called **discourse functions.** One main discourse function is to give information to our listeners (readers). To communicate this purpose, we use a **declarative** clause, as illustrated in (1).

> (1) The cat ate the dog's food.
> Mushrooms grow in damp soil.
> The house needs a new roof.

Another function of communicating is to get information from our listeners; for this function we typically use an **interrogative** clause, as illustrated in (2).

> (2) Did you cancel your subscription?
> Why doesn't she return my calls?
> Does the gym have a running track?

A third reason we use language is to get people to behave in certain ways, for which we use commands. The grammatical structure associated with this discourse function is the **imperative,** illustrated in (3).

> (3) Be kind to your sister.
> Give me your phone number.
> Don't guess on the exam.

A fourth discourse function is the **exclamative,** used to express a judgment or a feeling with added emphasis, as in the clauses in (4).

(4) What a nice person you are!
How considerate he was!
How she works!

As you can see, English uses a variety of means to signal these different discourse functions. We might rearrange the order of elements, add a special word, change the form of a word, or leave something out. In writing, we may alter the punctuation, and in speaking we may alter the intonation. The rest of this chapter will explore the particular means we use to signal each of these discourse functions.

DECLARATIVES

The *declarative*, the clause type designed to give information, is the most basic clause type. It is the one most often used in expository writing and probably in ordinary communication as well. Typically, the order of the elements in declarative clauses is subject + verb + object (when there is an object), which is why English is sometimes referred to as an SVO language. Most of our examples up to this point have been declarative. There is no special marking to indicate that a clause is declarative, except for the period that we put at the end of a declarative sentence in writing. In speaking, the intonation, or pitch, falls at the end.

DISCUSSION EXERCISES 9.1

1. Which of the following are declaratives?

    Don't be a fool.
    Why didn't you stop them?
    ✓ I have no time to talk right now.
    Save me a seat.
    He decided to run for office.
    The organization is poorly run.
    Did you see them arrive?
    How calmly she received the news.
    What an interesting person he is.
    The golf course was flooded for days.

2. Can you change the discourse function of the following declarative clauses by changing the order of elements?

    You are ready to leave.
    He has seen the light.
    They didn't like the speech.

(continued)

3. Now change the discourse function of the declarative clauses in 2, by changing the intonation.

4. Declaratives can be in the active or the passive voice. Turn each of these active declaratives into their passive equivalents.

A semi hit the bicycle.
The instructor dismissed the class.
Everyone loves mimes.
Her sister has seen her.
The new tenants repaired the sidewalk.

INTERROGATIVES

Yes-No Questions

There is much to say about *interrogatives,* those clauses that are designed to get information. There are several different types of interrogatives, because the type of interrogative we use depends on how much we already know and what kind of information we are trying to obtain. For example, suppose I have reason to think that Mary left town this morning, but I need to get verification from someone who knows. I might ask the question in (5).

(5) Did Mary leave town this morning?

In this case, my question has supplied all the relevant information about the event. All I'm asking of my listener is to tell me whether it is true or false. In other words, my listener can satisfy my curiosity merely by saying *yes* or *no.* For this reason this type of interrogative is called a **yes-no question.**

Yes-no questions are very complicated structures in English, much more so than in many other languages. Let's see what we do to change a declarative clause into its corresponding yes-no question. Consider the following declarative statements and think about how you would turn them into yes-no questions if you needed to find out if they were true or not.

(6) She can do it tomorrow.
I must leave early.
Those girls were laughing at him.
Your computer is making a funny noise.
Dana might leave before dinner.
The children have eaten already.
He had considered the consequences.
Classes will be over on Friday.
You will meet him today.
He would do it for me.

You undoubtedly noticed several things that you must change to create a yes-no question: the intonation, the punctuation, and the order of elements. The falling intonation of the declarative must change to a rising intonation for the question. In writing we replace the period with a question mark. What about the ordering change? So far it looks like the subject noun phrase and the verb change places. That's not very complicated, you must be thinking. The following set of exercises will demonstrate to you that there is more to this question-type than first meets the eye.

DISCUSSION EXERCISES 9.2

1. Write out the yes-no question that corresponds to each of the following declarative clauses.

   The show starts in five minutes.
   Her father taught her to fish.
   You like to eat strawberries.
   They seemed very nervous.
   The fork goes on the left.

2. How do these differ from the ones you formed from the statements in (6)?

3. What determines whether we simply reverse the subject and the verb or add the verb *do*?

You were able to figure out from these exercises that English yes-no questions are sensitive to whether the statement on which they are based has a helping verb or not. We can give the following as a rule for making yes-no questions.

If there is a helping verb, reverse the order of the helping verb and the subject noun phrase.

If there is no helping verb, add the auxiliary verb *do* to serve as the helping verb.

How do we know what form of *do* to add? You will notice in the following that the form of *do* varies from question to question.

(7) They left: *Did* they leave?
    Water takes a long time to boil: *Does* water take a long time to boil?
    Those people own that store: *Do* those people own that store?

The appropriate form of *do* has the same tense and number as the main verb in the declarative. Then what happens to the main verb in the yes-no question? As you can see, it seems to lose its tense and number and reverts to its base form. So we can think of the main verb as giving over its tense and number to the auxiliary verb *do*.

DISCUSSION EXERCISES 9.3

1. Revise the rules given for forming yes-no questions to make them more complete.
2. Make yes-no questions from the following:

   He has been making a mess.
   She could have been telling the truth.
   They will be taking the first train tonight.

   Which helping verb changes place with the subject if the clause has more than one helping verb?

3. Consider the following yes-no questions.

   Are you happy?
   Is Chicago in Illinois?
   Am I friendly?

   What kind of verb is *be* in these sentences, helping or main? How do we have to revise our definition of helping verb for the purpose of making yes-no questions?

4. Yes-no questions can be in the active or the passive voice. What is the passive equivalent of each of the following yes-no questions?

   Did the wind destroy the barn?
   Do the students respect the teacher?
   Does that university reject too many students? *is the teacher respected by the student?*

   Why doesn't the verb *do* appear in the passive form of the question?

Wh-Questions

There is a different kind of question we ask when we are missing a piece of information. In each of the following, for example, we are seeking some specific item of information that we need to complete the thought.

(8) Who is going?
    Whom did you call?
    What does he want?
    Whose did he borrow?
    Which do you like?

You will recognize the first words of each as the interrogative pronouns we discussed in Chapter 5. We also mentioned in that chapter that there are other interrogative words that elicit bits of information: *where, when, how,* and *why.* Collectively these question words are known as *wh-words* and the type of question they form is called a **wh-question.** Answers to *wh-questions,* of course, cannot be *yes* or *no.* Rather, the listener is required to supply the missing piece of information as indicated by the interrogative word you have chosen. That missing information might be a noun phrase, in which case you will use *who, whom,* or *whose* if it is human, *what* if it is nonhuman, and *which* if a choice is implied.

DISCUSSION EXERCISES 9.4

1. What determines whether we use *who, whom,* or *whose* if the missing information is a human noun phrase?
2. What type of information is sought by *where, when, why,* and *how?* Give an example of each.
3. Some of the interrogative words can also be used as interrogative determiners to ask a wh-question. Which ones can do this? Give examples.

Wh-questions are even more complicated to form than yes-no questions. We have already seen that they require the addition of a special interrogative word designed to elicit a particular kind of information. So, one part of the job of asking a wh-question is figuring out which wh-word to use. Another part of the job is deciding where to put it in the question. If you look at the examples in (8) or consider the examples you made up for the previous exercises, you will see a consistent pattern: the wh-word always appears at the beginning of the clause. So far that seems easy enough, but then we notice that sometimes the rest of the clause gets rearranged when we put an interrogative word in front. Compare the examples in (9) with those in (10).

(9) Who is blaming us?
    What is making that terrible noise?

(10) Where may I sit?
     How can we help you?
     Why would they remember that?

In (9), the clause retains its SVO order, but in (10), the subject and verb trade places. The difference between (9) and (10) is that in (9) the missing information is the subject; in (10) it is something other than the subject. So we can give the following two rules for forming wh-questions:

If you are questioning the subject noun phrase, simply insert an interrogative word in the subject position.

If you are questioning something other than the subject, place the interrogative
word at the beginning of the clause, then reverse the order of the subject and
the verb in the clause.

DISCUSSION EXERCISES 9.5

1. What is the wh-question you would ask to complete each of the following
   thoughts?

   (someone?) is knocking at the door
   They are going (sometime?)
   You are saying that (for a reason?)
   Shelly can park her car (somewhere?)
   Paul must respond (somehow?)

2. Which of the above require the subject and verb to switch places? Why?

3. Suppose you wanted to elicit the following information:

   You have been talking to (someone?)   *With what was he cutting it?*
   He was cutting it with (something?)   *What was he cutting it with?*
   They were waiting for (someone?)

   How would you form the questions? Do you have some choice? (You might
   want to consult Chapter 7.) How is the second rule that we gave affected by
   these examples?

The observant reader will realize that we are not finished yet. Notice that
the previous examples were carefully chosen to avoid an additional problem
that becomes evident in the questions in (11).

(11) They wanted (something?):   What did they want?
     The train leaves (sometime?):   When does the train leave?
     You do that (somehow?):   How do you do that?
     She found the answer (somewhere?): Where did she find the answer?

What you see should be familiar by now. The earlier questions all had helping
verbs, and so the order of the subject and helping verb was reversed. But what
if the statement on which the question is based has no helping verb? Then we
must insert a form of *do* as the helping verb, transfer all the grammatical information from the main verb to *do* and leave the main verb in its base form.
In other words, if we are questioning something other than the subject, we
move the interrogative word to the front of the clause and treat the rest of the
clause like a yes-no question.

DISCUSSION EXERCISES 9.6

1. Make a wh-question out of each of the following. Which require the insertion of the auxiliary verb *do.* Why?

   You have been (somewhere?)
   They traveled to Europe (sometime?)
   Stu is stalling (for a reason?)
   (Someone?) likes to sit in front
   Rebecca managed to do it (somehow?)
   (Someone?) has been using my razor *who has been using my razor?*
   The company hired (someone?)
   This is (someone's?) raincoat
   Art turned his back (for a reason?)
   The watchman heard (someone?)

2. Complete the following rules for forming wh-questions in English.
   1. Decide which wh-word to use:
      a. use *who* when the missing information is ___*subject*___.
      b. use *whom* ___*To Whom are you speaking?*___.
      c. use *whose* ___*Whose pencil is that?*___.
      d. use *which* – *choice* ___.
      e. use *what* – *Non human* ___.
      f. use *where* – *location* ___.
      g. use *how* – *manner* ___.
      h. use *when* – *time* ___.
      i. use *why* – *reason* ___.
   2. If the wh-word is a subject, place it *begin* ___.
   3. If the wh-word is not a subject, place it ___.
   4. If the wh-word is preceded by a preposition ___.
   5. If a nonsubject interrogative word is moved to the front, and the rest of the clause contains a helping verb,

   _____.

   6. If a nonsubject interrogative word is moved to the front and the rest of the clause does not contain a helping verb,

   _____.

   7. When *do* is added as an auxiliary verb, it derives its tense and number from _____.
   8. When *do* is added as an auxiliary verb, the main verb becomes

   _____.

(continued)

3. Give a wh- question to illustrate each rule you complete in 2.

4. One other difference between oral yes-no and wh-questions is in the into-nation. We said earlier that our pitch rises at the end of a yes-no question. What happens to our pitch in a wh-question?

5. It is possible to have more than one wh-word in a question. Suppose you knew the following: *(Someone?) did (something?) to (someone?)* What question would you ask to fill in the missing information?

6. Wh-questions can be in the active or the passive voice. Give the passive equivalents of the following wh-questions:

What did the fight accomplish?
When did the storm knock down the power lines?
How did the manager calm the angry crowd?
Which did you discover?
Who brought the chips?

The last has several different passive versions. Why?

Tag Questions

You will probably agree by now that interrogative-formation in English requires significant mental work, although as adult native speakers of English we do it without conscious effort. But you will notice that people learning English as a second language will have trouble mastering the fine points of questions, as do children who are learning English as their first language. It will be easier to grasp the other types of questions we are about to discuss if you remember some basic principles of question-formation in English: it is often sensitive to the difference between helping verbs and main verbs, it often involves some shift of word-order, and it typically makes use of some alteration of pitch (or intonation). In writing, the question mark signals an interrogative, but this does not necessarily reflect differences in pitch. For many questions we also add a word that specifically marks the clause as an interrogative. We have seen that all these features come into play in the formation of yes-no and wh-questions. We see them again in other types of questions.

Another type of question, closely related to the yes-no question both in form and purpose, is illustrated in (12).

(12) That woman is your cousin, <u>isn't she?</u>
      Monkeys can't speak, <u>can they?</u>
      The boys haven't returned yet, <u>have they?</u>
      You are listening, <u>aren't you?</u>

The underlined portion of each example is known as a **tag question.** One purpose of a *tag question* is the same as that of a yes-no question: to find out if a statement is true or false. Tag questions can have other conversational pur- poses as well: to get reassurance, to keep a conversation going, to get someone to admit to something that you believe is true, among others.

DISCUSSION EXERCISES 9.7

1. Finish off each of the following statements with its appropriate tag question.

    It's a nice day.
    You don't love me anymore.
    He's pretty smart.
    They've left already.
    Nancy shouldn't smoke.

2. What is the most likely conversational purpose of each of these tag questions?

We can see similarities in the formation of yes-no and tag questions if we compare those in (12) with the following:

(13) Jan wrote you a letter, didn't she?
     Your children play the piano, don't they?
     That nurse doesn't have any experience, does she?
     The equipment didn't function right, did it?

Both question types are sensitive to the difference between statements with helping verbs and those without. Both require the insertion of the auxiliary *do* as the helping verb when there is no other. Both have the grammatical information from the main verb transferred onto *do,* and both require reverse order of the subject and the helping verb. There are two additional requirements for the tag question:

The subject is a personal pronoun that agrees with the subject of the statement in person, number, and gender.
The tag question reverses the negativity of the statement: affirmative to negative and negative to affirmative.

DISCUSSION EXERCISES 9.8

1. Give the appropriate tag question for each of the following:

    Christmas falls on Monday this year.
    Having money isn't important.
    The movie starts in an hour.
    The meal isn't ready yet.
    You bought a new car.
    Pete didn't see the train.
    Bobbi practices law.

(continued)

Computers save us a lot of time.

This car can't run on diesel fuel.

Those pretzels are making him thirsty.

2. There is another kind of tag question that does not reverse the negativity of affirmative statements.

You're insulted, are you?

She left early again, did she?

What is the conversational effect of these tag questions?

3. Complete the following incomplete steps for forming a tag question. The completed list should enable someone who has not fully mastered English to predict which tag follows which statement.

   1. For the subject of the tag choose a personal pronoun that matches ____*in number and gender*____.
   2. If the statement has a helping verb, ____*Use helping verb in Tag*____.
   3. If the statement has no helping verb, _____.

   4. If the statement is affirmative, _____.

   5. If the statement is negative, _____.

   6. The order of elements in the tag is as follows: _____.

4. Not everyone agrees on the appropriate tag questions after statements like the following:

There is hardly any sugar left.

He seldom visits us.

You rarely get to see her.

Why do you think we have trouble agreeing on the form of these tag questions? Would studying the rules help us?

5. Why do you think some grammatical purists object to the tag question *aren't I?* as in *I'm included, aren't I?* In what way does it violate the rule for making tag questions? What are our choices if we don't choose *aren't I?*

6. The following do not conform exactly to the rules that we have developed for tag questions. In what way does each stray from those rules? Why do you think this happens?

Everyone is coming, aren't they?

Someone let the cat out, didn't they?

(continued)

> The baby is cute, isn't it?
> There are some left, aren't there?

7. What is the tag question associated with each of the following passive statements?

> Selma was arrested by the police.
> Selma got arrested by the police.

How are *be* and *get* different with respect to tag questions?

Minor Question Types

There are several other question types that have more limited use than the three we have discussed. One is used in response to a statement and basically echoes the structure of the statement, as in (14).

(14) I closed down my bank account.
      You closed down your bank account?

      Mary ran off to Australia.
      Mary ran off to Australia?

For this reason, they are called **echo questions.** (Some grammarians call them **declarative questions.**) The intonation and punctuation is that of a yes-no question, but the structure remains that of a declarative statement. Questions like this often signal surprise or disbelief rather than a true interest in getting information. It is also possible to form an echo question in response to a wh-question, as illustrated in (15).

(15) I faxed the letter to the president of the company.
      You faxed the letter to whom?

      We're going to live in Texas.
      You're going to live where?

Again you see that the basic structure of the declarative remains intact, and we use a wh-word to register what it is that surprises us. The questions in (14) are called **yes-no echo questions**; those in (15) are **wh-echo questions**.

DISCUSSION EXERCISES 9.9

1. Form an echo question as a response to the following statements. You will have a range of options because it is possible to register disbelief about the whole statement (yes-no echo) or about individual parts of it (wh-echo).

   I'm moving to Canada with my accountant.
   She bought a Jaguar to keep in her living room. *(continued)*

2. It is also possible to register disbelief or surprise about several different parts of a statement at once. Try it with the following statement:

Sandi is going to the opera with Placido Domingo.

3. The question *Who is going?* could be a simple wh-question or a wh-echo question. How do we signal which meaning is intended when we say it?

Another minor question type is not recognized as a question by everyone. It is embedded inside a sentence and is used when we have questions like the following in mind:

(16) I wonder (did she go?)
She doesn't know (did she pass the exam?)
They asked (could they ride with us?)

I wonder (what did she say?)
She doesn't know (how did she do that?)
They asked (where were we staying?)

Although some dialects of English express these questions just as they appear in (16), formal standard English requires that they retain their declarative structure, inserting *if* or *whether* before a yes-no question and a wh-word before a wh-question. These structures , as they appear underlined in (17), are called **embedded questions.**

(17) I wonder <u>if she went.</u>
She doesn't know <u>whether she passed the exam.</u>
They asked <u>if they could ride with us.</u>

I wonder <u>what she said.</u>
She doesn't know <u>how she did that.</u>
They asked <u>where we were staying.</u>

DISCUSSION EXERCISES 9.10

1. Embed each of the following questions into a larger sentence, changing the form as required by standard English.

Why did they change the date? *I wonder why they change d the date*
Are they still friends? *I wonder if they're still friends*
When will this job be finished?
Am I still in the running?
Did the class meet yesterday?

(continued)

2. Name the question type in each of the following:

Who is calling my name?
You're always right, aren't you?
Are you having a good time? *Yes/no*
She wonders if the paint will cover the stains. *embedded*
He hasn't studied for the exam? *echo question*
You told her what? *Wh-echo*

IMPERATIVES

Imperatives are those clause types designed to get people to behave in certain ways. They don't necessarily require a verbal response, but we hope for some action or some change in mental state when we utter them. Because they are designed to give orders directly to the person we are addressing, the grammatical subject is always *you* (singular or plural), but the most noticeable characteristic of imperative clauses is that they do not require the grammatical subject to be expressed at all, giving us the notorious "understood *you*." The following pairs are equivalent in intent, although they may differ slightly in force or emphasis.

(18) You leave this instant!
      Leave this instant!

      You bring me a cup of coffee!
      Bring me a cup of coffee!

As indicated by the examples, written English often punctuates imperatives with exclamation points.

DISCUSSION EXERCISES 9.11

1. Create an imperative clause with each of the following verbs: *read, stay, speak, jump.*
2. Which of the Discussion Exercises in this chapter use the imperative to get you to do something?
3. The verb in the imperative looks as if it could be the present tense or the base form, since they are often identical. But consider the verb *to be* in its imperative form. Does that help you decide which it is?
4. Imperatives with the *you* subject expressed could also be analyzed as declarative statements. Give the two possible interpretations of *You plan to be out of here by tonight.*
5. Imperatives do not readily combine with the passive voice, although it is possible. Can you think of an example? (Don't be fooled by the question!)

EXCLAMATIVES

Exclamatives are a minor clause type that, as we said earlier, allow us to express a judgment or feeling with added emphasis. You'll notice that they use some of the same signals as interrogatives: the addition of *how* or *what,* and re-arrangement of word order. In writing, they are often punctuated with an exclamation point. Below are some additional examples of exclamatives.

(19) What a fine job you've done.
     What an intricate pattern she's woven.
     What a silly idea that is.

(20) How ordinary he seems.
     How selfish you've become.
     How petty they are.

(21) How carefully they've scrutinized the report.
     How intensely they love each other.
     How neatly you write.

(22) How she trembles at the sight of him.
     How they studied before that exam.
     How they laughed that night.

What are the things we can exclaim about, grammatically speaking? In (19) it is a noun phrase, in (20) an adjective, in (21) an adverb, and in (22) a verb. For noun phrases, we ordinarily use *what* and for all the others we use *how.*

DISCUSSION EXERCISES 9.12

1. You'll notice that in three of the four previous sets of examples, we bring forward the thing we are exclaiming about. In which set does the word order remain the same as for declaratives?

2. Turn each of these into an exclamative to emphasize the underlined element.

   They dance <u>well</u> together.
   The sky looked <u>beautiful</u> that night.
   This is <u>a disorganized mess.</u>
   I <u>envy</u> you.
   He is <u>a fine physician.</u>

3. We are restricted in the kind of noun phrase we can exclaim about in this fashion. What is the only determiner that may appear?

(continued)

4. How do we exclaim about noun phrases with quantities as determiners, such as the following? How do these examples complicate our description of exclamatives?

   She made <u>many</u> mistakes. *How many mistakes she's made*
   We have <u>little</u> time.
   They have lost <u>much</u> money.

5. Some people think exclamatives sound old-fashioned. Others think they mark speech specifically addressed to children. What is your own opinion about the use of exclamatives?

CROSSOVER FUNCTIONS OF CLAUSE TYPES

We have seen throughout this chapter that there are certain clause types designed for certain discourse functions. When we choose one of these with its characteristic markings, we signal to our listener what our purpose is in communicating at that moment. But, as we have seen before, categories in English tend to be slippery and there is a tendency for elements of one category to shift into another. Such is the case for clause types. We find in normal everyday communication that clause types designed for one purpose can sometimes fulfill another. For example, consider the clauses in (23).

(23) What do you think you're doing?
     Do you think I'm stupid?
     Where are your brains?

As we can see, these all have the form of an interrogative, and they may be interpreted literally: *I think I'm teaching grammar; Yes, I think you're stupid; My brains are in a jar on my desk* (said by one anatomy student to another). But, as speakers of English, we know that these can also have the force of a declarative statement that means something different from the literal meaning: *You're doing something wrong; You're insulting my intelligence; You've done something stupid.* As declaratives, they do not require answers, and attempts to answer the literal question may be seen as inappropriate. Questions such as these are often called *rhetorical questions*.

Can we ever do the reverse, use a declarative statement to get information? Consider the following:

(24) I have to know your name.
     I need to know the capital of France.

Although these are literally declarative statements reporting on a need of the speaker, it would not be conversationally inappropriate to interpret them as requests for information and provide the answers: *It's Fran; It's Paris.*

The most interesting of the crossover functions of clauses involves the imperative. Although there is a specific clause type designated for giving commands, use of that clause type is often viewed as too blunt or too aggressive. Direct imperatives work well under urgent circumstances.

(25) Watch out!
     Duck!
     Follow that car!

But under normal, non-urgent circumstances we look for ways to soften the effect of the imperative. We may simply add the word *please,* but that is not the only strategy we employ. Often what we do instead is use another clause type. For example, we might use a declarative statement expressing our own needs, rather than issue a direct command.

(26) I wish you would stop talking.
     I need you to read those files by tomorrow.
     I expect you to be on time.
     I'd like you to call your grandmother.

Or we might use the interrogative with a modal verb.

(27) Can you help me?
     Would you close the door?
     Could you wait here a moment?
     Will you give me a pencil?
     Must you talk so loud?

Or we might use a declarative with a modal verb.

(28) You might want to check your oil more often.
     You could be a little nicer.
     You will arrive on time from now on.

All of these, of course, have literal interpretations, but they are not the ones that first come to mind. The softened imperative is the more natural interpretation: an action is a more appropriate response than the receiving or giving of information.

DISCUSSION EXERCISES 9.13

1. Give a literal answer to each of the following. Under what circumstances might they be considered rhetorical?

   Do you have two hands?
   Am I your maid?

(continued)

Can't you see that I'm busy?

Where is your sense of decency?

Why don't you stop talking?

2. Give a softened version of each of the following imperatives. Under what circumstances might the direct imperative be used?

Lend me fifty dollars.

Shut the window.

Write me a letter of recommendation.

Hand over that gun.

Don't vote for that amendment.

3. Can you find Discussion Exercises in this chapter that tell you to do things by means other than the direct imperative? Is this one of them?

Clause type, as we have seen in the last two chapters, is determined by voice—active versus passive—and by discourse function. There is another factor that determines clause type: affirmative versus negative. This will be the focus of the next chapter.

REFLECTIONS

1. There are two ways of asking someone for the time.

Do you have the time?

Have you the time?

What does it tell you about how the verb *have* is treated in yes-no questions? Does one sound more natural to you than the other?

2. You might hear a child say *Did he be happy?* What part of the rules for yes-no questions has she not yet figured out?

3. You might hear a child say wh-questions like *What daddy can do?* or *Where mommy put the ball?* Which part of wh-question formation has he not mastered yet? If you have regular access to a child learning English, a good project would be to record the child's questions over a period of a few days and then analyze them to see which rules have been mastered and which haven't.

4. Consider these questions, which appear in Shakespeare's *Julius Caesar.*

What mean'st thou by that?

What means this shouting?

Why stare you so?

Think you to walk forth?

Comes his army on?

In what respect has question formation changed since Shakespeare's time?

5. There are two possible tag questions for this statement: *He has a lot of money.* What are the two? What does it tell you about the classification of the verb *have* for the purposes of tag question formation?

6. One of the amazing facts about tag questions is that all children learning English go through the trouble to learn the rules for making them even though we have one word that can substitute for all of them, similar to the French *n'est-ce pas?* What is that word?

7. Are sentences containing embedded questions punctuated with a question mark or a period? If you don't know the answer, consult a style handbook.

8. There are two other structures that are also considered to be imperatives of sorts.

Somebody get the phone.

Let each man fend for himself.

Let's go to the movies.

In what ways are these different from the imperatives we have discussed? Why do you think they are called imperatives?

9. The verb *look* often precedes the exclamative without changing the intent of the utterance: *Look what a nice job you've done!* Can you think of another verb that acts like *look* in this respect?

10. It is interesting to think about how we learn that some statements are not to be taken literally, especially softened imperatives. If you have the opportunity, you might want to observe how adults give orders to children. (Is there an imperative in this paragraph?)

11. If you have the opportunity, learn how to make yes-no questions in another language. Are they grammatically more or less complicated than in English? Explain.

12. Each discourse function described in this chapter has a specific clause type associated with it. There are many other minor discourse functions that are signaled by the use of a verb that explicitly tells the function of the utterance. Some examples are *I promise not to talk* and *I warn you not to lie.* You'll notice that the first statement functions as a promise, and the second functions as a warning. What other discourse functions are signaled in this way? (Hint: some of the more formal ones are often preceded by the word *hereby.*

PRACTICE EXERCISES FOR CHAPTER 9 (Answers on p. 232)

1. Name the clause type in each of the following: *declarative, interrogative, imperative,* or *exclamative.* Provide the appropriate punctuation at the end.
   1. What an interesting course this is
   2. How can I help you
   3. Leave me alone
   4. She's thinking of buying a hamster
   5. Let's settle our differences
   6. How easily you judge others
   7. Does rice have a lot of calories
   8. When did the race begin
   9. That teacher taught me how to think
   10. Everyone remain calm

2. Make a yes-no question corresponding to each of the following declarative statements.
   1. We need to rotate the tires.
   2. Help is on the way.
   3. You can give me an estimate on the costs.
   4. He did the assignment before class.
   5. The laborers rested after lunch.
   6. Word-processing saves us a lot of time.
   7. We must observe the rules.
   8. They are aware of the danger.
   9. I spelled the word wrong.
   10. This dog won't fetch.

3. Formulate the standard English wh-question that will elicit the missing information in each of the following.
   1. You borrowed (someone's?) book
   2. (Someone?) needs a ride
   3. They can do (something?) for me
   4. I can find good corned beef (somewhere?)
   5. She was asking for (someone?)
   6. (Something?) fell on my head
   7. She ordered (one of several?)
   8. He remained silent (for a reason?)
   9. You wish to speak with (someone?)
   10. The scandal destroyed (someone?)

(continued)

4. Which of the previous questions required the insertion of the auxiliary verb *do?* Why didn't the others require *do*-insertion?

5. Form the appropriate tag question for each statement.
    1. The tornado hit the center of town.
    2. Bees communicate by dancing.
    3. We can't respond to that inquiry.
    4. Medical school is difficult.
    5. The children had a good time.
    6. You went sailing yesterday.
    7. The plants have all died.
    8. I have ink on my face.
    9. Stanley has lost the tickets.
    10. Barbara looks good.

6. Which tag questions in the preceding exercise required the insertion of the auxiliary *do?* Why?

7. What makes it awkward to follow the rules for tag-formation for each of the following statements?
    1. She can barely read it.
    2. No one likes housework.
    3. Someone called here yesterday.
    4. That baby is smart.
    5. They hardly ever get to see each other.

8. Name the question-type in each of the following:
    1. You haven't done it yet?
    2. I wonder if I need a raincoat.
    3. What's for dinner?
    4. You're upset, aren't you?
    5. To whom shall I direct your call?
    6. We're having dinner with whom?
    7. Can you spare a dime?
    8. Kenny didn't show up, did he?
    9. Tell me what you saw.
    10. Why can't we stay?

9. Turn each of these into an exclamative clause that emphasizes the under-lined element.
    1. Al is <u>a wonderful parent.</u>
    2. That building is <u>ugly.</u>
    3. My heart <u>aches</u> for you.
    4. They have <u>a cute baby.</u>

(continued)

5. She complained <u>bitterly.</u>
6. This is <u>awful</u> for you.
7. He <u>boasts</u> about his children.
8. Senta performed <u>well</u> in the recital.
9. Kara and Jan were <u>proud</u> of her.
10. Kara and Jan were <u>proud of her.</u>
11. This is <u>a tiresome discussion.</u>

10. Give two softened versions of each of the following imperatives, one using a declarative and one using an interrogative.
    1. Take the dog for a walk.
    2. Pick up some milk on your way home.
    3. Talk to me about your concerns.
    4. Help me with these groceries.
    5. Clean up this mess.
    6. Look for a job.
    7. Rethink your demands.
    8. Host a reception for them.
    9. Consider your alternatives.
    10. Get there on time.

11. Find an example of each of the following in the *Believers* selection that follows.
    a full passive
    a truncated passive
    a compound past participle
    a wh-question
    a yes-no question
    a rhetorical question
    an adverb of manner
    a transitive verb
    an intransitive verb
    a compound infinitive
    a reflexive pronoun
    a present perfect tense

The storm, empty of content, tucks itself toward the east and is being replaced even now by one of those insincere Midwestern blue skies.

Mary Esther begins to cry and wail as Patsy jogs toward Saul. Gordy Himmelman follows along behind her.

When she is within a hundred feet of Saul's beehives, she sees that the frames have been knocked over, scattered, and kicked. Saul lies, face down, where they once stood. He is touching his tongue to the earth

(continued)

momentarily, where the honey is, for a brief taste. When he rises, he sees Patsy. "All the bees swarmed," he says. "They've left. They're gone."

She holds Mary Esther tightly and examines Saul's face. "How come they didn't attack him? Did they sting him?"

"Who knows?" Saul spreads his arms. "They just didn't."

(Baxter: "Saul and Patsy Are in Labor," p. 118)

12. Identify the violations of formal standard English in the following letter:

Dear Chris,

I wonder did you get my last letter? My mother, she said to tell you that we was thinking about another vacation. Her and I been looking at brochures, and we found the most perfect place! I know you like the cold less than me, but don't Alaska sound exciting? There's glaciers and icebergs and beautiful mountains everywhere. I'm getting too anxious, aren't I? I'm suppose to ask you will you consider it.

Love,
Pat

TEN

CLAUSE TYPE: AFFIRMATIVE VERSUS NEGATIVE

WHAT IS NEGATIVITY IN GRAMMAR?

In addition to having voice and discourse function, clauses in English are generally marked as being either **affirmative** or **negative.** The *affirmative,* or positive, clause has no special marking for this feature, but the *negative*—that which negates or expresses a "no" answer—is marked in a variety of ways. Being able to say *no* is a very important feature of communication, so language provides us with many different ways to get this meaning across. As you can imagine, it would be highly inconvenient for us if the grammatical markings for negation were so inconspicuous that people would be inclined to miss them in our conversation. English grammar allows us to make it clear that we *don't* want to buy swampland or cemetery plots, even if there is static on the telephone; that the new VCR we are returning *doesn't* record accurately; that we *can't* serve on still another committee; and that the report *won't* be ready until tomorrow. No one likes to sound negative, but being able to express negativity is essential to our well-being.

VERB NEGATION

Negation in English is expressed by attaching it to different lexical categories. One of these categories is the verb. You can see how this works in the clauses in (1):

(1) You may not leave yet.
    The letter has not arrived.
    The secretary could not reach the client.
    A child cannot sit still for that long.
    The door must not be opened.
    I shall not be here tomorrow.
    Nancy is not coming to the party.
    They should not allow that to happen.
    The class will not meet tomorrow.
    The train might not be on time.

So far, there appears to be a very simple procedure for **verb negation:** add the word *not* after the verb.

DISCUSSION EXERCISES 10.1

1. As speakers of English, you know that in less formal usage a contraction of the verb and *not* can occur. Which of the sentences in (1) have corresponding contractions? Which contractions are irregular?

2. Express the following with a contraction:

   I am not allowed to smoke.

   How is this different from the contractions you made for the previous question?

3. The notoriously nonstandard *ain't* is a contraction of a verb and *not*. What, specifically, is it a contraction of in each of the following?

   I ain't going.
   She ain't happy.
   They ain't laughing.
   We ain't seen it.
   He ain't left yet.

4. Why can't the following affirmative statements be made negative by the simple insertion of *not* after the verb?

   The ship sails at noon.
   My parents speak Spanish.
   The dog ate its food.

If you were able to answer Discussion Exercise question 4, then you know that verb negation is sensitive to the difference between helping and main verbs, a distinction you are familiar with by now. Just as is the case for many interrogatives, verb negation requires the insertion of the auxiliary verb *do* if a main verb is negated and no helping verb is present. (The verb *be* is treated as helping regardless of whether it is actually main or helping.) If we negate the verbs in question 4, the results are as follows:

(2) The ship does not sail at noon.
    My parents do not speak Spanish.
    The dog did not eat its food.

We may also use the contractions *doesn't, don't,* and *didn't,* respectively. The form of *do* is dependent on the tense and number of the verb in the affirmative, and once the affirmative verb hands over its information to *do,* it reverts to its base form. This probably sounds more orderly than it did when we first came across this arrangement for interrogatives. Although there is a complicated set of adjustments involved in making verbs negative, the process is essentially the same as that used to turn declaratives into interrogatives.

DISCUSSION EXERCISES 10.2

1. Make the following clauses negative by negating the verb:

   I might see that film.
   The answers are in the book.
   The club has met recently.
   They are enjoying the course.
   My boss will let me have Saturday off.
   Jane sees the robin.
   Steve cooked dinner last night.
   She withdrew her funds in time.
   The rebels won the battle.
   Aerobics makes her energetic.

2. Complete the following rules for negating clauses by negating the verb:
   1. If there is a helping verb _____.
   2. If there is no helping verb, insert _____.
   3. *Do* derives its tense and number from _____.
   4. The main verb becomes _____.
   5. Insert *not* after _____.

NEGATION OF INDEFINITES

Another important way we have of expressing negation is to use the negative form of an indefinite word that begins with *some-*. We call this **indefinite negation.** The affirmative statements in (3) can be made negative by using the corresponding negative form of the indefinite, as illustrated.

(3) I need <u>something</u>.　　　　I need <u>nothing</u>.
　　 She went <u>somewhere</u>.　　　She went <u>nowhere</u>.
　　 <u>Somebody</u> called.　　　　　<u>Nobody</u> called.
　　 He saw <u>someone</u>.　　　　　He saw <u>no one</u>.

In many instances, you can get the same meaning across by negating the verb, but if you negate the verb, standard English requires that the indefinite word begin with *any-*. (But see Reflection 7.)

(4) I do not need <u>anything</u>.
     She did not go <u>anywhere</u>.
     He did not see <u>anyone</u>.

DISCUSSION EXERCISES 10.3

1. Make the following clauses negative by using negative indefinites.

   I have somewhere to go.
   She said something to someone.
   Somebody showed up.
   He loves someone.
   Something made me nervous.

2. Make the same clauses negative by negating the verb and using an *any-* indefinite. Which of the above cannot be made negative in this way?

3. Here is another grammatical connection between interrogatives and negatives. Negate the following by negating the verb. Then turn those same sentences into yes-no questions. What are the similarities in the two processes?

   He saw something.
   This is leading somewhere.

4. The adverbs *ever* and *never* behave similarly to indefinites, but they are placed differently in sentences. How is their placement different from other indefinites?

5. Clauses can be interrogative and negative at the same time. What is the negative interrogative that corresponds to each of the following?

   Ben saw someone.
   Natalia suspected something.

6. Clauses can be interrogative, negative, and passive at the same time. Can you turn your answers in question 5 into the passive voice?

A restriction on standard English negation in modern times is that we may not have two negatives in one clause, the so-called *double negation*. As we discussed in Chapter 1, this is part of the legacy from the eighteenth-century grammarians, who reasoned that two negatives would cancel each other out and become an affirmative. Since the eighteenth century, clauses like the following have been considered nonstandard:

(5) He didn't see nothing.
     I'm not going nowhere.
     They don't need nothing.

Utterances such as those in (5) are common in many dialects of English and are understood by everyone to be negatives, not affirmatives. They normally do not mean he sees something, or I'm going somewhere, or they need something. In ordinary language use, negatives reinforce one another rather than cancel one another out, regardless of the rule that says otherwise.

DISCUSSION EXERCISES 10.4

1. Many people still want to argue that two negatives make a positive in English. How could you demonstrate to them that this isn't the case in ordinary usage?

2. There is one interpretation of the sentences of (5) that is affirmative, where the negatives do cancel each other out. Can you put them in a context in which they would have affirmative meaning? How do we signal that we want the sentence to have the affirmative interpretation?

3. Are the following examples of multiple negation considered to be standard English or not?

   I don't never have no money.
   We don't never travel nowhere.

   According to the eighteenth-century grammarians' reasoning, should they be standard?

4. Although not part of standard English, negations like the following are used in some dialects of English:

   Can't nobody help me now.
   Don't nobody move!

   What are the rules for forming these negations? In what ways are they different from the standard English rules?

NOUN NEGATION

Nouns are another lexical category that can be negated. **Noun negation** is accomplished by using the determiner *no*. You'll notice in the pairs of sentences in (6) that some verb negations can also be expressed as noun negations.

(6) I don't have any time.
I have no time.

There isn't any milk left.
There is no milk left.

In the second of each pair, *no* works as a determiner in the same way that *the* and *some* do. (*Some* changes to *any* when the verb is negated.)

DISCUSSION EXERCISES 10.5

1. Turn each of the following into an equivalent statement by negating a noun.

   There isn't any point to this conversation.
   I do not see any reason to continue.
   She does not expect any compensation.
   This restaurant does not serve any liquor.
   That teacher doesn't have any patience.

2. Can verb negation and noun negation be used in the same clause in standard English? Give a sentence that illustrates the two used together.

ADJECTIVE AND ADVERB NEGATION

Still another way that we can express negation in English is by using a negative prefix on an adjective or an adverb, called **adjective negation** and **adverb negation.** The following pairs illustrate this alternative to verb negation.

(7) They are not lucky.
     They are unlucky.

     She is not satisfied with the results.
     She is dissatisfied with the results.

     He did not speak truthfully.
     He spoke untruthfully.

     You do not write legibly.
     You write illegibly.

There are many different negative prefixes in English and, for the most part, we cannot predict which adjective or adverb will be assigned which prefix. Probably the most common is *un-*, and it is often the one that people use instead of the less common ones required by standard English, for example, *unattentive* for *inattentive*.

One special feature of adjective and adverb negation is that it may occur in standard English together with verb negation, and when the two occur together they do have the effect of canceling each other out, just as the eighteenth-century grammarians said they would. Consider the examples in (8).

(8) I am <u>not unhappy</u> with the results.
     She spoke <u>not insincerely</u>.
     They are <u>not intolerant</u>.

Although we might quarrel about the exact meanings (see Reflection 4), the sentences in (8) are roughly the equivalents of those in (9).

(9) I am happy with the results.
     She spoke sincerely.
     They are tolerant.

DISCUSSION EXERCISES 10.6

1. Make each of the following adjectives negative by adding a prefix. Is there disagreement on any of these? *regular, secure, possible, courteous, legal, imaginable, violent*

2. Although there is very little predictability in these prefixes, there is some. For example, can you think of a reason that the following adjective and adverb roots all take the prefix *im-* as opposed to *in-? mobile, maturely, material, politely, pious, probably?*

3. What is the requirement on the roots that permit the prefix *ir-?* What about *il-?*

4. Express each of the following as a combination of verb negation and adjective negation.

    They are honest.
    His attention is flattering.
    These facts are relevant.

NEGATION OF COMPOUNDS

Compounds of constituents can be negated with the correlative coordinating conjunction *neither . . . nor.* Many different constituent-types can be negated in this way.

(10) We are neither sorry nor ashamed.   (adjectives)
      They neither sang nor danced last night.   (verbs)
      She neither helped the victim nor called the police.   (verb phrases)
      I'll have neither the pie nor the ice cream.   (noun phrases)
      You spoke neither convincingly nor eloquently.   (adverbs)
      He is neither for nor against the proposal.   (prepositions)
      We expected neither him nor her.   (pronouns)

When compound clauses are negated in this way, a curious thing happens, as you can see in the sentences in (11).

(11) Neither can he speak nor can he walk.
      Neither will they read the books nor will they return them.
      Neither have you answered my question nor have you proven me wrong.

You noticed, of course, that the subject and verb of the clauses change places, and you also undoubtedly noticed that the verbs are helping verbs. What do you suppose happens if there is no helping verb? The sentences in (12) illustrate what you were surely able to figure out.

(12) Neither did he speak nor did he walk.
      Neither do they read the books nor do they return them.
      Neither did you answer my question nor did you prove me wrong.

Here is still another instance in which English grammar is sensitive to the distinction between the presence or absence of a helping verb, requiring the insertion of *do* when no helping verb is present.

It is also worth pointing out here that *nor* can function independently of *neither*, just as *or* can function independently of *either*. Most commonly it occurs preceding the second of two conjoined clauses when the first is negated in some way, as illustrated in (13).

(13) We can't admit the truth, nor can we face the shame.
      The child is not happy, nor is she healthy.
      I never sleepwalk, nor do I have nightmares.
      She expects nothing, nor does she get anything.

DISCUSSION EXERCISES 10.7

1. Give an example of a *neither . . . nor* compound for each of the following constituent-types: noun phrase, verb phrase, adjective, pronoun, clause. Do all these constructions occur in your everyday spoken English? Do any seem especially formal?

2. *Neither* can function alone without *nor*. What does it mean in the sentence *I want neither?* What category of negative would you put it under?

3. Why do you think *anything* (as opposed to *nothing*) is required in the second clause of the last sentence of (13)?

PARTIAL NEGATION

One form of negation that we have mentioned before is what might be called **partial negation.** This is achieved through the use of the partially negative adverbs *seldom, rarely, barely, scarcely,* and *hardly.* You will remember from our discussion of tag questions in Chapter 9 that these adverbs lend some negativity to a clause but do not negate it entirely. That is why we have difficulty forming a tag question, which requires that we reverse the negativity of the statement it follows. Notice again how odd either tag sounds in the examples in (14).

(14) You hardly spoke to him, didn't you?
                              did you?

    She seldom gets out, doesn't she?
                         does she?

There is another interesting feature of these partially negative adverbs. Because they are adverbs, there is some flexibility in their placement in sentences. In addition to following the subject, as in (14), some of them may also precede the subject. But notice what happens when they precede the subject.

(15) Rarely can I find good pasta sauce.
Seldom will you encounter true friends.
Scarcely had the lecture begun, when he got up and left.

(16) Seldom does one hear pleasant news.
Just barely do I get my work finished.
Rarely did she get a raise in those days.

Yet again, we see a grammatical situation in which what you do depends on whether the sentence has a helping verb or not. If there is a helping verb, we reverse the subject and verb. If there is no helping verb, we add a form of *do,* taking all the information from the main verb and leaving the main verb in its base form. You may not ever say sentences like those in (15) and (16), but by now you can probably describe their formation with speed and eloquence!

DISCUSSION EXERCISES 10.8

1. Which of these have a corresponding sentence with the adverb before the subject?

They hardly ever visit us.
We can barely hear you.
You seldom long for company.
He scarcely made a living.
She rarely does her homework.

(continued)

2. These same placement rules operate for some other adverbs as well. Show how the adverb *often* can appear before or after the subject. What adjustments are necessary to the sentence if it appears before the subject? Can you think of other adverbs that behave this way?

3. What are the yes-no questions corresponding to the statements in question 1? Do you think they sound odd? Why? How would you answer them?

4. As we noted earlier, negation is independent of voice and discourse function. Clauses have all three, so we can refer to the following clause as an *active, declarative, affirmative* clause:

The police arrested the thief.

For purposes of grammatical description, this type is often considered the most basic clause type, from which the others are derived. What clause type is each of the following?

The police did not arrest the thief.
The thief was arrested by the police.
The thief was not arrested by the police.
Did the police arrest the thief?
Didn't the police arrest the thief?
Was the thief arrested by the police?
Wasn't the thief arrested by the police?
Arrest the thief!
Don't arrest the thief!

Up until this point, our discussion of English grammar has focused on clauses and their components, or constituents. For the most part, our examples have been single clauses, which we have sometimes called *sentences*. What we will see in the next chapter is that clauses and sentences are not the same thing. The sentence is a larger unit of language organization that is made up of clauses. A sentence might be made up of just one clause, and so it was not wrong of us to refer to our sample clauses as sentences. But sentences are often made up of more than one clause. Our next task is to learn how clauses can be arranged to make up sentences, which will complete our study of English grammar from its lowest to its highest levels of organization.

REFLECTIONS

1. Why do you think so many people use the contraction *ain't* even though everyone knows that it is nonstandard? Can you think of any popular songs that use *ain't* in the lyrics? What purpose does it serve? Have you ever heard any other versions of *ain't?* Here are some examples:

"The pint is grand, Tommy, and I'm the champion of all pint drinkers, amn't I?"

Frank McCourt, *Angela's Ashes: A Memoir* (Scibner: New York, 1996, p. 255)

"They an't seen you in more than ten years."

Dorothy Allison, *Cavedweller* (Plume: New York, 1999, pp. 5–6)

"An't nothing wrong with me." (Ibid, p. 191)

2. Consider the following from Chaucer's *Man of Law's Tale:* See Larry D. Benson, Editor, *The Canterbury Tales,* based on *The Riverside Chaucer,* Third Edition (Boston: Houghton Mifflin Company, 2000, p. 70).

And therfore he, of ful avysement

Nolde (would not) nevere write in none of his sermons . . .

How did negation in Chaucer's time (fourteenth century) differ from modern English negation?

3. Some languages typically use more than one word at a time to signal negation, such as French and Spanish, as illustrated.

French: *Je ne sais pas*

I -not- know- not

Spanish: *Yo no sé nada*

I -not- know- nothing

Do you know any other languages that use more than one negative per clause?

4. It can be argued that verb negation and adjective negation do not produce exactly the same meaning. For example, the two following sentences are not necessarily equivalent in meaning.

He is not lucky.

He is unlucky.

What is the difference between them? Similarly, it can be argued that the following are not strictly equivalent.

He is not unlucky.

He is lucky.

What is the difference between these? It is interesting to note that these differences are associated only with gradable adjectives. For nongradable adjectives, the affirmative and the doubly negated ones mean the same thing. For example, *reversible* and *not irreversible* have the same meaning.

5. It says in the Declaration of Independence that "all men are created equal, that they are endowed by their Creator with certain unalienable rights." In what way is this different from modern English usage?

6. Here is some dictionary work:

1. In what sense is *irregardless* a double negative? Is it considered to be standard English?

2. What is the function of the prefix *in-* in *inflammable?*

7. In the chapter we said that *some-* words must change to *any-* words when the verb is negated. Strictly speaking, it is possible to leave the *some-* words in the negative, but there is a slight difference of meaning. What is the difference in meaning between these two sentences?

Do you need any money?

Do you need some money?

8. These are some negative statements from Shakespeare's *Julius Caesar.* How are they different from modern English negation?

Knew you not Pompey?

Forget not in your speed.

Fear him not, Caesar.

I know not what you mean by that.

Review Reflection 4 in Chapter 9. Can you make a more general statement about questions and negatives in Shakespeare's time compared with those of today?

9. Some verbs can be negated with the prefix *dis-*, as in *disconnect.* Can you think of others? How is the meaning different from verb negation with *not?*

PRACTICE EXERCISES FOR CHAPTER 10 (Answers on p. 234)

1. Express each of the following using a contraction. Which are irregular? Which would you never say?
   1. You should not speak ill of the dead.
   2. Karel cannot cope with the situation.
   3. Bill may not play today.
   4. Sal is not listening to you.
   5. We were not expecting you.
   6. I am not surprised.
   7. We shall not be daunted.
   8. They must not think we are ungrateful.
   9. He will not be allowed to perform.
   10. That would not help me.
2. Which of the following statements require the insertion of *do* in the negative? Why?
   1. The games have begun.
   2. She needs to consider the alternatives.
   3. The milk is sour.

(continued)

    4. We could meet you after class.

    5. I do my chores in the evening.

    6. Reading puts me to sleep.

    7. Expect the worst.

    8. The felon was acquitted.

    9. This music is making Ben sleepy.

    10. I ordered the cake for the party.

3. Express the negative of each of these in two different ways.
   1. The printer has ink.
   2. A reasonable person would tolerate this behavior.
   3. I have an idea.
   4. She received compensation for the job.
   5. He got love from his grandparents.

4. Which of the following conform to the rules of standard English negation?
   1. He doesn't eat neither meat nor chicken.
   2. I never did see no thief.
   3. Nothing can be done about it.
   4. I can tolerate no alcohol.
   5. We didn't expect no visitors.
   6. They are neither tired or hungry.
   7. Can't nobody blame him for his actions.
   8. That doctor doesn't give no free samples to nobody.
   9. She neither cooks nor sews.
   10. My handwriting is not illegible.

5. Give an equivalent negative statement for each of the following by negating a noun.
   1. I don't see any people.
   2. Doesn't any proposal suit you?
   3. She won't accept any cash.
   4. There isn't any reason to stay.
   5. Why weren't there any police at the event?

6. Give a one-word negative for each of the following adjectives or adverbs: *happily, decent, proportionately, advisable, politely, relevant, literate, savory, toxic, remarkably.*

7. The following compound clauses have been negated with verb negation. For each, use *neither . . . nor* to express the same meaning.
   1. We are not proud and we are not arrogant.
   2. I didn't clean the garage and I didn't sweep the driveway.
   3. She didn't speak clearly and she didn't speak accurately.

(continued)

    4. They won't tolerate your laziness and they won't tolerate your impudence.

    5. Smoking is not good for you and drinking is not good for you.

8. Make each of the following statements partially negative by using a partially negative adverb. For which can the adverb be placed in front of the subject?

    1. I go to the movies during the week.

    2. Marie studies with Ken.

    3. We arrived on time.

    4. The farmers were able to support their families.

    5. He remembers their meeting.

    6. The patient could speak.

    7. There is enough time for this exam.

    8. The tenants complained to the landlord.

    9. The beams held up the roof.

    10. There is some food in the refrigerator.

9. Make each of the following negative in at least two different ways.

    1. This food is edible.

    2. We went somewhere last night.

    3. Our approach is confrontational.

    4. There is some reason to worry.

    5. These reviews are spectacular.

    6. She bought some bonds.

    7. I'll read it sometime.

    8. There is paint in the garage.

    9. A car can travel this road.

    10. That star has fan clubs.

10. Describe each of the following sentences according to its voice, negativity, and discourse function.

    1. Did you lose your keys in the parking lot?

    2. The broadcast was interrupted by the storm.

    3. The students weren't permitted to talk during exams.

    4. Don't be misled by false advertising.

    5. Did the soup taste salty?

    6. You didn't understand my question.

    7. Arrive on time for your next appointment.

    8. Can't the purchase be returned by the customer?

    9. I am uneasy about the truce.

    10. Don't call me before ten o'clock.

(continued)

11. Find an example of each of the following in the *Believers* selection that follows.

   verb negation with *do* as a helping verb

   verb negation with a modal

   uncontracted verb negation

   a partially negative adverb

   a missing relative pronoun

   an infinitival phrase

   have used as a main verb

   a prepositional phrase

   a subject complement

   a compound noun

My mother is exasperated with me again. I don't always enjoy provoking her, but our battles are sometimes the most intimate moments we share. I want to pat her hand, but it's not the right moment for that. "I shouldn't have to explain this to you. I had a music box near my bed. It was carved like a little Swiss chalet. And your father wound it up. He played it for me. He listened to it before he left. It went like this."

   To my horror, and amazement, my old mother starts to hum the tune that her music box used to play. There is something terrible about this, and I can hardly bear to listen to her, but I do. (Baxter: "Believers," p. 218.)

12. Identify the violations of formal standard English in the following letter:

   Dear Chris,

   I still haven't heard nothing from you. I'm wondering do you want me to stop writting? I seen you at the bank last week, and I had the feeling you seen me too. If I was more sensitive, I would think you was trying to avoid me. There's so many good times we had together. Maybe the amount of my letters are annoying you. I will write less letters in the future. My sister invites you to join her and I at the rock concert next week. I hope you will consider it and not hold no grudges.

   Sincerely,
   Pat

ELEVEN

COMBINING CLAUSES INTO SENTENCES: COORDINATION

HOW IS A SENTENCE DIFFERENT FROM A CLAUSE?

It is now time to take a closer look at the highest level of grammatical organization, the **sentence.** As we said at the end of Chapter 10, sentences are made up of combinations of *clauses,* those constituents that are themselves made up of a noun phrase and a verb phrase. Sentences consist of one or more clauses that bear certain relationships to one another. The simplest kind of sentence is the one made up of only one clause. It is, in fact, called a **simple sentence.** You may have noticed that until now we have used the terms *clause* and *sentence* more or less interchangeably, since most of the examples in the preceding chapters consisted of one clause; that is, they were *simple sentences.* In this chapter, we will be more careful to distinguish between clauses and sentences, so that we may accurately describe the processes of sentence building.

SENTENCE BUILDING THROUGH COORDINATION

We have already talked about how we combine like constituents by *coordination* (or *conjoining*) to form compounds. You will recall that in this process we use the coordinating conjunctions, either *simple* (*and, but, or, nor, yet, so, for*) or *correlative* (*both . . . and, not only . . . but, either . . . or, neither . . . nor*). Clauses, like other constituents, commonly combine to form compounds. A sentence made up of two or more such clauses is referred to as a **compound sentence.** The relationship between, or among, the clauses is determined by the choice of coordinating conjunction. For example, if *and* is used, it may simply link two facts together in a neutral way, as in (1).

> (1) Chicago is in Illinois and Utica is in New York.

The use of *and* may also suggest that the events happened in the order that they appear, as in (2).

> (2) She graduated and she got a job at the local bank.

Or it may suggest a causal relationship, as in (3).

> (3) Do that again and you're history.

So allows the first clause to give a reason for the second.

> (4) He was exhausted, so he went to bed.

On the other hand, *but* and *yet* imply that the second clause is contrary to the expectations of the first.

> (5) Bob worked very hard, but he didn't get a Christmas bonus.
> The plane had been thoroughly inspected, yet it crashed.

Or, as you know, creates a disjunction, presenting the clauses as alternatives.

> (6) You should put your money in the bank or you should invest it.
> Speak now or forever hold your peace.

For allows the second clause to offer a reason for the first.

> (7) He returned the wallet, for he was an honest man.

Nor follows a negative clause and means "and not."

> (8) The water is not safe to drink, nor is the food edible.

DISCUSSION EXERCISES 11.1

1. Simple sentences are by definition made up of one clause, but that does not mean they have to be "simple" in any ordinary sense of the word. What can you say about the grammatical structure of the following simple sentence?

    The small fluffy kitten with a ribbon around its neck and a twinkle in its eye did enormous damage to the sofa in our living room.

2. As a group exercise, start with the simple sentence *The girl threw the ball* and keep adding new structure to it without adding any additional clauses. What new structures are you adding?

3. What is the relationship between the two clauses in each of the following compound sentences?

    Show up for work tomorrow or you're fired.
    Potatoes are good with chicken and rice is good with lamb.

(continued)

↳add additional info

He's very strong, but he can't lift that boulder.
The child ran into the room and she began to cry.
They refuse to leave, for they love their country.
The economy is getting better, yet the work force is shrinking.
Study hard and you'll pass the test.
You cannot take piano lessons nor can you take up the saxophone.

4. What is the connection between the two clauses joined by the correlatives in the following sentences?

   Either we must contact the police or we must take the law into our own hands.
   Neither did he return my calls, nor did he acknowledge my letter.

5. Make the following clause compounds negative by using the correlative coordinating conjunction *neither . . . nor*. What adjustments must be made in the clauses?

   The baby is not hungry and the baby is not thirsty.
   She wouldn't leave and she wouldn't participate in the discussion.

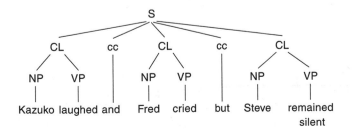

The baby is not hungry, nor is he thirsty.
She would neither leave, nor would she participate in the discussion.

As with other kinds of compounds, there may be more than two clauses conjoined in a sentence, as in the following:

(9) Kazuko laughed, and Fred cried, but Steve remained silent.
    They were upset, but they met anyway, and they solved the problem.

When sentences have combined clauses, it may become more difficult to visualize their structure mentally. It is sometimes useful to use the tree structure we have used elsewhere in this book to lay out the clauses graphically. The first sentence in (9) has the following corresponding tree structure, where S is a sentence, "cc" is a coordinating conjunction, CL is a clause, NP is a noun phrase, and VP is a verb phrase.

```
                              S
        ┌──────────┬──────────┬──────────┬──────────┐
        CL         cc         CL         cc         CL
       /  \        │         /  \        │         /  \
     NP    VP      │       NP    VP      │       NP    VP
      │     │      │        │     │      │        │     │
   Kazuko laughed and     Fred  cried  but     Steve  remained
                                                        silent
```

DISCUSSION EXERCISES 11.2

1. Draw tree structures for the following compound sentences:

    Spelling programs are useful, but they do not fix all spelling errors.
    His wife died years ago, yet he still dreams about her.

2. Add a third conjoined clause to each of the following compound sentences:

    Ken got there early but he couldn't find a parking space.
    My friends came to my party and they cheered me up.
    He didn't give money to charity nor did he volunteer his time.

3. Create a compound sentence with the correlative coordinating conjunction *either . . . or.* Then make the sentence negative. What further adjustments are required?

4. Tell whether each of the following sentences is simple or compound.

    The long winding road at the bottom of the canyon led to a stream with pure clear water and schools of fish.
    The baby cried but no one heard.
    Candy disliked her name, so she changed it to Bertha, yet she didn't tell her parents, for their feelings would be hurt.

5. There is some difference of opinion about the punctuation of conjoined clauses. What is the rule you were taught? And is it acceptable to begin a sentence with a coordinating conjunction?

As suggested in Exercise 11.2 question 5, handbooks may differ on the rule for placement of commas between clauses that are conjoined. But there is another troubling aspect of formal written English about which handbooks agree: sentences with conjoined clauses are punctuated differently from similar looking sentences with sentence adverbs. Compare, for example, (10) and (11):

(10) The lawn is a mess, but I refuse to mow it one more time.
(11) The lawn is a mess. However, I refuse to mow it one more time.

Example (10) is a compound sentence in which the two clauses are linked together by the coordinating conjunction *but.* Here we may or may not place a comma before *but.* Example (11) is not a compound sentence. Rather, it is two separate sentences, and *however* is a sentence adverb that begins the second one. You will remember from Chapter 6 that sentence adverbs like *however, therefore, furthermore, nevertheless,* and *moreover* often appear at the beginning of the sentence and are set off from it with a comma. Formal English offers a second option for punctuating sentences with sentence adverbs, as seen in (12).

(12) *The lawn is a mess; however, I refuse to mow it one more time.*

A semicolon may follow the first sentence, and when it does, the sentence adverb is not capitalized. These spelling conventions are often violated because coordinating conjunctions and sentence adverbs don't seem to be very different in purpose. To remember this rule, it might help to keep in mind that coordinating conjunctions link two clauses together but are not considered to be grammatically part of either one. Sentence adverbs, on the other hand, normally are grammatically part of the second sentence.

DISCUSSION EXERCISES 11.3

1. Punctuate the following according to standard English punctuation rules:

   I studied therefore I did well on the test.
   It was dry all summer so the crops didn't grow.
   We attended the show but we missed the reception afterwards.
   You need to turn on the machine furthermore you must boot up the disk.
   Her remarks were unnecessary moreover I thought they were hurtful.
   Our first stop will be Madrid and then we will go to Seville.

   Which have coordinating conjunctions and which have sentence adverbs?

2. Give another acceptable option for punctuating each of the following:

   The water was cold, but we jumped right in.
   She prepares delicious soups. However, she doesn't use enough seasoning.

CLAUSE COORDINATION AND ELLIPSIS

The process of conjoining gives us enormous power to combine ideas when we communicate. But when we conjoin whole clauses we find a great deal of potential redundancy as well, as evidenced by the sentences in (13).

(13) The man left the bar and the woman left the bar.
      I washed the dishes and I dried the dishes.
      She wrote a poem and she wrote a short story.
      They bought the house and they renovated the house.
      Bob studied physics and Millie studied engineering.
      Cary bought the present and Steve wrapped the present.

When there is repetition in conjoined clauses, English allows us to eliminate the repeated elements without changing the meaning. This elimination of redundancy is called **ellipsis.** Each of the sentences in (13) can be expressed in a shorter, more efficient manner.

(14) The man and the woman left the bar.
I washed and dried the dishes.
She wrote a poem and a short story.
They bought and renovated the house.
Bob studied physics and Millie engineering.
Cary bought and Steve wrapped the present.

not compound sentences any more

No meaning has been lost, but certain material in each sentence has been omitted. The omitted material may be referred to as "ellipted." When ellipsis occurs, the remaining elements may reorganize into compounds. *The man and the woman* in the first sentence in (14) is a conjoined noun phrase, for example. But you will notice that in the last two sentences of (14), no new compounds are formed. You will also notice that sometimes material is omitted from the first clause and sometimes from the second. As speakers of English, we always know which elements to leave out, but it would not be obvious to someone who is not a native speaker of the language. (See Reflection 2 for more on this.)

To summarize, when we conjoin two clauses we may also make them more compact by leaving out the repeated information. This may raise some questions about how to describe the structure of clauses that have ellipted material. In some cases, even after ellipsis, the clause structure remains fairly well intact, as in *Bob studied physics and Millie engineering.* For these, *ellipted clause* would be an appropriate designation. In other cases so much has been left out and rearranged that the sentence no longer looks compound, as in *She wrote a poem and a short story.* There is no harm in calling this second a simple sentence with a compound noun phrase, as long as we keep in mind that the listener must restore the missing information mentally to understand the sentence.

DISCUSSION EXERCISES 11.4

1. What has been omitted in each of the following? (i.e., restore the original conjoined clauses)

   She studied mathematics and Al biology.
   Joe washed and Ed dried the dishes.
   Karen cut and sewed the dress.
   Martha Gray and her sister are married.
   I like pie and ice cream for dessert.

2. You will notice that the last sentence can mean two different things, but only one of the meanings can be derived from clause coordination followed by ellipsis. Which one?

(continued)

3. Which of the following *cannot* be derived from clause coordination and ellipsis? Which have more than one interpretation?

Ed and Nancy are happy together.
Ed and Nancy are married.
Ed and Nancy met in Reno.
Ed and Nancy dance well.

4. Reduce the following conjoined clauses and describe the structure that remains.

Phil signed the letter and Marge signed the letter.
We identified the problem and we solved the problem.
The assistant collected the data and the assistant wrote the report.
Dan wrote the music and Mike wrote the lyrics.
Mildred cooked the chicken and Jack cooked the fish.

5. What final adjustment must be made in conjoined clauses reduced by ellipsis of a verb phrase? Use the following as a test.

The governor is studying the matter and the mayor is studying the matter.

As we have seen in this chapter, clauses can combine, with the help of coordinating conjunctions, to form compound sentences. The relationships expressed among the clauses will differ depending on the particular coordinating conjunction(s) used. What is important to understand, though, is that no matter what the meaning relationship is between the clauses, grammatically they are of equal status. They are two (or more) separate clauses, independent of each other. This will make more sense as you begin to read the next chapter, where we look at a kind of clause combination, called **subordination,** in which the clauses do not share equal grammatical status.

REFLECTIONS

1. Consult two different style manuals on the punctuation of compound clauses. Is there any disagreement? Does either differentiate between ellipted and full clauses, as in the following:

The teacher taught drama and she coached the football team.
The teacher taught drama and coached the football team.

2. There tends to be a pattern for clause ellipsis: elements on the right in their constituents are eliminated from the first clause; elements on the left in their constituents are eliminated from the second clause. Compare the following:

Fred [caught the fish] and John [cleaned the fish].
Fred [caught the fish] and John [caught the rubber tire].

Look again at the sentences in (13) and (14). Draw brackets around the constituents containing the omitted elements. Does the pattern hold?

3. Sometimes transitive verbs may have implied objects, which gives the appearance of clause ellipsis: *I washed the dishes and Jim dried [the dishes]*. These will not necessarily follow the pattern described in Reflection 2. Which of the following follows the pattern for clause ellipsis and which merely has an implied direct object?

Sue typed and Mary Jo proofread the manuscript.

Sue typed the manuscript and Mary Jo proofread.

4. There are restrictions on what kinds of clauses can be conjoined to form a compound. What makes the following compounds unacceptable in ordinary conversation?

*The weather is nice and what time is it?

*Go to the store but what a nice man you are!

*Neither did they leave their names nor what did they want?

5. One of the most pervasive punctuation errors in written English is the enclosure of a sentence adverb between commas, as in

*The furnace broke, therefore, the house was cold.

*The tomatoes grew well, however, the squash died.

Why do you think this type of error is more resistant to correction than other kinds of punctuation errors?

PRACTICE EXERCISES FOR CHAPTER 11 (Answers on p. 236)

1. Tell whether the underlined word in each sentence is a coordinating conjunction or a sentence adverb. Punctuate the sentence accordingly.
   1. The sky is cloudy <u>but</u> it won't rain.
   2. The class was delayed <u>for</u> no one had a book.
   3. My cousins were ill <u>nevertheless</u> they visited me.
   4. The roast was ready <u>so</u> I took it out of the oven.
   5. We had a good time <u>therefore</u> we exchanged phone numbers.
   6. Cats are affectionate <u>moreover</u> they are loyal.
   7. The elections were over <u>and</u> our party had won.
   8. Our trip to Quebec was tiring <u>however</u> we enjoyed it.
   9. I'm giving you the day off <u>furthermore</u> I'm increasing your salary.
   10. Turn yourself in <u>or</u> I will have to report you.

(continued)

2. Perform ellipsis on each of the following clause coordinations. Indicate which redundant material is omitted.
   1. The boy fished in the pond and his sister fished in the pond.
   2. Mary baked the potatoes and Mary baked the squash.
   3. Bill bought a house and his brother bought a condo.
   4. The squirrel ran up the tree and the squirrel ran down the tree.
   5. All children need love and all children crave attention.
   6. Her teeth are strong and her teeth are white.
   7. The customer called the company and the customer threatened to sue.
   8. All my friends came to our party and all her friends came to our party.
   9. Convertibles are nice in summer and hardtops are nice in winter.
   10. The man looked in the drawer and the woman looked in the cupboard.

3. Create compound sentences with each of the following coordinating conjunctions: *or, so, for, yet.*

4. Give the negative of this sentence: Either he played golf or he swam in the pool.

5. Which of the following sentences have (unreduced) compound clauses?
   1. They planned a party for all their friends but no one came.
   2. I like cities with parks and public sculptures.
   3. Frank and Connie are kind people.
   4. Every day he either burns the toast or overcooks the eggs.
   5. The economy is slowing down yet the stock market continues to do well.
   6. Neither does he drink nor does he swear.
   7. She neither writes nor telephones.
   8. Not only do they work on Sundays, but they also work on Christmas.
   9. Ben sleeps all day and is awake all night.
   10. Chris keeps calling Pat, but Pat won't respond.

6. Draw tree structures for the following:

   The boys played basketball and the girls played soccer.
   Everyone left but Bill stayed for he had lots of time.

7. Find an example of each of the following in the *Believers* selection that follows.

   two compound sentences
   a compound noun phrase
   a prepositional phrase
   a deferred preposition
   a sentence adverb
   a noun with an irregular plural

(continued)

an intensifier

an adverb modifying an adjective

an embedded question

a past perfect tense

She and Walton continued their job-and-castoffs hunt, and it was Walton who found a job first, at the loading dock of a retailer in the suburbs, a twenty-four hour discount store known for shoddy merchandise. The job went from midnight to 8 A.M.

She thought he wasn't quite physically robust enough for such work, but he claimed that he was stronger than he appeared. "It's all down here," he said, pointing to his lower back. "This is where you need it."

She didn't ask him what he was referring to—the muscles or the vertebrae or the cartilage. She had never seen his lower back. However, she was beginning to want to.

(Baxter: "Kiss Away," p. 17.)

8. Identify the violations of formal standard English in the following letter:

Dear Chris,

I was happy that you went to the rock concert with my sister and I, however, I still have the feeling that she was the one you preferred to be with. I felt left out of you guys' conversation. Maybe next time you and me can go ourself. I sure hope there ain't no bad feeling between you and I. I've always thought that we have the most perfect friendship, so if I have did anything to offend you, please let me know. Not having anything specific, the problems between us can't be fixed.

Hopefully,
Pat

TWELVE

COMBINING CLAUSES INTO SENTENCES: SUBORDINATION

SENTENCE BUILDING THROUGH SUBORDINATION

In the last chapter we talked about how clauses can combine into sentences by forming compounds. That is, through the process of coordination, clauses of equal status join together to form what are known as compound sentences. But there is another way that clauses can combine, and that is through the process of **subordination.** *Subordination* allows one clause to become a grammatical part of another. In this case the relationship is unequal, as the name of the process suggests, with one clause subordinate to another. Consider the following clauses, for example:

(1) The clown arrived. The children squealed with joy.

A much more natural way to express these two thoughts, as one sentence, is shown in (2).

(2) When the clown arrived, the children squealed with joy.

In this case, we have incorporated the first clause of (1) into the second, making the first a **subordinate clause.** The second clause is the main idea that we are expressing, while the first is used to tell the time of the action of the second. In other words, it functions in much the same way that an adverb of time, such as *yesterday,* might. In this sense we say that it has become a grammatical part of the second clause. Sentences that contain a least one subordinate clause are known as **complex sentences.**

English has a number of different ways in which one clause might be incorporated into another; this chapter will explore some of them in detail, showing the different grammatical roles that clauses can play and the unequal relationships that can exist among clauses of the same sentence. It will be helpful to have some terminology with which to refer to the clauses within a sentence. Unfortunately for us, many different terms for the same thing are current in grammatical description. For example, the clause that expresses the main idea is known as the **main clause** or the **matrix clause** or the **superordinate clause** or the **independent clause.** A subordinate clause may also be called an **embedded sentence** or a **dependent clause.** In this chapter we will refer to them as *main clauses* and *subordinate clauses.* In our examples, we will sometimes use brackets to mark off the boundaries of clauses within a sentence and to show how clauses can nest inside other clauses, as in (3).

(3) [[When the clown arrived] the children squealed with joy]

When we are analyzing the clauses of a sentence, it is important to keep in mind that subordinate clauses don't necessarily look exactly the way they would look if they were main clauses. They are clauses by definition as long as they have their own subjects and predicates, but they often undergo some distortion when they are subordinate. An introductory word may be added, a word may be replaced, or the verb may change its form. These distortions are very useful in helping listeners sort out the various clauses of the sentence, since they serve as red flags to alert listeners to the fact that the clause must be related grammatically to another clause that contains it. We will have more to say about these red flags as we continue our discussion of subordinate clauses.

DISCUSSION EXERCISES 12.1

1. Place brackets around the subordinate clause in each of the following sentences:

   I realize [that you have been waiting a long time.] *do*
   Rob bought the book [after Connie had recommended it.]
   He was not the same person [to whom I had spoken earlier.] *Rel.*
   subj [That coffee contains caffeine] is no secret.
   [Although Sam wanted to leave] Ben convinced him to stay.
   Barry said [that he would visit next week.] *obj.*
   We arranged [for Mary to telephone her sister in Kansas.] *obj.*
   [Before you fly off the handle] let me explain.
   subj [For the men to leave without the women] would be foolish.
   We discovered the baby [whose parents had abandoned him.] *Rel.*

2. Which do you think people understand faster (a) or (b)? Why?
   (a) They admitted you were right.
   (b) They admitted that you were right.

(continued)

Clue helps process idea

3. Which of the underlined sentence parts are subordinate clauses? What is your reasoning?

Theresa found the bone that her dog had buried in the sand. *Not sub.*

For Jake to announce his candidacy now would be a mistake. *Sub clause - subject*

Jane finished the novel although she was exhausted. *Not sub.*

After the first act, Jim fell asleep. *Not sub.*

I understand that you can't come to my party. *Sub. / relative clause*

Each type of subordinate clause has its own identifying characteristics. In the next few sections we will look at some of the most common types of subordinate clauses.

ADVERBIAL CLAUSES

We began our discussion of subordinate clauses with the **adverbial clause,** the type of subordinate clause illustrated in (2). Any clause that behaves like an adverb falls under this category. We have seen throughout this book that there are several different types of constituents that can perform adverbial functions: single adverbs and adverb phrases, as illustrated in (4),

(4) The boy ran <u>quickly</u>.
   The boy ran <u>rather quickly</u>.

and prepositional phrases, as in (5).

(5) A rabbit jumped <u>into the hole</u>.
   I'll meet you <u>at noon</u>.

One of the most important adverbial functions is to modify a verb, giving further information about the action, such as time, place, manner, or reason. What we now see is that whole clauses can serve the same purpose. Adverbial clauses all modify the verb of the main clause in some way: they may tell time, place, reason, or some condition placed on the action. There is always an introductory word, called a **subordinating conjunction,** that tells you the specific adverbial function of the clause. Some of these are shown in (6).

(6) I'll see you [before the night is over].
   She left [because she was angry].
   He'll go [wherever life takes him].
   We stayed [although we should have left].

Adverbial clauses are easy to spot. The subordinating conjunctions are reliable indicators of the function of the clause and, except for the introductory word, they look just like main clauses. They also move around relatively freely. All of the adverbial clauses in (6) could just as easily appear at the beginning of the sentence rather than the end. They might even interrupt the main clause, as in (7).

(7) My sister, because she lacked confidence, failed at most things.

Adverbial clauses are often set off from the main clause by commas, particularly if they are long or if they appear at the beginning of the sentence or interrupt the main clause.

DISCUSSION EXERCISES 12.2

1. Identify the adverbial clause in each of the following sentences:

    Since you have the time, you can proofread my paper.
    We stopped to eat because we were hungry.
    After the storm had passed, we surveyed the damage.
    I haven't stopped thinking about you since you left.
    We should look before we leap.
    Although he is competent, he never finishes a job.
    The men in my family, because they have big feet, have trouble finding shoes to fit.
    While he was gone they hired someone to replace him.
    All my children, since they are grown, support themselves now.
    We waited until the parade passed through the town.

2. Replace the adverb or adverb phrase in each sentence with an adverbial clause.

    I want to go now *before it rains —(reflects time)*
    She agreed very reluctantly. *although she didn't want to -*
    Let's go home. *where you want to go. (location)*

3. Replace the prepositional phrase in each sentence with an adverbial clause.

    Ben complained for a good reason. *because he waited so long.*
    After the storm all was calm. *★ Since the stormed ended*
    The deer fled into the woods. *where no one could see it.*

4. Subordinating conjunctions are sometimes made up of more than one word. Find the multiple-word subordinating conjunctions in the following sentences:

    He will remain provided that we raise his salary.
    I feel sorry for him even though he is mean.
    Some people die so that others may live.

    Can you think of any others?

    (continued)

5. What lexical category is *before* in the following sentence?

    I'll meet you before the game. ⌐ *Prep.*
    Why isn't it a subordinating conjunction? *No Sub-clause*

One of the most fascinating features of English is that there is no technical limit on the number of subordinate clauses in a sentence; they are permitted to nest within other subordinate clauses indefinitely. Consider the following set of sentences with adverbial clauses:

(8) Because you complimented her, she was surprised.
    Because you complimented her although she looked tired, she was surprised.
    Because you complimented her although she looked tired when she arrived, she was surprised.

Although we begin to find this kind of nesting stylistically cumbersome, we should recognize the fact that such nesting is an important feature of human language. Tree diagrams are an especially useful tool for visualizing the structure of sentences in which there is multiple nesting of clauses. Those of (8) might look like this:

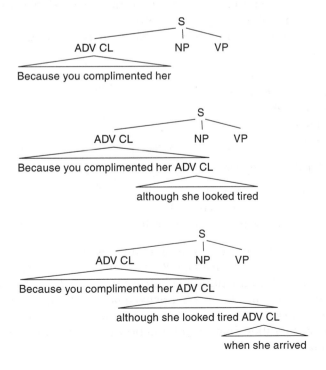

DISCUSSION EXERCISES 12.3

1. What is the clause structure of the following sentence?
   I complained [because [when the children played in the yard they left a mess.
2. Draw a tree diagram or use brackets to illustrate the structure graphically.
3. Can you insert another adverbial clause inside the most deeply embedded clause of the sentence in question 1?

NOUN CLAUSES

There is another type of subordinate clause, one that behaves like a noun phrase. We call this type a **noun clause.** It will help to identify a *noun clause* if we refresh our memories about the functions that noun phrases perform in sentences. You will remember that most often they are either subjects of the clause, direct objects, indirect objects, objects of prepositions, or complements. Noun clauses perform some, but not all, of these functions. We find them occurring as subjects, direct objects, and complements. Let's look at the direct object function first. If we have a transitive verb like *know* in a sentence, it has to be followed by a noun phrase or a pronoun as its direct object. So all the sentences in (9) are possible, with *know* taking different kinds of direct objects.

> (9) I know the answer.
>   I know the whole truth.
>   I know my limits.
>   I know Jim.
>   I know them.

Now consider the sentences in (10).

> (10) I know [that you like me].
>   I know [that the world is round].
>   I know [that grammar can be difficult].

You'll notice that in each of these sentences the direct object is a whole clause, introduced by the word *that.* Because these subordinate clauses play the same role as a noun phrase in the sentences, they are called noun clauses. Because the specific role happens to be direct object, they are called **object noun clauses.** Noun clauses are often introduced by the word *that,* also considered a subordinating conjunction (but sometimes referred to as a *complementizer.*)

DISCUSSION EXERCISES 12.4

1. Which of the following sentences have object noun clauses and which have adverbial clauses? How do you know? (Hint: a noun clause can be replaced with the word *something*.)

   We heard that you were leaving.
   She turned up the heat because she was cold.
   Let's buy food so that we can feed the baby.
   He suggested that I not ask questions.
   We regret that we cannot return the favor.
   I'll continue provided that you stop talking.
   Fay understands that the men will not help her.
   Joe anticipates that his team will win.
   Her husband resents that she earns more money.
   I've known her since she was a little girl.

2. Sometimes object noun clauses may omit their introductory *that.* Which of the following permit this omission? Do people disagree?

   We know that air travel has become more dangerous.
   She regrets that she can't attend the meeting.
   I resent that he never speaks directly to me.
   We fear that the warring parties will never seek peace.
   He suspects that someone stole his keys.

3. Find one object noun clause and two adverbial clauses in the last paragraph before this exercise set.

4. Noun clauses may have special markings other than *that.* What marks the noun clauses in the following sentences?

   I wonder if they will arrive on time.
   Jan expected Steve to call her.
   Who knows whether the operation was a success?
   We arranged for Judy to receive the package.
   Lois doesn't know what will happen next.

   Can you think of others?

Now that you can identify object noun clauses, it should be easy for you to identify **subject noun clauses:** they are noun clauses that play the role of subject in a sentence. We see in (11) a variety of different subject noun <u>phrases</u>.

(11) The answer is evident.
The truth seems obvious.
Your attitude was disturbing.
Mary's anger was apparent.

Again, we can replace any of these subject noun phrases with an entire clause.

(12) [That he knows the answer] is evident.
[That she needs attention] seems obvious.
[That the project failed] was disturbing.
[That Mary was angry] was apparent.

In each case, the subject of the sentence is an entire clause, called a *subject noun clause.* Like adverbial clauses, noun clauses can be conveniently represented by tree diagrams, as illustrated.

Object Noun Clause

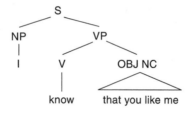

Subject Noun Clause

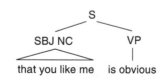

DISCUSSION EXERCISES 12.5

1. Identify the subject noun clause in each of the following sentences. Notice that they may be introduced by *that* or altered in some other way: Look for the NP + VP combination that defines a clause.

    [That they are angry] is evident.
    [For you to leave now] would be sensible.

    (continued)

sub) [Whether the plan will work] remains to be seen.
subj [What will happen next] is anybody's guess.
[That our resources are disappearing] is sad.

2. Which of the following sentences have subject noun clauses and which have adverbial clauses? How do you know?

Adv [When you get there] give me a call. — indicates time
Adv [If she finds my sweater] she can keep it. Condition
Subj [That they have finally met] is amazing.
Subj [For you to wait for me] would be impractical.
Adv. [Because he waited so long to seek advice,] no one pitied him. — Reason
Adv [Whether or not you want me to be there,] I will certainly show up. Reason
subj [Whether the tornado touched down] is still unknown.
subj [That Bud longs for the old days] puzzles me.
subj [For all of us to go] would be silly.
subj [Why you said that] is a mystery.

3. Identify the subject and the object noun clauses in the following sentences. Draw a tree diagram to illustrate the first sentence.

That you criticized her caused Karen to turn red.
Subj [That you didn't wait for me] suggests [that you didn't want me to come.] obj

4. What is the structure of each of the following sentences? Use brackets or a tree diagram to show the subordinate clauses.

subj [That you answered before I could answer] bothered me.
Tom knew [that Jerry would come [when he called.]] obj

You may be thinking that subject noun clauses sound very stilted and formal, maybe even awkward. You probably don't use them much in ordinary conversation, although you might use them more in writing. English provides us with another way to say these subject noun clauses so that they sound more conversational. We may move them to the end of the sentence, as illustrated in (13).

(13) ____ is evident [that he knows the answer].
____ seems obvious [that she needs attention].
____ was disturbing [that the project failed].
____ was apparent [that Mary was angry].

Of course, when we do this, we leave the subject position vacant. English permits this only in the imperative; in all other situations, as we mentioned in

Chapter 3, we must fill the subject position with a placeholder, or expletive. In this case we use the word *it,* giving us the sentences in (14).

(14) It is evident that he knows the answer.
It seems obvious that she needs attention.
It was disturbing that the project failed.
It was apparent that Mary was angry.

These are still subject noun clauses. They haven't changed their function, only their position in the sentence. They are now called **extraposed subject noun clauses,** literally "put outside."

DISCUSSION EXERCISES 12.6

1. Identify the extraposed subject noun clauses in the following sentences:

   It is imperative [that you remain on board.]
   It would be futile [for Holly to follow us.]
   It was important [that he learn the truth.]
   It wasn't necessary [for you to give me your seat.] subj
   It is evident [that the tomato plants won't survive.] sub

2. Put each of the extraposed clauses in the previous sentences back in its original subject position.

3. Which of the following sentences contain object noun clauses and which contain extraposed subject noun clauses? How do you know?

   John found [that he couldn't talk to Alice anymore.] obj
   It was necessary [for Jean to find work.] Extraposed subj
   It was surprising [that the stadium didn't fill for the home game.] Subj Extr.
   My relatives learned [that they couldn't visit without an invitation.] obj
   It startled her [that the baby could talk at such an early age.] Subj Ext.

4. What is the structure of each of the following sentences? Place brackets around the subordinate clauses. Draw a tree diagram of the first one.

   subj [That you ate dinner [before I arrived] is obvious.]
   It is clear [that he won't speak to me until I finish my homework.]

5. Name the type of subordinate clause in each of the following sentences:

   The teacher knew [that the students were tired.] Obj. (something)
   It was important [for Linda to take that course.] Adv.

   (continued)

Adv [After the crowd dispersed,] the city workers swept the streets.
Subj [That snakes eat mice] isn't surprising.
Let's party [until the neighbors complain.] *Adv. time*
Subj [For Ollie to admit his guilt] was a big step in his rehabilitation.
We expected [that you would be surprised.] *Obj. (something)*
It didn't bother me [that we had no money.] *Adv. Reason*
Chuck learned [that his friends loved him.] *Obj. (something)*
Lulu kept smiling [even though she was enraged.] *Adv*

There is one other common function of a noun clause. You can probably figure it out by comparing the sentences in (15) and (16).

(15) My excuse is <u>insufficient funds</u>.
The reason she gave for resigning was <u>ill health</u>.

(16) My excuse is <u>that I have insufficient funds</u>.
The reason she gave for resigning was <u>that her health is failing</u>.

You will recognize the underlined portions of the sentences in (15) as subject complements, since they follow a linking verb and describe the subject. You can see that in (16) the underlined portions are also complements, playing exactly the same role in the sentence as the noun phrases in (15). But since they are complete clauses, we call them **complement noun clauses.**

DISCUSSION EXERCISES 12.7

1. Which of the following have complement noun clauses and which have object noun clauses? How do you know?

   My answer is that I'm staying home.
   Renee answered [that she would not speak before a big crowd.] *Obj (something)*
   verb be — Joe's excuse [is that he is shy.] *be subj. com.*
   Mike said [that he would hook up my computer.] *Obj (something)*
   The fact [is that I can't face him.] *Complement*

2. Name the type of noun clause in each of the following: *subject*, *object*, *extraposed subject*, or *complement*.

   I accept [that you won't ever marry me.] *Obj*
   It is reasonable [that we should save some money.] *Subj extraposed.*
   [That diamonds appreciate in value] is a fact. *Subj*
   The fact [is that we are all dismayed.] *Complement*
   Nicole knew [that the jig was up.] *Obj.*

RELATIVE CLAUSES   *— Function as an adjective*

One other important kind of subordinate clause is the one that behaves like an adjective, in the sense that it helps describe or identify a noun phrase. We know that various types of constituents can perform this function. In (17) we see that this descriptive function can be performed by a simple adjective, an adjective phrase, a prepositional phrase, or a nonfinite verb phrase, respectively.

> (17) He is the architect. Which architect?
>   The <u>famous</u> architect.
>   The <u>extremely competent</u> architect.
>   The architect <u>with the right skills</u>.
>   The architect <u>designing the building</u>.

A whole clause can also perform an adjectival function, and when it does it is called a **relative clause.** You will remember that we first encountered this clause type in Chapter 5, where we discussed pronouns. To review, consider the two sentences in (18).

> (18) He is the architect. The architect designed the building.

English provides us with a way of incorporating the second into the first by creating a relative clause, which describes a noun phrase in the main clause. This noun phrase is known as the *head* of the relative clause. Relative clauses, you will remember, use relative pronouns that replace the repeated noun phrase. The choice of pronoun depends on whether the noun phrase it replaces is human or not, and if it is human, whether it is a subject, an object, or a possessive within the relative clause. By those criteria, each of the following will require a different relative pronoun.

> (19) He is the architect.   The architect designed the building (who)
>   The firm hired the architect (whom)
>   The architect's brother was hired by the firm (whose)
>
>   This is the building. The architect designed the building (which)

You will also remember that the relative pronoun *that* can often be used in place of *who, whom,* and *which.* (But see Reflection 12 in Chapter 5 and <u>the next section on restrictive and nonrestrictive clauses</u>.) Finally, when we form relative clauses, we must put the relative pronoun at the beginning of the clause.

Again, a tree diagram is a useful device for describing the structure of a relative clause in visual terms. For example, the architect who designed the building, might be represented as follows:

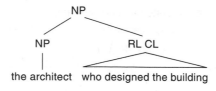

This shows us that the head of the relative clause, *the architect,* and the relative clause *who designed the building* together form a noun phrase.

DISCUSSION EXERCISES 12.8

1. Create sentences with relative clauses by incorporating the second of these clauses into the first. The relative clause always comes directly after its head.

   She forgave the woman. ~~The woman~~ *who* insulted her.
   My uncle is the person. ~~You met the person.~~ *whom you met*
   The child is absent. The child's seat is empty.
   the child whose seat is empty is absent

2. What is the head of the relative clause in each of the following?

   The <u>person</u> who just left is a foreign dignitary.
   Fran identified <u>the thief</u> who stole the computer.
   The <u>lawyer</u> whom you consulted is the best in town.
   <u>Children</u> who have bad colds should not be in school.
   Carl dreamed of <u>a woman</u> who would accept him for himself.

3. Complete the following instructions for making relative clauses:
   1. Replace the repeated noun phrase with ___*relative pronoun*___.
   2. If the replaced noun phrase is a human subject, use the relative pronoun ___*who, whose, whom*___.
   3. If it is a human object, use the relative pronoun ___*whom*___.
   4. If it is a human possessive, use the relative pronoun ___*whose*___.
   5. If it is nonhuman, use the relative pronoun ___*which*___.
   6. You can use the relative pronoun *that* in place of ___*which, who*___.
   7. Make sure the relative pronoun is positioned *after the noun phrase it modifies*.

4. How would you need to revise the above rules to accommodate the following?

   He is the man to whom you were speaking.
   This is the book for which I was waiting.
   This is the scientist with whom she collaborated.

5. What are some less formal ways of expressing the relative clauses illustrated in question 4?

Although most of our examples so far suggest that relative clauses typically occur at the end of the sentence, they can occur following any noun phrase in the sentence and may interrupt the main clause to do so.

Restrictive Rel. clauses (handwritten, left margin)

(20) The person [who left this note] has a sense of humor.
The animals [that suffered the most] were the bears.
The artist [to whom you are referring] lives in New Mexico.

And, as you have probably figured out, relative clauses can nest inside other clauses, relative or otherwise, as seen in the sentences in (21).

(21) This is the house that the architect whom you hired built.
I know that you hired me because the architect whom you hired quit.

DISCUSSION EXERCISES 12.9

1. Describe the clause structure of the sentences in (21). Draw tree diagrams for the two sentences.

2. Which are relative clauses and which are noun clauses in the following? How do you know?
   We know [that you are sad.] – *noun phrase / object*
   He recognized the man [that you described.] *Relative describes man*
   They found the child [that ran away.] *Relative close · child*
   I find [that too much work makes me irritable.] *noun clause*
   Paul used the coffeemaker [that makes ten cups.] *Rel. mod · coffee maker*

RESTRICTIVE AND NONRESTRICTIVE RELATIVE CLAUSES

One thing we have not acknowledged yet is that there are actually two different kinds of relative clauses. All the examples we have given so far are of one type: they help to identify the head noun phrase. Without the relative clause our listeners would not have enough information to know what the head noun phrase referred to. These relative clauses are called **restrictive relative clauses**, because their job is to restrict the head noun phrase enough so that you can identify it. But now consider the sentences in (22).

(22) We visited Greece, which is a lovely country.
My friend Val, whose brother competed in the Olympics, is a good athlete.
That doctor, whom I called repeatedly, refused to renew my prescription.

In these sentences, the head noun phrase has already been fully identified. The relative clause gives more information about it, but that information is not required for me to know what you're talking about. For example, in the first sentence, I would know which Greece you are talking about even with-

non restrictive (handwritten, bottom left margin)

out the relative clause. You are just telling me, additionally, that it is a lovely country. These relative clauses are called **nonrestrictive relative clauses.** As you can see, nonrestrictive clauses are set off from the rest of the sentence by commas (at least in written American English), while restrictive clauses must not be set off by commas. If we take out a nonrestrictive relative clause, the basic meaning of the sentence remains intact, but if we remove a restrictive relative clause, the meaning changes. You can see this by comparing the two sentences in (23) and imagining what they would be like without their relative clauses.

(23) The person who played Gandhi in that movie is a wonderful actor. — Rest.
      Ben Kingsley, who played Gandhi in that movie, is a wonderful actor. Non Rest.

One other difference between restrictive and nonrestrictive relative clauses is that the relative pronoun *that* can only be used with restrictive clauses. So we could use *that* in the first sentence in (24), but not the second. key

(24) The person that played Gandhi in that movie is a wonderful actor.
      *Ben Kingsley, that played Gandhi in that movie, is a wonderful actor.

It is very important to recognize that most of the time whether a clause is restrictive or not is not purely a matter of grammar; it depends on what you mean to say and what you think your listener already knows. For example, look at the pair of sentences in (25).

(25) The Americans who have a lot of money travel extensively. — some americans Rest.
      The Americans, who have a lot of money, travel extensively. — All Americans Non Rest.

In the first sentence, I am talking only about a certain subset of Americans. But in the second I am talking about all Americans. The relative clause is the same, but I am using it for two different purposes.

DISCUSSION EXERCISES 12.10

1. Consider the following sentence:

   Students who are intellectually curious love this course.

   What would be the change in meaning if the relative clause were nonrestrictive?

2. Is this relative clause more likely to be restrictive or nonrestrictive?

   The Joe Louis Arena [which is in Detroit] hosts many sporting events.

   Under what circumstances could it be interpreted as the other one?

   (continued)

3. Identify all the relative clauses in the following sentences. Set off the ones most naturally interpreted as nonrestrictive with commas.

My sister Mary who lives in Florida is coming to visit.
The girl who had the most points won the contest.
Vancouver which is in British Columbia is a lovely city.
Ulysses S. Grant whom we studied in history class was a general.
All the people to whom you gave tickets can now see the show.
The thing that bothers me most is the humidity.
The child whose mother was late was getting nervous.
My parents who own a hardware store know how to fertilize lawns.
His new computer which he bought last week doesn't work.
The books that are on the shelf are for you.

REDUCED RELATIVE CLAUSES

Relative clauses may be reduced, or shortened, in two different ways. The first is that the relative pronoun may be omitted, provided that it is an object within the relative clause. In the sentences in (26), for example, the relative pronoun is optional.

→object pronoun can be omitted

(26) We visited the museum (which) we read about.
I contacted the lawyer (whom) you recommended.
He cooked the meat (that) we brought.

In each of the above sentences, the relative pronoun stands for an object in the relative clause and can therefore be omitted. Subject relative pronouns cannot ordinarily be omitted, as you can see in (27).

(27) We visited the museum which has the Mona Lisa.
*We visited the museum has the Mona Lisa.

I contacted the lawyer who handled your case.
*I contacted the lawyer handled your case.

He cooked the meat that was in the refrigerator.
*He cooked the meat was in the refrigerator.

DISCUSSION EXERCISES 12.11

1. Which of the following relative clauses can be reduced?

Here is the book which I read last night.
The man whom she married is a good husband.
The person who delivers our mail is late again.

(continued)

The doctor whose patient survived the operation was elated.
The plan that you proposed was accepted by the board.

2. Does this reduction apply equally to restrictive and nonrestrictive clauses? Test it out with the following:

Lora, whom you met in Kentucky, is my cousin.
The Eiffel Tower, which we visited on our European tour, is magnificent.

The other way in which a relative clause can be reduced is by the elimination of the relative pronoun and a following form of the verb *be*. The pairs of sentences in (28) show how this reduction works.

(28) I like the person <u>who is</u> sitting next to you.
  I like the person sitting next to you.

  A man <u>who was</u> leaving the building noticed the fire.
  A man leaving the building noticed the fire.

Because the words eliminated from the clause are often *who is,* this reduction is sometimes called **whiz-deletion.** But the reduction can apply to any relative pronoun followed by any form of *be,* as illustrated in (29).

(29) Omit the words (which are) underlined in red.
  They finally bought the house (that is) on the hill.

DISCUSSION EXERCISES 12.12

1. Does whiz-deletion work for nonrestrictive clauses as well as restrictive? Use the following as a test:

Montreal, which is a large and beautiful city, is located in Quebec.
My friend Alice, who is the first in her family to attend college, is very smart.

2. Which of the following relative clauses can be reduced?

The woman who is rearranging your furniture looks worried.
I studied the documents that you sent to me.
My friend Max, whom you met last summer, just won the Nobel prize.
This is the child who has chicken pox.
I translated the letter that was originally written in German.

3. For the ones in question 2 that cannot be reduced, explain why not.

(continued)

4. Can you find an example of whiz-deletion in the paragraph preceding this exercise set?

5. What additional step must be taken if all that is left after reduction is an adjective, as in the following?

The horse that is brown won the race.

You'll notice that reduction of relative clauses gives us two ways to describe some sentences. If you describe a sentence such as (30) as a reduced relative clause,

(30) They visited the ruins in the ancient city.

then you are implying some comparison to another sentence in which the clause is not reduced: *They visited the ruins which are in the ancient city.* You are also making reference to some mental process that leads from one to the other. But it is also possible to describe the end result of this process. In that case, we would say that *in the ancient city* is a prepositional phrase that serves to modify the noun phrase *the ruins.* We saw the same possibilities for different kinds of description when we talked about ellipsis in clause coordination in Chapter 11. When something is omitted that listeners can restore in order to understand the sentence, we can describe the relationship between the restored and unrestored version, or we can describe the structure of what people actually say. Using both kinds of description gives us a fuller, richer picture of how the language works.

DISCUSSION EXERCISES 12.13

1. Describe each of the following sentences in relation to another more complete sentence to which it is related.

The person sitting next to me is breathing heavily.
The house on the corner is vacant.
A woman rejected by that employer filed a discrimination suit.
The baby, startled by the noise, began to cry.
The startled baby began to cry.

2. Describe each of the sentences in question 1 in terms of its structure as it is said, without reference to mental processes.

So far we have described three different types of sentences that we form by combining clauses in a variety of ways. If the sentence contains only one clause, we say it is a *simple* sentence. If it is made up of at least two clauses linked together by a coordinating conjunction, it is called a *compound* sentence. If it contains at least one subordinate clause, it is a *complex* sentence. But how will we describe a sentence like the following?

(31) The girl that won the spelling bee stood up and the audience cheered.

We know that it is a compound sentence, because it is made up of two compound clauses linked together by *and*. But it is also complex because it contains the subordinate clause *that won the spelling bee*. The term used to describe such sentences is **compound-complex sentence.**

DISCUSSION EXERCISES 12.14

1. Identify the subordinate clauses in the following sentences:

    The student who was ill came to class because she knew that the assignment was due.

    One person who was waiting noticed that the doctor that was on duty expected patients to pay their bills before she examined them.

    It amazed Alice that the puppy which she just adopted had already learned that she would feed him before she prepared her own dinner if he wagged his tail.

2. Which of the following sentences are compound and which are complex?

    I knew the answers but I froze on the exam.

    Everyone laughed when they came on stage.

    The boys who collected the most money were praised by the principal.

    The salad is wilted and the bread is cold.

    Although it was still early, Vickie felt that she should leave.

    That she became a doctor reflects well on her family.

    The nurse said that the patient who had malaria recovered.

    The concert was long over, yet the crowds remained.

    Either you should use the gift or you should return it.

    Until she pays her dues she should not expect that the union will support her.

3. Which of these sentences are complex and which are compound-complex?

    We agreed that you would fix the faucet.

    Karan knew the words to the song, but she forgot them when she started to sing.

(continued)

Tom did not file a tax return nor did he alert the IRS that he was leaving the state.

The weather that we encountered was rainy, yet we had a lovely vacation.

The man who took the job never learned that he was considered temporary help.

4. Tell whether each of the following sentences is simple, compound, complex, or compound-complex. Draw tree diagrams if they help you to visualize the structures.

Cheryl found the jacket that she had lost before she moved to Florida.

Neither will she accept responsibility nor will she recognize that we are displeased.

The long, winding road to the top of the hill provides a beautiful view of the valley.

Algebra is interesting but geometry is more challenging.

Whenever she sees her mentor they have a discussion that lasts until midnight.

Everyone loves clowns but mimes are not universally appealing.

I left my job, for I always knew that I could do something more interesting.

The reason that I'm late is that my alarm didn't go off so I overslept.

The weary traveller regaled us with tales of far away lands and unfamiliar cultures.

Expect the worst so that you will not be disappointed.

Combining clauses by coordination and subordination gives us infinite variety in the kinds of sentences we can construct. Even everyday conversation exhibits an amazing amount of complexity and linguistic virtuosity on the part of speakers and listeners alike.

We have now completed our study of English grammar. At this point you should be able to describe any English sentence, from its highest level of organization to its lowest. You can determine how the clauses are arranged and what roles they play within the sentence. You can identify the constituents within each clause and describe the relationships they bear to one another, and you can identify the individual parts of speech that are the building blocks of sentences. You are also in a position to recognize many of the differences between standard English and its various nonstandard varieties and to understand the array of factors that lead people to use nonstandard grammar in their own usage. In the following concluding remarks, we will reflect on some of the ways in which your new-found knowledge can be put to use in your everyday life.

REFLECTIONS

1. There is still some controversy over the use of the words *like* and *as*. *Like*, traditionally, is a preposition, and *as* is a subordinating conjunction. Why do you think many people were upset years ago over the advertising slogan "Winston tastes good like a cigarette should"?

2. There is another kind of noun clause that we did not discuss in this chapter, sometimes called a *relative nominal*. Examples appear underlined:

> Whoever did this good deed should be praised.

> I'll accept whatever you offer me.

> He'll go with whoever invites him.

Why do you think the last sentence uses *whoever* rather than *whomever*, even though the preceding word is a preposition? To help your explanation, consider the following sentence, which does require *whomever*:

> He'll go with whomever he invites.

3. A common complaint among grammatical purists is the following sentence type:

> The reason I am tired is because I worked late last night.

What do you think is the basis for the complaint? What would make this sentence strictly grammatical?

4. A common definition of an independent clause is "a clause that can stand alone." Can you show why this definition does not work well for sentences that contain noun clauses?

5. Can you explain the ambiguity of the following sentence?

> The philosophical Greeks valued learning.

6. The following sentence contains a relative clause reduced by whiz-deletion:

> The man tossed the ball tossed the ball.

What makes it so odd?

7. In *if . . . then* sentences like the ones that follow, which clause do you think is the subordinate one? Why? What kind of subordinate clause is it?

> If you were in my shoes, then you would do the same thing.

> If she follows my instructions, then she will get there.

8. A character in Wally Lamb's *I Know This Much is True* (HarperCollins: New York 1998) p. 382 asks, " 'You got a brother works on this work crew too? Right?' " What is nonstandard about his rule for reducing relative clauses?

9. Here are some additional examples of sentences with extraposed subject noun clauses:

> It appears that you haven't taken my advice.

> It seems that the conflict has escalated.

What would these sentences be if the subject noun clauses were not extra-posed? How are *appear* and *seem* different from other verbs?

10. What makes the following sentence ambiguous?

The teacher is making us memorize *Hamlet,* which is a tragedy.

11. Sally's homeowner's insurance policy states the following:

"All major improvements, which require permits, must be reported to the insurance company." Sally installs a fence but does not need a permit to do this. Do you think she needs to report it to her insurance company?

12. Find one piece of writing in which simple and compound sentences dominate the prose. Find another in which complex and compound-complex sentences dominate. What is your sense of the comparative difficulty of the two pieces?

13. What is the clause structure of the third sentence in Discussion Exercise 12.14, question 1, repeated here for convenience?

It amazed Alice that the puppy which she just adopted had already learned that she would feed him before she prepared her own dinner if he wagged his tail.

Read this sentence just once to someone and see if he or she (they!) can answer the following questions:

What amazed Alice?

Which puppy am I talking about?

What had the puppy learned?

Under what condition would Alice feed him?

When would she feed him?

Would it surprise you to learn that people can understand sentences like these fairly quickly and easily?

14. How many clauses are in the sentence *Politicians who trust people who buy them presents are foolish?* Create another sentence in which this sentence is the direct object of the verb *believe*. How many times can we repeat this embedding process? How would you respond if someone asked you how many sentences there are in the English language?

15. Sentences like the following are not considered compound even though they contain a compound clause.

We knew that Len would succeed and Glen would fail.

Why do you think they are not considered compound?

PRACTICE EXERCISES FOR CHAPTER 12 (Answers on p. 236)

1. Which of the following clauses are combined by coordination and which by subordination?
    1. Jerry lost his wallet, but he had some spare change in his pocket.
    2. Michelle bought things on sale, for she was a thrifty woman.
    3. We stayed overnight, since we missed the last train.
    4. Neither could she sleep nor could she eat.
    5. Judy worked hard although she expected no reward.
    6. Park your car somewhere else or you will get a ticket.
    7. Bill was happy because he won the prize.
    8. We missed the train, so we booked a hotel.
    9. The dogs sleep in the barn and the cats sleep in my bed.
    10. I'll sign the contract if you delete the first paragraph.

2. Tell whether the underlined word is a coordinating conjunction, a subordinating conjunction, a sentence adverb, or a preposition.
    1. Jill stopped <u>before</u> she got to the corner.
    2. My uncle played the guitar, <u>but</u> he hated the banjo.
    3. Read this book <u>and</u> you'll see what I mean.
    4. Politicians can't all be trusted; <u>however</u>, we must rely on them.
    5. Let's have a drink <u>after</u> the meeting.
    6. They danced <u>until</u> they fell to the ground.
    7. She was very intelligent; <u>moreover</u>, she had good judgment.
    8. The children were excited, <u>yet</u> they were reluctant to participate.
    9. He's sad <u>because</u> his dog ran away.
    10. I stayed up <u>until</u> dawn.

3. Identify the noun clause in each of the following sentences. Tell whether it is a subject noun clause, an object noun clause, or an extraposed subject noun clause.
    1. It amuses me that you like doing housework.
    2. For Karen to quit now would be foolish.
    3. That she loves her children is apparent.
    4. Betty knew that I was busy.
    5. It would not make sense for your associate to redo your work.
    6. My brother likes his friends to entertain him.
    7. It seems clear that the plan is unworkable.
    8. We regret that we can't see you more often.
    9. The heat caused the animals to sleep a lot.
    10. It is fitting that she receive the award.

(continued)

4. Which of the following sentences contain noun clauses and which contain adverbial clauses?
   1. The apartment is clean although it isn't elegant.
   2. Liz accepted that she would never be a great opera singer.
   3. For the crew to set sail tomorrow would be smart.
   4. I'll participate provided that you listen to me.
   5. The conductor knew that the train would be delayed.
   6. We waited until the sun had set.
   7. It would be wise for the children to remain in school.
   8. Deb expected that the foundation would collapse.
   9. The trash spilled because you forgot to seal the bag.
   10. The interviewer will hire him if he makes a good impression.

5. Which sentences contain object noun clauses and which contain complement noun clauses?
   1. Ted knew that Irene would pack a lunch.
   2. The plan is that we will meet in New York.
   3. My reason for being late is that my alarm didn't go off.
   4. All teachers expect that students will learn.
   5. His biggest fear is that no one will show up.
   6. The president claimed that he would attend the reception.
   7. Our expectation is that the paint will peel before long.
   8. The sad part is that they used to be good friends.
   9. Her sister found that the house had been destroyed.
   10. The students decided that they would prefer a take-home exam.

6. Identify the relative clauses in the following sentences. What is the head of each relative clause?
   1. I went to the branch library that is located in my neighborhood.
   2. The person to whom you were speaking is a sailor.
   3. The doctor whose patients complained was fired.
   4. The painting that I mentioned is not for sale.
   5. I need to consult with someone who understands my problem.
   6. The baby that is crying needs to be fed.
   7. One example that I gave you is wrong.
   8. They identified the man whom she had accused.
   9. This is the zoo which houses the pandas from China.
   10. We met the couple who adopted the twins.

7. Identify the subordinate clause in each of the following sentences and tell what kind it is.
   1. Since you're already here, I don't need to call you.
   2. Chuck wanted Bill to play soccer.

(continued)

3. It is imperative that you refrain from smoking.
4. The annoying thing is that I can't go home until spring.
5. That she admires you is obvious.
6. Carolyn said that she would support our decision.
7. Call me if you have the time.
8. The stranger who accosted you is now in jail.
9. That is the story that my grandparents told me.
10. For Chris to lie about her age would be silly.

8. Which of the following restrictive relative clauses could also be nonrestrictive? How would the meaning of the sentence change?
    1. My cousin who lives in Denver is coming to visit me.
    2. The boy that threw the stone apologized.
    3. The young man who sat in the front row never smiled.
    4. He spoke to his friend who raises sheep in Australia.
    5. Toby fed the cat which he found in his barn.

9. Which of the following relative clauses can be reduced by whiz-deletion? Which by omitting the object relative pronoun? Which cannot be reduced at all? Why?
    1. Nancy, who is a very good dancer, just opened a studio.
    2. She disapproved of the man whom her daughter married.
    3. My aunt Charlotte, whom you've met, turns ninety this month.
    4. Is he the actor who is starring in your new movie?
    5. Mr. Jenkins, who was seated next to me, began to snore.
    6. Every child that plays this game loves it.
    7. The trees that are marked with red dots will be cut down.
    8. The spider, which was caught in its own web, began to struggle.
    9. Can I borrow the necklace that you wore last night?
    10. This quilt, which she made by hand, is beautiful.

10. Reduce the following relative clauses and describe the structure that remains after reduction.
    1. The boy who was standing on the corner laughed at me.
    2. A woman who was insulted by the remark left the room.
    3. The shelters which were in the park were torn down.
    4. The nervous man, who was expecting a call, paced the room.
    5. The hat which is made of straw is my favorite.

11. Place brackets around the subordinate clauses in each of the following sentences. Which have subordinate clauses nesting inside other subordinate clauses?
    1. That you never smile suggests that you are sad.
    2. The sweater which the clerk showed me had a tear in it.

(continued)

3. People who are rich often do not appreciate the problems of those who are poor.

4. The boy whose mother died said that he wanted to live with his uncle.

5. The rules had been established before they arrived.

6. I consulted the lawyer whom you recommended because I knew that she would give me sound advice.

7. When you get to town, I suggest that you visit the library that was just built.

8. The girl that laughed when you entered the room didn't realize that you were upset.

9. It is necessary for Bob to understand that we meant no harm.

10. My relatives will shop wherever they can find the best bargains.

12. Which of the following sentences are *compound* and which are *complex?*

1. The gift that you bought me for my birthday is beautiful.

2. She knows that you left because you were tired.

3. We sometimes like to ski in winter, but we prefer to keep warm.

4. Either he will call or he will write.

5. That you drive so fast worries me, because I love you.

6. Judy expected Tom to show up for rehearsal.

7. Pat thinks that grammar is easy and algebra is difficult.

8. Call your mother and tell her the news.

9. It is unlikely that you will get special treatment.

10. You may not have a cookie nor may you eat potato chips.

13. Label each of the following sentences as *simple, compound, complex,* or *compound-complex.*

1. Everyone in my family appreciated your kind hospitality last night.

2. It bothers us that we can't earn more money at this job.

3. Although it rained, we all had a good time at the picnic you planned.

4. My cousin Sue, who is also my best friend, stayed until everyone left.

5. The cup broke when the cat landed on the table, but I was able to fix it.

6. His excessive frankness will get him in trouble with his coworkers.

7. Lend me fifty dollars and I'll never ask for another loan.

8. Her instincts told her that she should get up and leave.

9. I need a rest, so I will spend a week in the mountains.

10. Since you're free and since you'll be around anyway, I'm inviting you to my party.

14. Find an example of each if the following in the *Believers* selection that follows.

a compound sentence

a compound-complex sentence

(continued)

a complex sentence

a relative clause

whiz-deletion

a simple sentence

an adverbial clause

noun negation

a subject complement

an inverted indirect object

a present perfect tense

an ellipted direct object

Saul can hardly stand to look at Gordy and Bob. There are no windows in the room where he teaches them, and no fan, and after half an hour of everyone's mingled breathing, the air in the room is foul enough to kill a canary.

Yesterday Saul gave the kids pictures clipped from magazines. They were supposed to write a one-sentence story to accompany each picture. For these ninth-graders, the task is a challenge. Now, before school starts, his mind still on Patsy and Mary Esther, Saul begins to read yesterday's sentences. Gordy and Bob have as usual not written anything: Gordy tore his picture to bits, and Bob shredded and ate his.

(Baxter: "Saul and Patsy are in Labor," p. 104.)

15. Identify the violations of formal standard English in the following letter:

Dear Chris,

I am glad you finally answered my last letter. But don't you see that your interest in grammatical rules are silly? We could of had a wonderful relationship. There's lots of reasons why we should stay together. I talked to my sister about you and I, and she thinks that we was meant for one another. Neither you nor I are to blame for our differences. People can help theirselves overcome obstacles if they want to. You are the one I want to spend my life with. We can do it if we want it bad enough. I feel terribly about losing you. I know you are more interested in grammer than me, but we can work it out. I can learn to use correct grammer. I will probably have less friends as a result, however, being with you, friends won't matter as much. I am your best friend, aren't I? You still have the chance to think of me as the one whom will be at your side forever.

Sadly,
Pat

THIRTEEN

WHY STUDY ENGLISH GRAMMAR? (ONCE MORE!)

At the end of an intensive study such as this one, it is a worthwhile exercise to reflect on what you have learned and on what use you think this knowledge will be to you. If you were hoping for definitive answers about grammatical correctness, you might be somewhat disappointed and feel ill at ease about what to tell your students or children about usage in English. That is a reasonable concern of anyone who assumes responsibility for bearing the standard of acceptable language use. By way of comfort, you should remember that most judgments about grammatical correctness in English are universal: you don't have to wonder about *I ain't got none* or *Him and me is friends.* Where there is indeterminacy, it is almost always a bi-product of language change or some unresolved awkwardness in the current system. There is no legitimate approach to the study of English that can ignore that fact, so questions about acceptable past tenses and past participles (*dreamed* or *dreamt?*), or the use of certain pronouns (*smarter than me* or *smarter than I?*), for example, can never be answered in the absence of a larger discussion about how English evolves. Arbitrary judgments about correctness shut down discussion and have the potential to generate anxiety and resentment. On the other hand, recognition of change and fluctuation opens up a conversation and invites all users of the language to participate. That doesn't mean that anything goes and there are no standards; we all know there are. It does mean that sometimes they are negotiable and sometimes they change. Keep in mind how educated users of English struggle to come to terms with the absence of a gender-neutral singular human pronoun, for example.

Ultimately, it is up to the individual to assess the usefulness and importance of what he or she (they!) learns. Such assessment necessarily occurs in stages and lasts a lifetime, with only some inklings at the end of a course, so you may not know at this point how useful it is to you. But here are some things this author hopes might happen to you down the line as a result of your having studied English grammar:

- When you hear people use nonstandard English, your first reaction will be to wonder what part of the grammar they are attempting to regularize or what gap in standard English they are trying to fill.
- When you observe people speaking English as a second language you will wonder how the grammar of their first language is influencing the English they produce.
- When you encounter a language other than English, you will marvel at how people can achieve the same communicative goals in such radically different ways.
- When you observe deaf people communicating with one another, you will marvel even more that all the complexities of oral language can be expressed using hand-movements and body gestures.
- When you read a grammar letter in Ann Landers' column, you might be inspired to respond to it.
- When a grammar question arises, you might be inspired to initiate a discussion, perhaps in *The Atlantic Monthly*, perhaps online.
- When an over-inflated ego hypercorrects, you will silently gloat.
- When you travel to places where the English is different from the English you speak, you will be curious about those differences.
- When you read the literature of earlier times, you will think in terms of patterns of change in English.
- When you drive past a billboard that advertises a "totally nude gentlemen's club," you will laugh your head off at the ambiguity.
- You will be filled with awe when a little child you love utters his first relative clause, apparently out of the blue.

And remember the words of the wise person who said, "When you go forth to seek your fame and fortune, it's not who you know that counts, it's whom."

Answers to Practice Exercises

Note: Answers are provided only for *odd-numbered* items within each question set, except for the last two sets in each chapter. For these *all* answers are provided. Some questions may have more than one possible answer; for these, only one of the answers is given.

CHAPTER 3

1.
1. calcium, element, bones
3. worker, factory, dissatisfaction, colleagues
5. animal, Minnesota, gopher; state is a noun functioning as an adjective

2.
1. *wind*-count; *hole*-count, *tent*-count
3. *mother*-count, *wine*-noncount, *meals*-count
5. *babysitter*-count, *baby*-count, *milk*-noncount, *cereal*-noncount

3.
1. *both my older sisters*
   pre det   head
3. *what an exciting event*
   pre det   head
5. *three boats*
   det head
7. *such a shame*
   pre det head

4.
1. *my:* possessive pronoun
3. *an:* indefinite article
5. *three:* quantity
7. *a:* indefinite article

5.
1. *the weekend:* subject
   my favorite part of the week: subject complement
   the week: object of a preposition

3. *Bob:* subject
   the doctor: direct object
   the answer to his prayers: object complement
   his prayers: object of a preposition

5. *the cashier:* the subject
   the receipt: direct object
   the woman in the fur coat: indirect object
   the fur coat: object of a preposition

6. 1. subject: *the child*
       direct object: *a present*
       indirect object: *her mother*
       object of a preposition: *Mother's Day*

7. All have indirect objects. 1 and 5 are inverted.

8. 1. *Mr. Allen taught the boy   geometry.*
       subject   indirect object   direct object
       2. *Mr. Allen considered the boy   an idiot.*
       subject   direct object   object complement

9. 1. *Winning a race:* gerundive subject
       3. *to hike in the woods:* infinitival direct object
       5. *not trying:* gerundive object of a preposition
       7. *all this whining:* gerundive direct object
       9. *waiting for the results:* gerundive subject complement

10. *The young woman's* is inside *The young woman's father*
        at the foot of the hill is inside *the farm at the foot of the hill*
        the foot of the hill is inside *at the foot of the hill*
        of the hill is inside *the foot of the hill*
        the hill is inside *of the hill*

11. compound subject: Barry and all his relatives showed up for dinner.
        compound direct object: I found a cat and the dead goldfish.
        compound indirect object: I gave my two best friends and both
          screaming monkeys a round of applause.

12. Is *my husband and lover* a compound noun or a compound noun
        phrase with a determiner omitted?

13. subject complement: the first thing she liked about him
        object of a preposition: the alley
        compound noun phrase: both the dog and the man
        noun phrase with indefinite article: an upstairs sleeping porch
        noun phrase with demonstrative determiner: these two

14. word's; less bags; them customs official's (two violations); a umbrella;
        a overcoat; a common phenomena; my travel agent, he. . . ;
        umbrella's; you coming with us

CHAPTER 4

1.   1. *to ask:* infinitive
     3. *considered:* past participle
     5. *having:* present participle
       been: past participle
       informed: past participle
     7. *to be:* infinitive
       like: infinitive
     9. *sitting:* present participle
       see: infinitive
       parked: past participle (used as an adjective)

2.   1. gerund
     3. present participle
     5. gerund—gerund
     7. gerund
     9. present participle

3.   N = nonstandard, S = standard
     1. N
     3. N
     5. S
     7. N
     9. S

4.   1. *can:* helping, modal
       leave: main

     3. *is:* helping, auxiliary
       running: main

     5. *have:* helping, auxiliary
       been: helping, auxiliary
       expecting: main

     7. *has:* helping, auxiliary
       had: main

     9. *must:* helping, modal
       stop: main

5.

simple present:	Mary goes home
simple past:	Mary went home
simple future:	Mary will go home
present progressive:	Mary is going home
past progressive:	Mary was going home
future progressive:	Mary will be going home
present perfect:	Mary has gone home
past perfect:	Mary had gone home

future perfect:	Mary will have gone home
present perfect progressive:	Mary has been going home
past perfect progressive:	Mary had been going home
future perfect progressive:	Mary will have been going home

6. 1. simple past
   3. simple present
   5. past perfect
   7. past progressive
   9. future perfect

7. 1. *flew:* intransitive
   3. *seemed:* linking
   5. *felt:* linking
   7. *saw:* transitive
   9. *landed:* intransitive

8. 3 is the only odd-numbered sentence with a dangling participle.

9. Of the odd-numbered sentences, 3, 7, and 9 are violations of subject-verb agreement.

10. For example:
   1. You may help yourself to a cookie.
   3. She felt the tension in the room.
   5. He must be there by now.
   7. They looked furious.
   9. I tasted the stew.

11. infinitive: to ponder
   be as linking: was (dimly visible)
   past perfect: had committed
   compound verb phrase: had created the wrong tone or put some element into the air. . . .
   direct object noun phrase: a terrible social blunder. . . .
   compound noun phrase: depth or extension
   simple past: drifted
   object of a preposition: an invisible black fabric
   modal verb: would
   past participle: created
   subject noun phrase: my Mickle Street story
   present participle: swirling

12. Having been to Paris before, . . . ; photo's; seen; went; less photos; have been there; variety . . . are

CHAPTER 5

1. 1. his/Max's, it/his book
   3. her/Alice

    5. my/speaker
    7. she/Sally, him/Joe
    9. he/my uncle, my/speaker, me/speaker

2.   1. I
      3. your
      5. him
      7. you
      9. our

3.   1. mine
      3. theirs
      5. hers

4.   N = nonstandard, S = standard
      1. S
      3. N
      5. N
      7. S
      9. N

5.   1. ourselves
      3. themselves
      5. myself

6.   1. subject and object refer to same entity
      3. alone
      5. subject and object refer to same entity

7.   1. who
      3. whom
      5. whom
      7. who

8.   1. what
      3. which
      5. whose

9.   1. universal
      3. relative
      5. indefinite
      7. indefinite
      9. relative

10.   1. *somebody:* indefinite human subject
       me: personal first person singular direct object

3. *whose:* interrogative human possessive subject complement
   this: singular demonstrative subject

5. *she:* personal third person singular feminine subject
   that: relative direct object
   they: personal third person plural subject

11.   subject pronoun: he
       possessive pronoun: his
       relative pronoun: that (caught)
       omitted relative pronoun: willow__he hadn't seen
       pronoun before antecedent: he . . . Father Pielke
       intransitive verb: stepped
       compound noun phrase: his temporary disorientation and his limp
       past perfect tense: hadn't seen
       simple past: emerged
       object of a preposition: the wood

12.   My uncle, he. . . ; than us; and I; whom; and myself; me and my
       father; you guys; mind; less complications; began; guidebook's;
       having waited so long; came

CHAPTER 6

1.   1. spectacular: more spectacular, most spectacular
         rigid: more rigid, most rigid
         mossy: mossier, mossiest
         verifiable: nongradable
         bland: blander, blandest

2.   illiterate, unacceptable, unfortunate, irreversible, immobile,
      dysfunctional, disconnected, impolite, indistinct

3.   1. *only:* nongradable, attributive
         depressed: gradable, predicate
         favorite: nongradable, attributive
      3. *incredible:* gradable, attributive
         stable: gradable, predicate
      5. *sour:* gradable, predicate
      7. *circular, square, rectangular:* nongradable, predicate
      9. *thoughtful:* gradable, attributive
         happy: gradable, predicate

4.   1. *very nervous:* subject complement
      3. *extremely lazy:* object complement
      5. *big colorful leafy:* attributive
      7. *highly impertinent:* object complement
      9. *very generous:* attributive
         overly needy: attributive

5.   1. *responsibly* /verb
    3. *extremely*/ adjective
    5. *yesterday*/ verb; *quite*/ adverb; *well*/ verb
    7. *so*/ adverb; *patiently*/ verb
    9. *happily*/ verb

6.   1. good
    3. bad (badly if feel is an action verb)
    5. well
    7. well (good if he did good things)
    9. soft

7.   1. quite impudently
    3. very easily
    5. better than her brother
    7. as civilly as I could
    9. as quickly as possible

8.   If the relatives are visiting, *visiting* is an adjective.
    If you are visiting the relatives, *visiting* is a gerund.

9.   adverb of manner: painfully
    intensifier: so (straight)
    attributive adjective: unusual
    noun used as an adjective: medicine
    adjective phrase: rather long
    subject complement: cleanshaven
    sentence adverb: instead
    personal pronoun: she
    possessive pronoun: his (face)
    linking verb: wasn't
    object of a preposition: a ruler
    intransitive verb: sat
    demonstrative determiner: this (distance)

10.   real; (could) of; badly; me and you; most favorite; very unique; best (of the two); (pretty) good; (if I) was; photo's; hopefully; memory's

CHAPTER 7

1.   1. the springtime
    3. you and me
    5. hook, crook
    7. my birthday
    9. class

2.   1. with the flea collar: adjectival

3. in the red helmet: adjectival
5. under the tree: adjectival
7. into the board: adverbial
9. before the judge: adverbial

3.   Meaning 1: He found the speeding motorist by means of an electronic sensor. The prepositional phrase is adverbial.

Meaning 2: He found the speeding motorist who had an electronic sensor. The prepositional phrase is adjectival.

4.   into a pipe; under the house; around the corner

on one reading: [into a pipe [under the house [around the corner]]]

5.   1. For whom are you looking?
3. Is this the pot in which I am supposed to cook it?
5. For which actor are you standing in?
7. Is this the channel on which the news is broadcast?
9. This is the hill down which we rolled as children.

6.   1. She turned the ignition off.
3. The teacher brought the books in.
5. Lois put her new dress on.
7. The children turned their parents in to the police.
9. They turned our offer down.

7.   1. particle
3. preposition
5. particle
7. preposition
9. preposition

8.   Among the odd-numbered sentences, 7 and 9 require particle movement because the direct object is a pronoun.

9.   1. adverb
3. preposition
5. adverb
7. particle
9. adverb

10.   a particle: up
a preposition: of (the park)
prepositional phrase: of the park
object of a preposition: the park
sentence adverb: however
noun used as an adjective: night (shot)
intensifier: terribly (blurred)
adjective complement: (delighted) to see that. . . .
subject complement: good enough to frame

11.   seen; who were you buying it for (two violations); my family and I; each . . . have; either . . . are; more than me; drivers; real horrible (two violations); you and me; where you want to drive to

CHAPTER 8

1.   1. Our house was sold by the realty company.

3. Great sensitivity is required by this job.

5. A new chancellor is being hired by a consulting firm.

7. A book was left at the circulation desk by the librarian.

9. A week's worth of groceries was purchased by the family with your gift.

2.   Of the odd-numbered sentences, 1 and 9 are candidates. Others are possible with some change in meaning.

3.   1. *the teller:* subject

the customer: indirect object

a roll of bills: direct object

3. *the stagecoach:* subject

the bandits: object of a preposition

5. *the customer:* subject

a roll of bills: direct object

the teller: object of a preposition

7. *your party:* subject

the fountain: object of a preposition

9. *the suspect:* subject

his rights: object of a preposition

the police: object of a preposition

4.   The nervous patient was given a clean bill of health by the doctor.

5.   1. The passive voice should be avoided.

3. You are expected to dress appropriately.

5. The trash is picked up on Tuesdays.

7. The Yankees were defeated.

9. A warrant was obtained to search the house. (or A warrant to search the house was obtained.)

6.   The doers can be inferred from the rest of the sentence.

7.   1. Lunch should be eaten by employees in the cafeteria.

3. Her cries for help were ignored by everyone.

5. The bell was rung one last time by the bellringer.

7. The rules of the competition were rarely understood by the participants.

9. Her gardens were planted in May by her gardener.

8.   the child: subject

the magician: object of a preposition

a handful of coins: direct object

coins: object of a preposition

9.   The magician gave the child a handful of coins.

    the child: indirect object (inverted)
    the magician: subject
    a handful of coins: direct object
    coins: object of a preposition

10.   Of the odd-numbered sentences, 1 and 5 are ambiguous. Each can be analyzed as a linking verb + adjective or as a truncated passive.

11.   truncated passive clauses:
    it was arranged; intermediaries were empowered. . . ; bishops and archbishops and cardinals were no doubt enlisted. . . .
    infinitival phrase as direct object: to let me look in those records
    compound determiner: each and every
    object of a preposition: the archdiocese
    present perfect tense: haven't gone
    interrogative pronoun: whom
    indefinite pronoun: anyone
    adverb: now

12.   run; fluent; pronounciation; you and I; real good (two violations); neither . . . were; badly; choice . . . were; couldn't order nothing; less mistakes; what are friends for?

CHAPTER 9

1.   1. exclamative (!)
    3. imperative (!)
    5. imperative (.)
    7. interrogative (?)
    9. declarative (.)

2.   1. Do we need to rotate the tires?
    3. Can you give me an estimate on the costs?
    5. Did the laborers rest after lunch?
    7. Must we observe the rules?
    9. Did I spell the word wrong?

3.   1. Whose book did you borrow?
    3. What can they do for me?
    5. For whom was she asking?
    7. Which did she order?
    9. With whom do you wish to speak?

4.   Of the odd-numbered sentences, 1, 7, and 9 require the insertion of *do*. The others have helping verbs.

5.   1. didn't it?
    3. can we?

    5. didn't they?

    7. haven't they?

    9. hasn't he?

6.   Of the odd-numbered sentences, 1 and 5 require insertion of *do* because the statements contain no helping verbs.

7.   1. *barely* is only partially negative so it is unclear how to reverse it

    3. *someone:* has indeterminate gender

    5. *hardly* is only partially negative (same as #1)

8.   1. yes-no echo

    3. wh

    5. wh

    7. yes-no

    9. declarative with the force of a question

9.   1. What a wonderful parent Al is!

    3. How my heart aches for you!

    5. How bitterly she complained!

    7. How he boasts about his children!

    9. How proud Kara and Jan were of her!

   11. What a tiresome discussion this is!

10.   For example . . .

    1. The dog needs to be walked; Can you take the dog for a walk?

    3. I want you to talk to me about your concerns; Won't you talk to me about your concerns?

    5. I suggest that you clean up this mess; I wonder if you might clean up this mess.

    7. You ought to rethink your demands; Might you rethink your demands?

    9. You might consider your alternatives; Won't you consider your alternatives?

11.   full passive: is being replaced even now by one of. . . .

    truncated passive: the frames have been knocked over

    compound past participle: knocked over, scattered, and kicked

    wh-question: How come they didn't attack him?

    yes-no question: Did they sting him?

    rhetorical question: Who knows?

    adverb of manner: tightly

    transitive verb: holds

    intransitive verb: rises

    compound infinitive: to cry and wail

    reflexive pronoun: itself

    present perfect tense: They've left.

12.   I wonder did you get . . . ; my mother, she . . . ; we was; her and I; been looking; most perfect; than me; don't Alaska; there's glaciers; anxious (some still think it is different from "eager"); aren't I?; suppose; will you consider it.

CHAPTER 10

1.   1. You shouldn't speak ill of the dead.

   3. —

   5. We weren't expecting you.

   7. We shan't be daunted.

   9. He won't be allowed to perform.

   Exceptions: *Mayn't* isn't used. *Won't* is an irregular form for *will not.*
   Shan't is rarely, if ever, used in American English.

2.   Of the odd-numbered sentences, 5 and 7 require *do* because they
   contain no helping verb.

3.   1. The printer has no ink; the printer does not have any ink.

   3. I have no idea; I do not have any idea.

   5. He got no love from his grandparents; he didn't get any love from his
   grandparents.

4.   N = nonstandard, S = standard

   1. N

   3. S

   5. N

   7. N

   9. S

5.   1. I see no people.

   3. She will accept no cash.

   5. Why were there no police at the event?

6.   unhappily, indecent, disproportionately, inadvisable, impolitely,
   irrelevant, illiterate, unsavory, nontoxic, unremarkably

7.   1. We are neither proud nor arrogant; neither are we proud, nor are we
   arrogant.

   3. She spoke neither clearly nor accurately; neither did she speak
   clearly, nor did she speak accurately.

   5. Neither smoking nor drinking is good for you; neither is smoking
   good for you, nor is drinking good for you.

8.   For example . . .

   1. I seldom go to the movies during the week.
   Seldom do I go to the movies during the week.

   3. We barely arrived on time.
   Barely did we arrive on time.

   5. He barely remembers their meeting.
   Barely does he remember their meeting.

   7. There is hardly enough time for this exam.
   Hardly is there enough time for this exam (??)

   9. The beams barely held up the roof.
   Barely did the beams hold up the roof.

9.   1. The food isn't edible; the food is inedible.
      3. Our approach isn't confrontational; our approach is nonconfrontational.
      5. These reviews aren't spectacular; these reviews are unspectacular.
      7. I'll never read it; I will not read it anytime.
      9. No car can travel this road; a car can't travel this road.

10.   1. active, affirmative, interrogative
      3. passive, negative, declarative
      5. active, affirmative, interrogative
      7. active, affirmative, imperative
      9. active, negative, declarative

11.   verb negation with *do:* I don't always enjoy. . . .
      verb negation with modal: shouldn't have to explain
      uncontracted verb negation: it's not the right moment
      partially negative adverb: hardly
      missing relative pronoun: moments__we share
      infinitival phrase: to pat her hand
      have as a main verb: I had a music box
      prepositional phrase: with me
      subject complement: the right moment for that
      compound noun: horror and amazement

12.   haven't heard nothing; wondering do you . . . ; writting; seen; if I was;
      you was; there's so many . . . ; amount of letters; amount . . . are; less
      letters; her and I; not hold no grudges

CHAPTER 11

1.   1. The sky is cloudy, but it won't rain. CC
      3. My cousins were ill; nevertheless, they visited me. SA
      5. We had a good time. Therefore, we exchanged phone numbers. SA
      7. The elections were over and our party had won. CC
      9. I'm giving you the day off; furthermore, I'm increasing your salary. SA

2.   1. The boy (fished in the pond) and his sister fished in the pond.
      3. Bill bought a house and his brother (bought) a condo.
      5. All children need love and (all children) crave attention.
      7. The customer called the company and (the customer) threatened to sue.
      9. Convertibles are nice in summer and hardtops (are nice) in winter.

3.   I'll see you tomorrow or I'll give you a call.
      He won the lottery, so he quit his job.
      Let's celebrate, for he's a jolly good fellow.
      She seemed irresponsible, yet we knew she would show up.

4.   Neither did he play golf nor did he swim in the pool.

5.   Of the odd-numbered sentences, 1 and 5.

6.

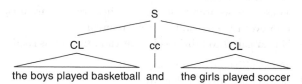

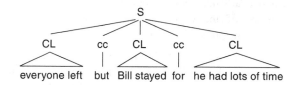

7.   two compound sentences:
   She and Walton . . . , and it was . . .
   She thought he . . . , but he . . . .
   compound noun phrase: the muscles of the vertebrae or the cartilage
   prepositional phrase: from midnight
   deferred preposition: referring to
   sentence adverb: however
   irregular plural: vertebrae
   intensifier: quite
   adverb modifying an adjective: physically
   embedded question: what he was referring to
   past perfect tense: had never seen

8.   my sister and I; however; to be with; you guys'; you and me; ourself;
   ain't no bad feelings (two violations); between you and I; most
   perfect; have did; not having anything specific

CHAPTER 12

1.   1. coordination
       3. subordination
       5. subordination
       7. subordination
       9. coordination

2.   1. subordinating conjunction
       3. coordinating conjunction
       5. preposition

   7. sentence adverb

   9. subordinating conjunction

3. 1. that you like doing housework: object noun clause

   3. that she loves her children: subject noun clause

   5. for your associate to redo your work: extraposed subject noun clause

   7. that the plan is unworkable: extraposed subject noun clause

   9. the animals to sleep a lot: object noun clause

4. 1. adverbial: although. . . .

   3. noun: for the crew. . . .

   5. noun: that the train. . . .

   7. noun: for the children. . . .

   9. adverbial: because. . . .

5. 1. object

   3. complement

   5. complement

   7. complement

   9. object

6. 1. that is located in my neighborhood (the branch library)

   3. whose patients complained (the doctor)

   5. who understands my problem (someone)

   7. that I gave you (one example)

   9. which houses the pandas from China (the zoo)

7. 1. since you're already here: adverbial clause

   3. Bill to play soccer: object noun clause

   5. that she admires you: subject noun clause

   7. if you have the time: adverbial clause

   9. that my grandparents told me: relative clause

8. 1. nonrestrictive if you have only one cousin

   3. nonrestrictive if the young man has already been identified in the conversation

   5. nonrestrictive if the cat has already been identified in the conversation

9. 1. whiz-deletion

   3. no reduction (nonrestrictives cannot omit object relative pronouns)

   5. whiz-deletion

   7. whiz-deletion

   9. omit object relative pronoun

10. 1. The boy standing on the corner laughed at me.

    standing on the corner is a participial phrase, a nonfinite verb phrase

   3. The shelters in the park were torn down.

    in the park is a prepositional phrase

      5. The hat made of straw is my favorite.

      made of straw is a participial phrase, a nonfinite verb phrase

11.   1. [That you never smile] suggests [that you are sad.]

      3. People [who are rich] often do not appreciate the problems of people [who are poor.]

      5. The rules had been established [before they arrived.]

      7. [When you get to town] I suggest [that you visit the library [that was just built.]]

      9. My relatives will shop [wherever they can find the best bargains.]

12.   1. complex

      3. compound

      5. complex

      7. complex (See Reflection 15.)

      9. compound

13.   1. simple

      3. complex

      5. compound-complex

      7. compound

      9. compound

14.   compound sentence: Gordy tore his . . . and Bob shredded. . . .

      compound-complex sentence: There are no windows. . . .

      complex sentence: Now, before school starts. . . .

      relative clause: where he teaches them

      whiz-deletion: (the air) in the room

      simple sentence: Saul can hardly stand. . . .

      adverbial clause: before school starts

      noun negation: no windows

      subject complement: foul enough to kill a canary

      inverted indirect object: the kids

      present perfect tense: have (as usual) not written

      ellipted direct object: shredded ___ and ate his

15.   interest—are; could of; there's lots; reasons why (some object to *where, when,* and *why* used as relative pronouns, but see previous passage); you and I; we was; one another; neither . . . are; theirselves; spend my life with; bad enough; feel terribly; grammer; than me; less friends; however; being with you; aren't I; whom

Glossary

Note: Numbers in parentheses indicate the chapters in which the term is either introduced or discussed.

abstract noun: a subcategory of noun that refers to ideas or concepts (**3**)

active voice: sentence structure that follows the order *doer* + *action* + *receiver* (**8**)

adjective: the lexical category that typically modifies nouns (**2, 6**)

adjective complement: an element following an adjective in an adjective phrase that completes the meaning of the adjective (**6**)

adjective negation: expressing negation by attaching a negative prefix to an adjective (**10**)

adjective phrase: a phrase with an adjective as its head (**6**)

adverb: the lexical category that typically modifies verbs, adjectives, or other adverbs (**2, 6**)

adverb complement: an element following an adverb in an adverb phrase that completes the meaning of the adverb (**6**)

adverb negation: expressing negation by attaching a negative prefix to an adverb (**10**)

adverb phrase: a phrase with an adverb as its head (**6**)

adverbial clause: a subordinate clause that plays the role of an adverb (**12**)

affirmative: describes a positive clause, one which contains no markers for negation (**10**)

affix: a bound morpheme attached to a root (**2**)

ambiguity: more than one interpretation of a grammatical structure (**6**)

animate noun: a subcategory of noun that refers to animals and humans (**3**)

antecedent: the noun phrase that a pronoun stands for (**5**)

article: a type of determiner; see **definite article** and **indefinite article** (**2, 3**)

aspect: a feature added to the time of an action to show its relationship to another time (**4**)

attributive adjective: an adjective within the same noun phrase as the noun it modifies **(6)**

auxiliary verb: a type of helping verb that carries no meaning of its own **(4)**

bare infinitive: the infinitive without *to;* also called the **base form** of the verb **(4)**

base form: see **bare infinitive**

case: the grammatical function of pronouns: subject (or subjective), object (or objective), and possessive **(5)**

category shift: see **conversion**

clause: a combination of a noun phrase (subject) and a finite verb phrase (predicate) **(2, 11)**

collective noun: a noun that is grammatically singular but has plural meaning **(4)**

common noun: a subcategory of noun that refers to general categories **(2, 3)**

comparative: the form of an adjective used to compare two entities **(2, 6)**

complement: a noun phrase or adjective that describes or renames another noun phrase in the same sentence **(3, 6)**

complement noun clause: a noun clause that plays the role of a complement in a clause **(12)**

complementizer: a term sometimes used to refer to a word that introduces a noun clause **(12)**

complex sentence: a sentence containing at least one subordinate clause **(12)**

complex tense: time combined with the perfect or the progressive aspect **(4)**

compound: the constituent that results when two or more like constituents are conjoined **(3)**; also used to refer to words that have more than one root

compound negation: the negation of a compound using *neither . . . nor* **(3, 11)**

compound sentence: a sentence consisting of two or more conjoined clauses **(11)**

compound-complex sentence: a compound sentence that contains at least one subordinate clause **(12)**

compounding: see **conjoining**

concrete noun: a subcategory of noun that refers to tangible or visible entities **(3)**

conjoining: creating a new constituent by joining together two constituents of the same type; also called **coordination** and **compounding** **(3, 11)**

constituent: words in a sequence that group together and function as a grammatical unit **(2)**

conversion: moving an element from one lexical category to another; also called **category shift** **(4)**

coordinating conjunction: a lexical category used to link together like constituents **(3, 11)**

coordination: see **conjoining**

count noun: a subcategory of noun that can be counted directly (3)

correlative: a two-part coordinating conjunction (3, 11)

cross-referencing rule: a grammatical rule that marks a relationship between two constituents (2)

dangling modifier: a nonfinite predicate that cannot be appropriately linked to a noun phrase in the rest of the sentence (4)

dangling participle: a dangling modifier that contains a past or a present participle (4)

declarative: the sentence type typically used to give information (9)

declarative question: see **echo question**

deferred preposition: a preposition that has been left behind when its object has been moved elsewhere in the sentence (7)

definite article: a determiner used to modify an already identified entity (3)

demonstrative: a determiner or pronoun that signals location of an entity with respect to the speaker (3, 5)

dependent clause: see **subordinate clause**

derivational affix: an affix that changes the lexical category or subcategory of a root (2)

determiner: one kind of modifier in a noun phrase (3)

dialect: set of characteristics within a language associated with a community of speakers (1)

direct object: typically the noun phrase that follows the verb and receives the action (3)

discourse function: the communicative purpose of an utterance (9)

disjunction: a coordinating conjunction that signals a choice between (or among) the conjoined elements; also used to describe the conjoined structure itself (3, 11)

echo question: an interrogative that retains the structure of a preceding declarative statement ; also called **declarative question** (9)

ellipsis: omitting repeated material, used in this book specifically to refer to omission in conjoined clauses (11)

embedded question: a question inserted within a main clause (9)

embedded sentence: see **subordinate clause**

exclamative: the sentence type used to express a feeling with added emphasis (9)

extraposed subject noun clause: a noun clause that has been moved to the end of its sentence (12)

finite verb form: a form of the verb that is marked for tense (4)

finite verb phrase: a verb phrase with a finite verb form as head (4)

flat adverb: an adverb that has the same form as its corresponding adjective (6)

full passive: a sentence in the passive voice that includes the doer of the action **(8)**

gender: grammatical marking on a pronoun to match the sex of its antecedent: masculine, feminine, or neuter **(5)**

gerund: a verbal noun formed by adding *-ing* to a verb root **(3)**

gerundive phrase: a noun phrase with a gerund as head **(3)**

gradable adjective: an adjective capable of expressing degrees and comparison **(6)**

head: the main or core word in a phrase; in a phrase containing a relative clause, it is the noun phrase that the clause describes **(2, 5)**

helping verb: a verb that supports a main verb, typically by carrying tense **(4)**

human noun: a subcategory of nouns; refers to human beings **(3)**

hypercorrection: nonstandard language that results when people misapply a grammatical rule in order to avoid a grammatical error **(1)**

imperative: the sentence type typically used to give orders **(9)**

inanimate noun: a subcategory of noun that refers to entities that are neither human nor animal **(3)**

indefinite article: the determiner used to introduce an entity into a discussion **(3)**

indefinite pronoun: a pronoun that refers to unspecified entities or quantities **(5)**

independent clause: see **main clause**

indirect object: typically the animate noun phrase that is the beneficiary of an action **(3)**

infinitival phrase: a noun phrase with an infinitive as head **(3)**

infinitive: the base form of the verb, or the base form preceded by *to* **(3)**

inflectional affix: an affix that conveys grammatical information and does not change the lexical category of the root **(2)**

intensifier: a type of adverb used to modify an adjective or another adverb **(6)**

interrogative: the sentence type typically used to request information **(9)**

interrogative pronoun: a pronoun used to elicit the identity of an unknown noun phrase **(5)**

intransitive verb: a verb that can stand alone in its verb phrase **(4)**

lexical category: a class of words that have similar grammatical functions and forms, also known as a **word class** or a **part of speech** **(2)**

linguistic ambiguity: see **ambiguity**

linking verb: a verb that connects a subject to a description of the subject **(4)**

main clause: the clause that expresses the main idea of the sentence and may contain clauses within it; also called **matrix clause (12)**, **independent clause (2)**, and **superordinate clause (12)**

main verb: the verb of a clause that expresses an action or a mental state (**4**)

mass noun: see **noncount noun**

matrix clause: see **main clause**

modal auxiliary: see **modal verb**

modal verb: a type of helping verb that adds additional meaning to the main verb; also called a **modal auxiliary** (**4**)

modifier: an element in a phrase that describes or limits the head (**2**)

negative: describes a clause that contains a marker for negation (**10**)

noncount noun: a subcategory of noun that cannot be counted directly, also called **mass noun** (**3**)

nonfinite verb form: a form of the verb that carries no tense of its own (**4**)

nonfinite verb phrase: a verb phrase with a nonfinite verb form as head (**4**)

nongradable adjective: an adjective with absolute meaning; has no degrees (**6**)

nonhuman noun: subcategory of nouns; refers to entities that are not human (**3**)

nonrestrictive relative clause: a relative clause that gives added information about an already identified head (**12**)

noun: the lexical category that names entities (**2, 3**)

noun clause: a subordinate clause that plays the role of a noun phrase, as subject, object, or complement (**12**)

noun negation: expressing negation by associating a negative word with a noun (**10**)

noun phrase: a phrase with a noun as its head (**3**)

number: the grammatical marking of quantity; in English the two numbers are singular (one) and plural (more than one) (**3, 4**)

object complement: a noun phrase or predicate adjective that describes the direct object of a sentence (**3, 6**)

object noun clause: a noun clause that plays the role of direct object in a sentence (**12**)

object of a preposition: the noun phrase that follows a preposition in a prepositional phrase (**3, 7**)

objective case: the case of pronouns used as objects (**5**)

part of speech: see **lexical category**

partial negation: effect of using one of the set of partially negative adverbs (**10**)

particle: the second element of a two-part transitive verb that can occur either before or after the direct object (**7**)

particle movement: the grammatical rule that moves a particle behind the direct object (**7**)

passive test: rearranging a sentence from active to passive voice to determine if a noun phrase is a direct object (**3**)

passive voice: sentence structure that follows the order *receiver* + *action* + *doer* **(8)**

past participle: a nonfinite verb form that typically consists of *-ed* or *-en* added to the base form; used in the perfect tenses **(2, 4)**

perfect aspect: a feature added to time to show that the action relates to a later time **(4)**

person: the grammatical feature that refers to the role of the participant in a conversation: speaker (first person), listener (second person), or entity spoken about (third person) **(4)**

personal pronoun: a pronoun that plays the role of subject, object, or possessive **(5)**

phrase: a constituent consisting of a single word (the head of the phrase) and all its modifiers **(2)**

possession: a grammatical marking on nouns and pronouns to indicate ownership and a variety of related concepts **(3)**

possessive case: the case of nouns or pronouns used as possessives **(5)**

possessive noun phrase: a noun phrase in which the head noun is in the possessive case **(3)**

possessive pronoun: a pronoun that expresses ownership; has both a determiner form and a free-standing form **(5)**

postdeterminer: one kind of modifier in a noun phrase **(3)**

predeterminer: one kind of modifier in a noun phrase **(3)**

predicate: the finite verb phrase of a clause **(2, 4)**

predicate adjective: an adjective that is outside the noun phrase of the noun it modifies **(6)**

prefix: an affix that attaches to the beginning of a root **(2)**

preposition: a word that indicates the relationship of a noun phrase to other noun phrases in the same sentence **(2, 7)**

prepositional phrase: a constituent that consists of a preposition followed by a noun phrase **(3, 7)**

present participle: a nonfinite verb form consisting of the base form + *-ing;* used in the progressive tenses **(2, 4)**

progressive aspect: a feature added to time to indicate ongoing or background activity **(4)**

pronoun: a word that typically stands for or takes the place of a noun phrase **(2, 5)**

proper noun: a subcategory of noun that refers to a specific, named entity **(2, 3)**

quantity: one kind of noun modifier in a noun phrase **(3)**

reciprocal pronoun: like a reflexive pronoun in purpose, but used with plural subjects to express mutual activity **(5)**

reduced relative clause: a relative clause that has lost either its object relative pronoun or a relative pronoun and a form of the verb *be* **(12)**

reflexive pronoun: a pronoun that typically is used to avoid repetition of the same noun phrase within a clause **(5)**

relative clause: a subordinate clause that modifies a noun phrase **(5, 12)**

relative pronoun: a pronoun used within a relative clause to replace the second occurrence of the head noun phrase **(5, 12)**

restrictive relative clause: a relative clause that restricts and therefore identifies the head noun phrase **(12)**

root: that part of a word that carries the core meaning **(2)**

sentence: a grammatical constituent consisting of one or more clauses **(2, 11)**

sentence adverb: an adverb that modifies an entire sentence, injecting commentary from the speaker **(6)**

simple sentence: a sentence consisting of only one clause **(11)**

simple tense: time with no aspect: present, past, and future **(4)**

split infinitive: an infinitive with something in between *to* and the base form of the verb **(3)**

standard American English: that form of English expected in public discourse in the United States: in newspapers and magazines, radio and television news broadcasts, textbooks, and public lectures **(1)**

subject: typically, the noun phrase of a clause that appears before the verb and performs the action **(2, 3)**

subject complement: a noun phrase or adjective that describes the subject of a sentence **(3, 6)**

subject noun clause: a noun clause that plays the role of subject in a sentence **(12)**

subject-verb agreement: the requirement that the subject and the verb of a clause must match in person and number **(4)**

subjective case: the case of pronouns used as subjects or subject complements **(5)**

subordinate clause: a clause that performs a grammatical function within another clause; also called **embedded sentence** and **dependent clause** **(2, 12)**

subordinating conjunction: lexical category that introduces certain subordinate clauses **(12)**

subordination: the process whereby one clause becomes a grammatical part of another **(12)**

suffix: an affix that attaches to the end of a root **(2)**

superlative: the form of an adjective used to compare more than two entities **(2, 6)**

superordinate clause: see **main clause**

tag question: an interrogative attached to the end of a declarative statement **(9)**

tense: the time of the action of the verb, or a combination of time and aspect **(4)**

time: the indicator of when the action occurred relative to the time of the utterance: past, present, or future **(4)**

transitive verb: a verb that must be followed by a direct object **(4)**

truncated passive: a sentence in the passive voice that omits the doer of the action **(8)**

universal pronoun: a pronoun that represents an all-inclusive noun phrase or entity **(5)**

verb: the lexical category that typically refers to actions or mental states **(2, 4)**

verb negation: expressing negation by associating a negative word with a verb **(10)**

verbal noun: a noun that is formed from a verb **(3)**

verb phrase: a phrase with a verb as its head and all modifiers of the verb **(4)**

wh-question: a question type that seeks a specific piece of information **(9)**

whiz-deletion: reduction of a relative clause by omitting a relative pronoun and a form of the verb *be* **(12)**

word: a combination of a root and all its affixes **(2)**

word class: see **lexical category**

yes-no question: a question type that can be answered *yes* or *no* **(9)**

Index

W

Y